Fast
Powerboat
Seamanship

Fast Powerboat Seamanship

The Complete Guide to Boat Handling, Navigation, and Safety

Dag Pike

International Marine / McGraw-Hill

Camden, Maine • New York • Chicago • San Francisco • Lisbon • London • Madrid
Mexico City • Milan • New Delhi • San Juan • Seoul • Singapore • Sydney • Toronto

The McGraw·Hill Companies

1 2 3 4 5 6 7 8 9 10 DOC DOC 0 9 8 7 6 5 4 3

Library of Congress Cataloging-in-Publication Data
    Pike, Dag.
      Fast powerboat seamanship : the complete guide to boat handling,
    navigation, and safety / Dag Pike.
         p.   cm.
    Includes index.
      ISBN 0-07-142209-9
      1. Motorboats—Handbooks, manuals, etc. 2. Seamanship—Handbooks,
    manuals, etc. I. Title.
      GV835.P554 2004
      797.1´25—dc22   2003025915

Questions regarding the content of this book should be addressed to
        International Marine
        P.O. Box 220
        Camden, ME 04843
        www.internationalmarine.com

Questions regarding the ordering of this book should be addressed to
        The McGraw-Hill Companies
        Customer Service Department
        P.O. Box 547
        Blacklick, OH 43004
        Retail customers: 1-800-262-4729
        Bookstores: 1-800-722-4726

Illustrations by Bruce Alderson unless noted otherwise.
Photographs by the author unless noted otherwise.

WARNING: Fast powerboating can expose you to potentially dangerous situations. In using this book, the reader releases the author, publisher, and distributor from liability for any loss or injury, including death, allegedly caused, in whole or in part, by relying on information contained in this book.

Contents

Introduction 1

Chapter 1 Fast-Boat Design 5
    Hull Designs 8
    The Technical Side of Fast Boats 29

Chapter 2 The RIB Concept 40
    Design and Construction of RIBs 41
    How the Inflatable Tube Affects Performance 42
    Alternative Tube Designs 45
    Interaction Between Tube and Hull 46
    Water Drainage 50
    Seating 53

Chapter 3 Fast-Boat Features 56
    Seating 56
    Footrests and Toe Straps 58
    Handholds 59
    Seat Belts 60
    Windshields (Windscreens) 61
    Helm Station 63
    Antennas 65

Chapter 4 Engines and Propulsion 66
    Engines 66
    Propulsion 79
    Gearboxes 97
    Slow-Speed Maneuvering 99

Chapter 5   Fast-Boat Controls 101
    Throttle 101
    Trim Tabs 109
    Interceptors 112
    Power Trim 116
    Steering 120
    Control of Directional Stability 124
    Balance 128

Chapter 6   Wind and Waves 129
    How the Wind Generates Waves 130
    Wave Basics 130
    Types of Waves 132
    Inshore Waves 136
    Sea Conditions and Fast Boats 146
    Weather 151

Chapter 7   Driving a Fast Boat 157
    Performance Reserve 158
    Driving in Head Seas 159
    Driving in Beam Seas 169
    Driving in Following Seas 173
    Running an Inlet 178
    Spinout 180
    Concentration and Special Skills 182
    Longer-Term Tactics 185

Chapter 8   Driver and Crew 187
    The Driver's Role 189
    The Navigator's Role 190
    The Rest of the Crew 191
    Communication on Board 192
    Personal Equipment 193
    Fatigue 201
    Seasickness 202

Chapter 9   Navigation 204
                Navigation Before You Leave 206
                Navigation on the Water 213
                Radar 217
                Steering a Course 223
                Visual Navigation 226
                Communications 232

Chapter 10   Emergencies 235
                Major Emergencies 236
                Towing 239

Chapter 11   The Future 240
                Monohulls 240
                Catamarans 241
                Trimarans 243
                Hovercraft 244
                Flying Machines 245
                Ride Control 246
                Fast-Boat Engines 249
                Fast-Boat Propulsion 249
                Into the Future 250

Index 251

Introduction

Fast powerboating is fun. It also carries responsibility, because the faster you travel, the greater the risk. Safety is in your hands, as the person at the helm and throttles. At a leisurely pace of 10 knots, you can proceed with hardly a care in the world—maybe even enjoying a hot drink—but at 20 knots things happen more quickly. Double this speed to 40 knots and you need absolute concentration on operating the boat (don't even consider that hot drink), and you must also be aware of the changing shape of the waves and of everything going on around you. At slow speeds your boat will probably do a pretty good job of looking after itself, even if you make a mistake, but from 40 knots upward, the pleasure of driving a boat can quickly turn to pain.

Driving at high speeds, you ride an increasingly narrow line between success and failure. The designer and builder have provided you with the tools for the job, but they rely on you—the driver—to make sure the boat travels safely. *Your* skill and awareness will enable you to assess the sea and weather conditions, *you* will trim the boat for optimum running and, most importantly, *your* hand on the throttles will dictate the boat's performance and level of safety.

When we consider fast boats, we tend to think of speeds in excess of 60 knots (about 70 mph), but a speed of 30 to 35 knots (35 to 40 mph) is also fast. The techniques for driving boats in this more moderate speed range are just as important as for the ultra-fast machines. For a driver who performs at the level of the offshore racer, the skill required is very high indeed: at 100 knots (115 mph) or more, there is no margin for error.

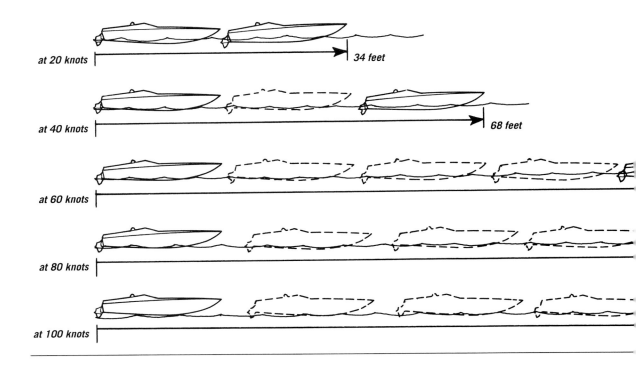

at 20 knots |————————————————————▶| *34 feet*

at 40 knots |——————————————————————————————▶| *68 feet*

at 60 knots |

at 80 knots |

at 100 knots |

Fast Powerboat Seamanship will guide you in the right direction for gaining the essential skills to drive a fast boat. This book explains how powerboats are designed and built and compares the effects of hull design on performance, so you will have a better understanding of your own boat. It discusses the all-important engines, propulsion systems, and controls. The techniques of fast-boat driving and navigating are explained, as are the measures you can take for your own comfort and safety. Finally, we look at the sea itself, and how its ever-changing waves are generated and how they move. The more you know about the medium in which you operate, the more satisfaction you will derive from fast powerboating.

Fast Powerboat Seamanship will also help you improve the performance of your boat so that you can enjoy the full range of its capabilities. The book cannot, however, give you experience: this you need to get on the water. With the solid foundation of information from the book, you will be able to analyze your boat's performance, while acquiring experience safely.

The word *seamanship* has been around for centuries, but it is no less relevant to modern fast boats. Fast-boat design has changed dramatically over the past twenty years, but the sea has not. It demands the same respect and understanding it has over

Drive Fast, Think Fast

There is little margin for error when driving at high speeds. One second is the average best-case response time. Suppose you've reached a marker and realize you have to turn. Here's how far past it you'll travel before you can react.

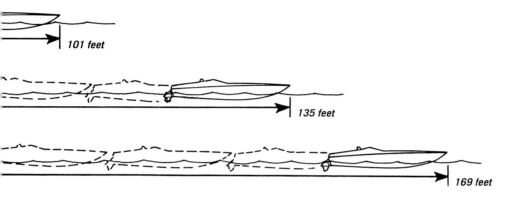

101 feet

135 feet

169 feet

the ages. Modern fast-boat design and driving techniques allow you to drive in the open sea at speeds unheard of a generation ago, but the water's surface is still unpredictable and constantly changing. Seamanship is the art of deciphering and respecting the sea environment and developing the skills to negotiate it, and this book will bring you a long way toward successful fast-boat seamanship.

In order to fully understand what happens when you drive your boat, you first need to know about its basic design, which strongly influences how the boat will perform. Therefore the book begins with an examination of hull designs. The text assumes that you have some boating knowledge and experience with navigation, winds, and tides. With that basic background, you will be able to use *Fast Powerboat Seamanship* to learn techniques of driving and navigating powerboats that can take you safely to the limits of excitement and performance.

1

Fast-Boat Design

Driving a fast boat well requires a partnership between boat and driver, a partnership made possible when you, the driver, understand your boat. This chapter examines fast-boat design so you can appreciate what the designer and builder of your boat were aiming to achieve.

Fast-boat design involves choices, compromises, and balances. Even within the confines of a single hull type, such as a deep-V monohull, a designer can choose a wide or narrow beam, a low or rising chine, and a moderately or extremely deep V, to name just a few options. Each choice is a compromise among competing objectives, all of them desirable, many of them mutually incompatible. The designer must find a good balance among these conflicting requirements in order to create the best design for the speeds, uses, and conditions under which a boat is intended to operate.

One boat might perform beautifully in calm water but be an absolute dog in rough seas. Another might perform well in waves but lose out in top-end flatwater speed. Still another might have a large internal volume for luxurious accommodations, but only after the designer compromised on that long, slim hull he originally wanted for speed and comfort in a seaway.

A boat based in Florida, with its normally clement conditions, can be optimized for performance more than seaworthiness, whereas a West Coast boat will likely have to cope with more frequent swells and rougher seas. Occasionally a hull is designed for particular conditions, but more commonly a boat is invested with a shape the designer hopes will perform acceptably

A Comparison of Hull Designs for Fast Boats

HULL DESIGN	APPROX. UPPER SPEED	CHARACTERISTICS
DEEP-V MONOHULL *deep V* *deep V with reverse chine*	90 knots*	22 to 28 degrees of deadrise at the transom. Good wave cushioning, but can become unstable at higher speeds. Good all-around performance. Average economy. *deep V with chine flats and with lifting strakes extending aft to transom*
SHALLOW-V MONOHULL	50 knots	As little as 5 degrees of deadrise at the transom, increasing forward. Can pound heavily in waves, so can give an uncomfortable ride with high hull stresses. Good economy.
STEPPED DEEP-V MONOHULL	105 knots	Good longitudinal (fore-and-aft) stability and wave cushioning. Good all-around performance for higher speeds. Average economy.
SEMIDISPLACEMENT MONOHULL	25 knots	May have a chine or a tightly radiused round bilge. Often has very little deadrise aft. Too heavy to attain true planing speeds; rarely exceeds a speed-to-length ratio of 3.0, thus not a focus of this book.
LONG, THIN MONOHULL (VERY SLENDER VESSEL, VSV)	50 knots	Excellent seaworthiness due to wave penetration, but limited onboard space. Probably the best design where ultimate seaworthiness is required, but otherwise the concept is not very practical.

*1 knot equals 1.15 miles per hour

Hull Design	Approx. Upper Speed	Characteristics
Cathedral Hull	45 knots	Good lift and load carrying. A good general-purpose design, but it has limitations in open-sea performance because of wave impacts. Notice extended chines that look like the start of small side hulls.
Trimaran	50 knots	Excellent seaworthiness and economy, but limited onboard space. Has many of the features of the long, thin monohull (very slender vessel), but better transverse (side-to-side) stability.
Displacement Catamaran	35 knots	Excellent economy and good seaworthiness until waves hit under the cross-deck. A good design for long-range cruising where high speed is not the prime consideration.
Planing Catamaran	130 knots	Good stability in waves, but can be flighty at higher speeds. Is the design for highest performance, but onboard accommodation can be limited. Economy not a consideration. Wave impact on the cross-deck can be a limiting factor for seaworthiness.
Wave-Piercer Catamaran	45 knots	Good seaworthiness due to wave penetration of bow, but this style of hull does not translate easily into small sizes. Good economy.
Foil-Assisted Catamaran	70 knots	Better efficiency than a standard catamaran, and the foils help to give a better ride. Good economy and seaworthiness comparable to other catamarans, with wave impact under the cross-deck being the limiting factor.

*1 knot equals 1.15 miles per hour

well under most conditions, even if better under some than others.

Prevailing sea conditions, desired speed, weight of crew and provisions, maneuverability, comfort, range—the designer must take all these factors and more into account, knowing that a change in one will usually affect others. Designers of fast boats first consider the various hull forms that can be used, such as deep V, cathedral, catamaran, and other, more exotic designs. This is the starting point for the compromises that follow, during which the designer will also consider the various controls available to the driver. Controls such as the throttles, flaps, and power trim can produce short-term changes in a fast boat's trim *and* attitude, altering its handling characteristics in predictably beneficial ways.

Hull Designs

We start where the design process starts, by considering the various basic shapes for high-speed boats. As in most classification systems, distinctions sometimes blur, and the hull shapes overlap. At one extreme, for example, a cathedral hull resembles a trimaran; at the other it starts looking a lot like a deep V.

Deep-V Monohulls

The deep V is by far the most popular type of fast-boat hull, outnumbering all other designs put together. The first deep-V de-signs, with their V-shaped bottom (when viewed in cross section), were produced in the late 1940s. They were commonly known then as Hunt designs, after Ray Hunt, who developed the concept.

The deep V was developed out of the hard-chine planing boats that were common in the 1930s—boats with a simple sharp corner or chine, where the bottom of the boat meets the sides, and a relatively flat bottom that permitted the boat to rise easily in the water onto a plane. Although these hard-chine monohulls produced good planing performance, their flat bottoms generated considerable wave impact stresses. These boats in smaller sizes simply didn't handle rough seas well—certainly not at high speeds.

Hard-chine hulls worked well in larger craft whose bows could cut through waves, leaving the flatter aft sections to generate lift for planing. A shallow-V hull is still used in some craft over 100 feet long. The deadrise angle might be as little as 5 degrees at the transom but increases steadily forward, making a transition to sharger bow sections that cut through waves rather than pounding. In larger sizes the hull never leaves the water, thus eliminating wave impact stresses. Smaller craft, however, must be able to withstand these stresses when they are driven hard, at which times the bow sections leave the water and the boat rides on its shallow aft section. On such vessels, the impact of the hull returning to the water in-

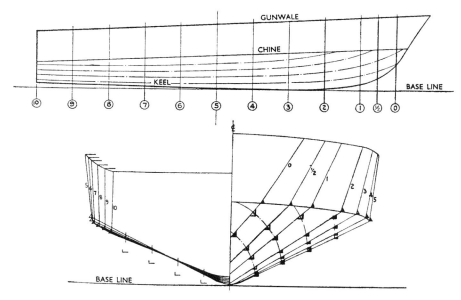

(Top) An early deep-V hull designed by Ray Hunt in the 1940s. This hull form was the paradigm for modern deep Vs, and is easily recognizable in the boat above. The photo shows more modern refinements, however, including a chine flat and lifting strakes. (Line art courtesy Ted Brewer, Understanding Boat Design*)*

troduces severe structural stresses on both boat and crew and can seriously limit overall performance.

The deep-V hull, on the other hand, cushions the wave impact and allows improved performance in smaller boats, considerably reducing stresses on hull and crew. Thus the seagoing performance of a deep-V hull is vastly superior to that of a shallow V. However, a V bottom generates less lift than a nearly flat bottom; therefore it requires more power to rise onto a plane and stay there. Modern lightweight engines have alleviated this problem, providing plenty of power to the less efficient V hull. A key difference between the deep-V hull and the shallow-bottomed hull is its deadrise—the angle at which the hull rises from keel to chine. The deadrise of a truly flat-bottomed hull is 0 degrees; a fast boat may have a deadrise of 24 degrees at the transom.

Over the years, deep-V hulls have been refined considerably to improve their performance, and they can be altered to meet different requirements. A deep-V monohull designed for high speed has a long, narrow hull with a cutaway forefoot and a fine entry. Its narrow beam reduces the concentration of lift toward the stern to reduce pitching, the up and down plunging of the bow, and the cutaway forefoot helps the hull cut cleanly through waves. This cutaway forefoot, where the bow is angled forward,

The design of the bow on this fast deep-V monohull provides additional last-minute buoyancy to prevent the bow nose-diving in following seas.

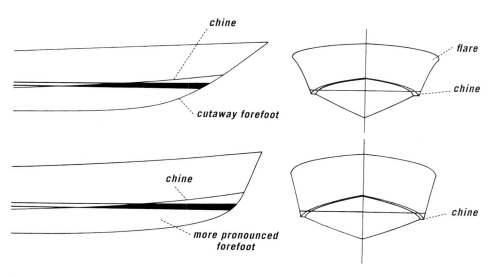

Bow shape for a high-speed boat with a cutaway forefoot to give a fine entry (top) and for a slower boat with a fuller hull shape.

along with the fine entry, reduces lift forward. Together these factors reduce the chance of the hull lifting and becoming unstable when it encounters a wave. This works well in head seas, but the hull needs to retain enough reserve buoyancy in the bow to generate adequate lift in a following sea. This can be achieved by introducing flare into the bow—essentially increasing the hull volume near and above the waterline—or by keeping the chine line a little lower at the bow.

In contrast, a deep-V hull designed to operate at lower speeds—in the 30- to 40-knot range of many pleasure and patrol craft—will have a wider beam and generally a lower chine line, which meets the bow only a little above the waterline. The wider hull creates a more efficient planing surface because it generates more lift. There will be less cushioning effect in waves, however, because the hull will not cut through cleanly, but rather will tend to lift and pound over the waves. The main purpose of the wider beam and the lower chine is to increase the internal volume of the hull, creating additional space for accommodations. Additionally, these designs have more initial stability, making them more stable at rest.

In designs for the slower deep-V boats, the deadrise angle at the transom is likely to be around 15 to 20 degrees, compared with 22 to 24 degrees in narrow, high-per-

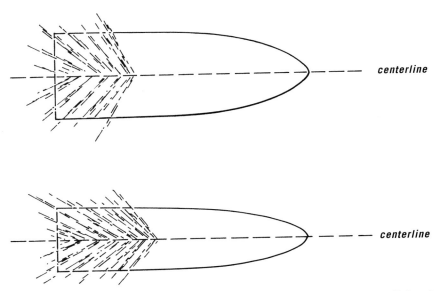

The planing surface (marked by the hatching) of a beamy deep-V hull (top) and a narrower deep-V hull (bottom). The beamier (wider) boat has a more efficient planing surface, but the narrower boat cushions wave impact better.

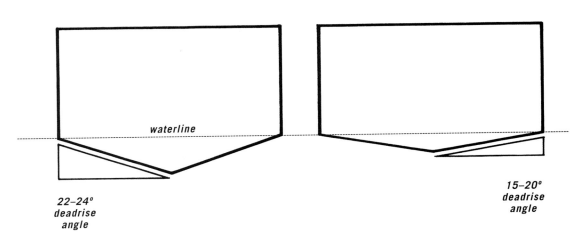

waterline

22–24°
deadrise
angle

15–20°
deadrise
angle

The stern shape of a deep-V hull with a high transom deadrise (left) and a moderate-V hull with lower transom deadrise (right).

formance hulls. Thus, we sometimes call these hulls intended for slower speeds moderate Vs rather than deep Vs, and since their deadrise increases forward they are also sometimes called modified Vs. At high speeds, where wave impacts can be especially severe, the designer has to find a compromise between the planing efficiency of a low-deadrise hull and the desirable cushioning effect of a high-deadrise hull. With plenty of engine power now available, it is possible to use a deeper V design without too much compromise in performance.

Lifting Strakes (Running Strakes)

Deep-V hulls have been refined by the use of lifting strakes (also known as running strakes or spray rails; in this book, "spray rails" refer to rails mounted on the topsides, which function to help deflect spray away from the deck). These are strips, triangular in cross section, that are added to the underwater part of the hull, running aft from the bow and usually lying parallel to the keel. The strakes generate additional lift. The flat lower surface of the lifting strake is more efficient than the angled V of the hull for generating lift, and this is helpful in getting the boat onto a plane so that it travels atop the water rather than through it.

The main purpose of lifting strakes, however, is to peel water away from the hull around the waterline. This decreases the area of the hull in contact with the water, thus reducing friction between hull and water. Lifting strakes usually end at around

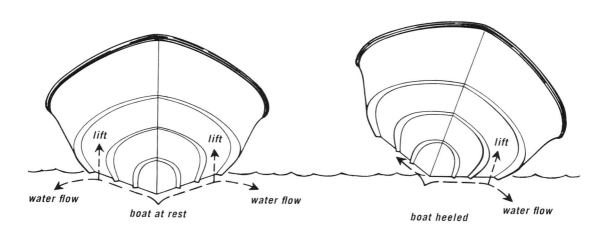

Lifting strakes help stabilize a deep-V hull when running on a straight course by increasing the lift on the lower side of the hull when heeled (right).

two-thirds of the length of the boat from the bow; the boat's stern remains in the water except at very high speeds, so strakes in this area would just create drag. Leaving the stern free of lifting strakes also avoids adding turbulence in the water flow to the propellers. On boats fitted with water jets, the designer needs to take great care in the location and extent of the lifting strakes to avoid introducing turbulence into the water-jet intakes.

Lifting strakes also have a balancing effect: when the hull heels to one side, the angle between the lifting-strake bottom and the hull becomes an inverted V that generates considerable lift, forcing the hull back into an upright position when traveling fast. This dynamic ability of lifting strakes is a main factor in maintaining deep-V hull stability at high speed.

lift as the boat is coming onto a plane. Once the boat is planing, the forward part of the chine flat (as these shelves are called) tends to ride clear of the water (except when the hull hits a wave), leaving the aft part of the chine to balance the hull by providing a concentration of lift at the outside extremities of the hull.

Chine flats tend to present a wider and flatter surface than lifting strakes; therefore they are an important aspect of hull stability. The wider the chine, the more effectively it will generate lift and create stability, but this benefit has to be balanced against the impact of waves against a wide, flat surface. If the chine is too wide, the boat will offer a harsh ride. On large deep-V hulls, chine surfaces that are 6 inches or more in width can bring harshness to what would otherwise be a soft-riding hull. One

Chines

Much like the lifting strakes, chine flats on a deep-V hull provide considerable lift and stability. The chines, marking the point where the bottom of the hull transitions into the near-vertical topsides, are designed on a deep V to provide a narrow flattened area along the edge of the hull bottom. This shelf, running from bow to stern, produces its greatest

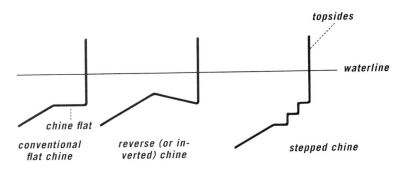

A midsection view of a deep-V hull showing various chine configurations.

chine flat

lifting strakes

A deep-V hull with a double chine arrangement to reduce chine slamming. Also note the lifting strakes, the two lower strips along the underside of the hull.

option is to have a stepped chine so that wave impact is staggered slightly and thus softened.

To generate more lift from the chine, some designs incorporate a chine that actually turns downward when the hull is running level, creating an inverted V. This so-called reverse or inverted chine produces extra lift, but it can also increase wave impact considerably. While it may produce an easy-planing hull, it also tends to generate a harsh ride. In developing a balanced hull, a designer looks for a smooth flow of water

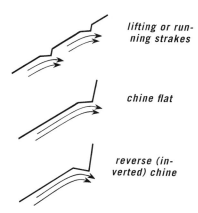

lifting or running strakes

chine flat

reverse (inverted) chine

Deflection of water to provide lift with (top to bottom) running strakes, a chine flat, and a reverse chine.

under the hull to give a smooth ride. This means creating hull surfaces that will not temporarily trap water—but the reverse chine can cause this problem. Water flowing under the hull should always have somewhere to go. If it gets trapped it can create great pressure and cause a pounding ride.

On some boats running at very high speeds, the chines lift fully clear of the water—even at the stern—and the stabilizing influence of the chine is lost. This problem can be counteracted by a lifting strake that extends all the way aft. This solution can work on a single-prop boat, where the lifting strake will not interfere with the flow of water to the propeller. On twin-screw boats, however, taking the lifting strake all the way aft may disturb water flow. In this case, when the chine clears the water at high speeds and the boat is riding only on its V, stability will be lost. Additionally, the chines can feed aerated water to the propellers, reducing efficiency. The boat will also have a jelly-like feeling, called chine wallowing, which should be interpreted as a warning that the boat is reaching its limits of safe operation.

Weight

The weight of a deep-V monohull boat, as with any fast-boat design, is critical to its performance. The heavier the boat, the deeper it rides in the water, which means that the wetted surface area is greater and

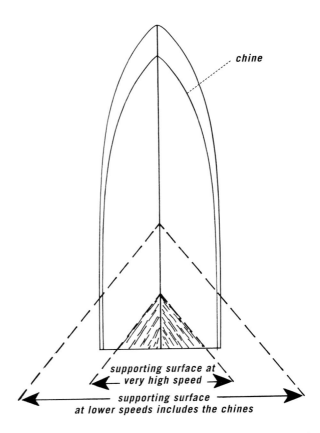

Chine stability on a deep-V hull, showing the loss of stability at very high speeds (represented by the smaller crosshatched area). This is also known as chine wallowing.

therefore the resistance of the hull is higher. As a result, more power will be needed for a given speed, and more powerful engines can add even more weight. This can become a vicious design circle, so in most high-speed designs, the designer takes every opportunity to reduce weight.

Making a boat as light as possible, however, may not always be the right solution. It can require exotic and expensive materials or paring the structure to its bare minimum, which can affect the boat's reliability. Although the alternative solution of simply providing more powerful engines can add weight, this weight will not necessarily increase in the same proportion as the extra power. In rough seas, a heavy fast boat will perform much better than a light boat. It will remain glued to the water and won't have the flighty performance of a light boat, which can leave the water with little provocation. In fact, a cruising boat could be twice the weight of a racing boat of similar length. The lightweight boat may be the best solution for racing and high performance, but for a fast, comfortable cruising boat there is no substitute for a powerful, relatively heavy design.

This design philosophy is used in many sportfishing boats, which are meant to perform in adverse conditions at speeds typically ranging from 30 to 40 knots. They are characterized by a hull with a moderate V, with perhaps a skeg or shallow keel added for directional stability. A pair of powerful diesel engines matched to conventional propulsion gives these boats adequate speed, but they are heavy craft designed for tough conditions, and it is almost impossible to drive them to the point where the hull leaves the water.

This sportfisherman is typical of a heavy, fully-powered type of fast boat. The hull is usually a moderate V, often fitted with a skeg for directional stability.

In creating a deep-V monohull, the designer analyzes all factors to arrive at the best compromise for specific performance requirements. A flatter hull with a low deadrise and sharp, wide chines combined with low weight will get on a plane easily and require less power, but it will tend to have a harsh ride and be less stable in rough sea conditions. A long, narrow hull with a high deadrise angle will need more power for a given speed and may be less stable at rest, but its performance in waves will be considerably enhanced. The long, narrow hull also tends to spread the lift over a larger area in the longitudinal (fore-and-aft) direction, and this produces better longitudinal stability, which means a reduced tendency to pitching. Increasingly, designs for fast deep-V monohulls are favoring the use of modern diesel power units that supply considerable power and don't require big sacrifices in overall boat weight (see chapter 4).

Stepped Deep-V Monohulls

The stepped hull—incorporating stepped breaks across a hull bottom when viewed in profile—is nothing new, but develop-

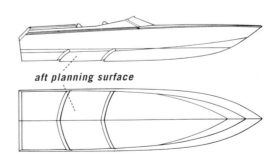

The stepped deep-V monohull rides on two or three short, wide surfaces, rather than on a long, narrow surface, which improves longitudinal stability. The areas behind each step run "dry," which reduces the wetted surface area. The Callan 55 (see photos) typifies this hull shape and is powered by twin surface-piercing props aft of twin trim tabs. (Photos courtesy Callan)

A stepped deep-V monohull showing two steps in the aft part of the hull and the strakes that run the length of the boat. Note the rounded deck edge of this design.

ment of the stepped deep-V monohull is relatively recent. Steps were originally designed to reduce the concentration of lift in the aft part of a hull when very flat hulls were in use, spreading the lift along the bottom. The hull was effectively riding on the two or three surfaces created by the steps.

Steps are used in modern deep-V designs for a similar reason. A short, wide planing surface is more efficient than a long, narrow one, and at high speeds it is also more stable. With the addition of steps, the hull rides on two or three short, wide surfaces rather than a single long and rather narrow surface. This design improves longitudinal (fore-and-aft) stability, and because the hull will not pitch so much, it will ride at a more constant angle. Decreased pitching also allows the propeller thrust to

be more constant and effective, and hull resistance is reduced.

A stepped hull creates areas immediately behind each step that will run "dry," which is thought to reduce the wetted surface area of the hull. Some designers also believe that the introduction of air as it is drawn into the area behind the step provides "lubrication" to the hull, which should further reduce resistance. Although these theories are difficult to prove, stepped hulls have a record of demonstrated success in race boats—and because of this, such hulls have become fashionable on many leisure boats. But a stepped hull offers no advantages at speeds below 30 to 40 knots and can, indeed, increase drag at these speeds. The benefits of stepped hulls become apparent only at speeds of around 50 knots and above.

Semidisplacement Monohulls

The semidisplacement hull has developed largely from the hard-chine hull. Instead of a hard angular chine, the semidisplacement hull has rounded chines that are used to soften the ride. These rounded chines are quite sharp aft to help generate lift from the flat bottom, but the hull fines away (narrows), reducing the hull volume as it runs forward to provide good wave penetration and a level ride. To improve planing performance and reduce spray, a pronounced flat chine is often incorporated into the rounded section.

A skeg or keel is frequently used with a semidisplacement hull to give good directional stability. Without this the hull would have little grip on the water and would tend to have poor directional stability. The semidisplacement hull design is an interesting compromise that takes something from other displacement mono-hull designs. A displacement hull moves mainly *through* the water while a planing boat rides more *over* the surface. A displacement boat is unlikely to run faster than 10 knots. The semidisplacement hull is part displacement hull and part planing hull, and it also includes aspects from the long, thin monohull. It will work reasonably well at speeds up to 25 knots, but above that the power requirements start to rise out of proportion to the speed increase, and the ride can be very wet. To enhance performance, earlier hulls tended to be narrow, which restricted the internal space. Modern versions work well by utilizing a wider beam.

Long, Thin Monohulls (Very Slender Vessels)

The long, thin monohull, or very slender vessel (VSV), is a new idea, although the idea of such a hull for fast boats has been around for some time in catamaran applications, where two hulls are used for stabil-

A semidisplacement boat at speed. Note the considerable spray that is generated by this type of hull when driven hard.

A long, thin monohull (or very slender vessel, VSV) at speed. The needlelike bow generates very little lift, so this hull is wave piercing and provides a wet ride.

ity. While the benefits and efficiency of a long, thin monohull have been recognized, the design tended to be rejected because it could not be stabilized enough for practical use. Today, new designs that feature a pronounced chine have been developed, and these show exceptional seaworthiness.

The VSV gains performance because the thin hull slips through the water with little resistance. Modern versions use a rounded, almost tube-shaped hull that is very strong. At high speeds the pronounced chine roughly along the waterline generates enough lift to reduce the wetted surface area, reducing resistance, and provides good stability. This chine also improves stability of the hull at rest by increasing buoyancy on the lower side of the hull if it heels.

The increased seaworthiness of the VSV comes from its ability to penetrate waves at high speed rather than riding over them. Because there is minimum buoyancy at the bow, the hull does not lift over waves, and it will ride almost level and true. This does mean that the ride can be very wet, with solid water running down the deck in any kind of a sea.

Driving a VSV is challenging and exhilarating, but the appearance of solid water rolling down the deck can be frightening, and it takes time to get used to it. Once it becomes clear that the boat is not going to self-destruct as it goes through the waves, it can give an exciting ride at 50 knots. These boats do present problems because it's difficult to see where you are going and internal space is limited. Still, for boats of equal length, the long, thin monohull will easily beat a standard monohull in rough sea performance. At present, however, these designs are mainly restricted to military applications.

Cathedral Hulls

Cathedral hulls (also known as gull-wing hulls) are usually based around a deep-V hull, but this is a deep V with a considerably modified chine that is designed to generate additional lift and increased stability. The reverse chine (see illustration on page 14) could be the basis of a cathedral hull design, with the chine continuing downward and beginning to look like the start of a small side hull. This enlarged reverse chine generates considerable lift. A major advantage of cathedral hulls is the way they rise quickly onto a plane, making

them excellent load-carrying designs.

A drawback to the cathedral hull is that the spaces between the main hull and the side hulls or chines can present surfaces that magnify wave impact. In some cathedral designs the side hulls are very noticeable, producing a boat that resembles a trimaran. In others the side hulls may be pronounced at the bow and dwindle aft to become small reverse chines. The side hulls or chines can run right up to the bow, level with the center hull, or they may start some distance back. With an almost infinite number of variations on the cathedral theme, hull features can be tailored to meet required characteristics.

Most cathedral hull designs have a mod-

A fast cathedral hull showing its pronounced chines that develop into embryonic side hulls underwater.

ified bow shape above the waterline, wider and more rounded than on a similar deep-V monohull. This fuller bow may perform poorly in following seas because it can present a virtually flat surface to the slope of a wave as waves are overtaken. The result can be a sudden increase in lift, or even a wave impact that brings the boat to a stop. The significant buoyancy at the bow also makes cathedral designs sensitive to waves when operating in head seas. These limitations in seaworthiness can cause a harsh ride in rough, open-sea conditions.

flat bow shape makes broad
impact on waves

The fuller bow shape of a cathedral hull may perform poorly in following seas because it presents a virtually flat surface to the waves as they are overtaken.

Despite their drawbacks, cathedral hull designs are extremely versatile. They have larger deck areas than similar-sized deep-V hulls, and they are good load carriers. Cathedral designs tend to be limited to hulls up to about 25 feet long; they are widely used as yacht tenders and harbor craft.

Trimarans

A trimaran represents an extension of either the cathedral hull or the deep-V monohull, depending on which direction the design is approached from. One type of trimaran has a long, slender center hull, with the two side hulls used mainly for stability. In this concept the side hulls are also very slender for minimal resistance, allowing this trimaran to perform in many ways like a long, thin monohull. The alternative concept utilizes fuller side hulls, which can be large enough to house the engines. These side hulls tend to be more integrated into the center hull to create additional internal volume. Unlike the cathedral hull, a trimaran has a distinct tunnel running between the main hull and side hulls, extending the length of the boat.

Trimaran development has been limited because there is little internal space in the hulls, making them generally unacceptable as leisure boats. But they confer considerable performance advantages. The main center hull is usually long and narrow, which provides efficient performance at high speed. This center hull offers good wave penetration, although lift may be restricted at the bow. This, in turn, could allow solid water to come down the deck in high-speed, rough-sea operations, particularly in following seas.

A fast trimaran powerboat that is both efficient and seaworthy. (Icemarine)

In modern trimaran designs, the side hulls tend to be attached well aft on the center hull to reduce the likelihood of wave impact in the tunnels. In high-speed trimaran designs, the side hulls are very narrow and contribute little to the dynamic lift of the hull, being incorporated principally to provide stability for the hull at rest. This means that the boat's machinery has to be concentrated in the center hull, which often has space for only one engine.

Trimaran design is still developing, and some patented concepts have been produced, but they do not have the general-purpose characteristics of the monohull or cathedral hull. These trimarans tend to be restricted to high-speed performance.

Catamarans

The sailing catamaran has been around for a long time, and power catamarans have been developed for both commercial and leisure use. The main advantages of a power catamaran are its wide beam, which allows generous internal and deck space, and its excellent stability both when under way and at rest. On the negative side, open-sea performance can be severely compromised if waves hit the underside of the cross-deck between the twin hulls. When this wave impact starts to occur, reducing speed would be the logical solution, except that reducing speed also reduces lift and thus lowers the boat in the water. This shrinks the clearance between the cross-deck and the water, which in turn increases the chance of more wave impact under the cross-deck.

This problem suggests that catamarans travel a fine line between being viable performance craft and requiring a dramatic reduction in speed for safe operation (even down to displacement speed levels when sea conditions deteriorate). Some modern designs gain improved seagoing ability by having deep hulls, staving off the point at which cross-deck wave slamming occurs.

Catamarans are the accepted form when very high speeds are required, because of their excellent stability. The fact that the boat rides on two long, thin hulls means that a catamaran runs much more level and true than a comparable monohull. This improves propulsion efficiency and gives improved safety when speeds reach 90 knots and more.

There are two principal types of power catamaran hulls: the displacement catamaran and the planing catamaran.

Displacement Catamarans

Displacement catamaran hulls are rounded and do not generate much lift. But because they are so long and narrow, they slip through the water easily and generally allow

A cruising catamaran based on long, thin displacement hulls.

speeds up to 30 knots. They have many of the characteristics of the long, thin monohull (or VSV, very slender vessel), though without the ability to go through waves with the same efficiency.

Displacement catamarans are extremely fuel efficient, offering low resistance to the water, and they are seen in many excellent long-range cruising designs that require low power for good performance. Though top speed is usually about 30 knots, the larger designs can reach higher speeds. Limited buoy-

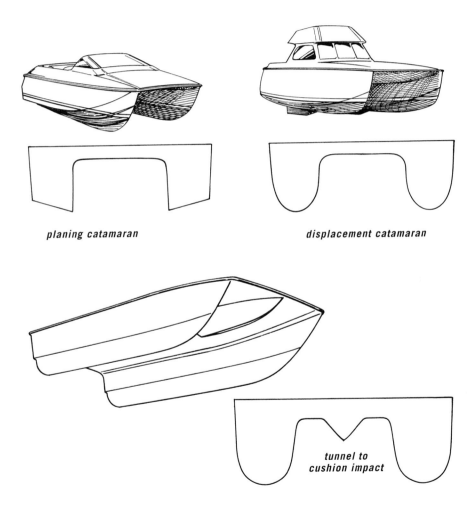

planing catamaran

displacement catamaran

tunnel to
cushion impact

Hull shapes for a planing catamaran (top left), displacement catamaran (top right), and displacement catamaran with a center tunnel pod (bottom) to cushion impact.

ancy at the bow can lead to excessive pitching, and many designs incorporate a tunnel pod—a kind of embryonic center hull—down the middle of the tunnel between the two main hulls. The tunnel pod adds buoyancy and reduces the impact of waves hitting the underside of the cross-deck.

Planing Catamarans

In contrast to the rounded hulls of a displacement catamaran, the planing catamaran runs on sharply angled surfaces. But because the hulls are long and narrow, these surfaces do not need as sharp a deadrise angle as on a deep-V monohull to cushion the ride. These characteristics make these hulls more efficient, and they are the design of choice for modern offshore racing boats.

These racing boats, and high-performance leisure craft based on the same designs, incorporate transverse steps into each hull to give the same benefits as found in a stepped deep-V monohull. There are usually two steps on each side, a configuration that increases the boat's efficiency and improves both longitudinal (fore-and-aft) and transverse (side-to-side) stability. With these steps, the planing catamaran is effectively on five points of support. This design makes the boat's propulsion system more effective, because the hull rides very level.

These high-performance planing catamarans have hulls that are asymmetric—with the inner side of each hull having a vertical surface down to the hull bottom and then the angled bottom taking the hull to the outer vertical surface. Another type of catamaran has symmetric hulls—basically two narrow deep-V monohulls joined at the cross-deck—for an efficient design that might be considered a cross between the displacement and the planing catamaran. The asymmetric design gives a clean flow of water and air down the tunnel, while symmetric hulls tend to have characteristics more similar to displacement catamarans.

A planing catamaran with its asymmetric hulls and chines.

Wave-Piercer Catamarans

Another catamaran design is the wave piercer, which has been used for large, fast ferries. There have been only a few attempts to bring the scale down to leisure-boat size. The wave piercer is virtually a trimaran, but the center hull rides clear of the water. The side hulls have the rounded displacement-catamaran shape, but they extend forward of the main center hull and are designed to pierce the waves. The vessel rides on these side hulls, but they have little or no reserve buoyancy, so the pronounced center hull is incorporated into the design and only comes into play if the craft starts to pitch. Advantages of the wave piercer are its good fuel efficiency and its limited pitching and rolling.

Foil-Assisted Catamarans

Yet another variation is the foil-assisted catamaran. One or more foils are fitted be- tween the two hulls below the waterline to generate lift as the boat moves through the water, raising the hull and reducing wetted surface area and resistance. The normal layout incorporates a full-width foil aft, where the main weight of machinery is located, and two canard foils forward. These canard foils extend out from the sides of the catamaran tunnel in the forward area of each hull. When adjustable canard foils are used they can control the trim of the boat, modifying its fore-and-aft angle relative to the surface of the water. The foils also serve to dampen some of the boat's pitching movements.

Power catamarans are still regarded as specialized craft and are not widely seen as recreational boats. One of the reasons for their limited use is that designers are rarely able to give a catamaran the sleek good looks of a traditional powerboat, even though catamaran designs can offer good

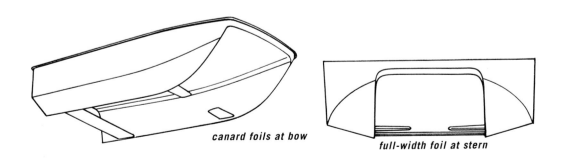

canard foils at bow

full-width foil at stern

A foil-assisted planing catamaran, showing the full-width foil aft and the shorter canard foils at the bow.

fuel efficiency. The catamaran is more widely used as a workboat, providing a solid, practical design.

Rigid Inflatables

The development of rigid inflatable boats (RIBs) introduced the factor of variable geometry into boat design. This means that the hull can change shape under wave impact, allowing it to adapt to changing sea conditions. This is an automatic process and it can have a considerable bearing on the way a boat performs, particularly in rough seas. Rigid inflatables are designed around one of the above-mentioned hull forms—usually a deep-V monohull—but design constraints and compromises are less severe. However, several new factors affect the performance of a RIB design, such as the inflatable-tube height, its pressure, and the material from which it is constructed.

Rigid inflatables are widely used in leisure boating—particularly in Europe—and other applications. The unique RIB concept will be discussed in detail in chapter 2.

The Technical Side of Fast Boats

So far we have looked at the various hull forms used for fast boats, but now it's time to get a bit more technical and consider what makes a fast boat perform. This sec-tion will concentrate on planing boats, because they form the vast majority of fast boats out on the water. Understanding what makes a fast boat tick will help you drive your boat and, perhaps more importantly, give you an indication of when you might be approaching the limits of performance.

Planing Surfaces

A planing surface is one that travels on the surface of the water at a slight angle. The interaction between the forward motion of the planing surface and the surface of the water generates lift—a force that is more or less at right angles to the planing surface, which usually means that it is nearly vertically upward. This upward force lifts the boat in the water, reducing the area of the hull in contact with the water and thus also reducing frictional and wave-making resistance. The boat's speed will increase until the thrust from the propeller and the resistance of the hull are in equilibrium.

The most efficient planing surface is a wide, flat surface. Something like a plank of wood would do a good job. Early planing boats had virtually flat bottoms, at least toward the stern, where it matters most. A flat plank board with a motor attached to one end, for example, would generate maximum lift, because all the lift would be concentrated upward. Because the plank is wide, the lift would be concentrated toward the rear so that much of the plank would be lifted clear of the water, reducing frictional resistance. As the early fast-boat designers discovered, however, a hull of this shape is not efficient in waves: it gives a rough ride with poor directional stability, and it is prone to instability from pitching.

To counteract these problems, a slight V shape was introduced into the hull bottom to give better directional stability and to reduce the impact of hitting waves. A skeg was sometimes added, its protrusion from the keel further aiding steering and directional stability. The lift generated by a V hull is partly dissipated outward, with the lift being reduced in proportion to the angle of the V (the hull's deadrise). Planing surfaces on modern fast-boat hulls are angled as steeply as 30 degrees, with a consequent reduction in lift—but powerful engines can compensate for this loss. The benefit of such a steep deadrise is its cushioning effect in waves: these boats can keep going at high speeds long after a flat-bottomed boat has had to slow down because of wave pounding.

A wide beam still affords the best planing efficiency, and all the early planing boats followed this style. The wide beam works well at speeds up to around 40 knots, because a fair amount of the hull still remains in the water to provide required stability. But as speeds increase, more of the hull leaves the water and the lift becomes concentrated aft. It becomes more difficult to find a point of balance where the various forces on the hull are in reasonable

equilibrium. The boat may then start to porpoise, with the bow sharply pitching up and down, or show other signs of instability, because it takes only a small change in the sea surface to create a fairly large change in the angle of the boat.

Modern high-speed hulls tend to have a narrower beam, which spreads the lift farther forward over a longer part of the hull, yielding better longitudinal stability as the hull lifts out of the water when speed increases. The introduction of the long, narrow hull and of deeper V hulls all contributed to moving the point of lift farther forward.

The need to spread the lift forward for stability becomes more critical at high speeds. A 45-foot-long high-speed hull might be stable up to a speed of about 90 knots; introducing steps into the hull can extend its range of stability up to 100 knots or more. These steps allow the hull to ride on two or three points of contact (see illustration on page 18), providing better fore-and-aft stability because the hull is less prone to pitching.

The location of the steps is critical, and their position will depend on the intended speed of the boat. For high speeds the steps will be well aft, probably in the last third of the hull, because this is the part of the boat that remains in the water. For lower speeds the forward step could be at the halfway mark. Slower boats have little need for steps; some designs incorporate steps simply to follow the fashion set by racing boats rather than to enhance performance.

A hull with a wide beam is naturally going to be more stable from side to side (transversely) than a hull with a narrow beam. When a deep-V hull heels over while planing, one side of the V assumes a much flatter aspect relative to the surface of the water, and the other a much steeper aspect. Consequently a lot of the lift is transferred to the lower, flatter side, and it is this transfer of lift that produces a corrective force to bring the hull upright. Obviously the wider the beam, the stronger the righting moment—and the more stable the boat. This has to be balanced against the fact that a boat with a wider beam will have a harsher ride because of the wider planing surfaces.

As a deep-V hull heels, the nearly flat surface of the lower side of the V can collide sharply with waves, producing a rough ride. If the boat is flying at the time, the return into the water when heeled can be very rough indeed because of the flat wave impact. With a narrow deep-V hull, just turning the steering wheel can cause the boat to heel over and introduce this rougher ride (see chapter 7, "Driving a Fast Boat").

Gravity and Buoyancy

Two basic forces acting on a boat are *gravity,* which is exerted downward through the boat's center of gravity, and *buoyancy,* which is exerted upward through the center of buoyancy. It's easy to take these forces for granted, but understanding them can help you become aware of what is going on as you drive your boat.

The center of gravity is the point at which, if you could support the boat at a single point, the vessel would balance. It is the point where all the weight in the boat is balanced and in equilibrium. The center of gravity is usually somewhere inside the boat and likely well aft, because this is where the weight of the engines is concentrated.

The center of gravity is fixed no matter what position the boat adopts. It is only when weight is moved, added, or taken away that the center of gravity changes position. When a crew member comes aboard or when the fuel tank is filled, the center of gravity moves toward the added weight. Similarly, if weight is removed, the center of gravity moves away from the point at which the weight is removed. If you fill a bow ballast tank, the center of gravity will move toward the bow (and the bow will drop); if you empty the tank, the center of gravity will move aft (and the bow will lift). As you drive the boat, the fuel tank steadily empties; because the tank is often located in the bottom of the boat, the center of gravity rises as fuel is burned.

The force of gravity acts vertically downward regardless of any changes in the boat's angle in the water. Balanced against this downward force is buoyancy, the upward force of the water that supports the boat when it floats. The force exerted by buoyancy acts vertically upward through the center of buoyancy, the geometric center of the underwater part of the hull.

To visualize this, think about what happens when the boat heels to one side. The center of buoyancy (B) moves toward this lower side, because now there is a greater volume of hull underwater on this side. Likewise, if the bow becomes immersed, the center of buoyancy moves toward the bow, because the underwater portion of the hull has increased in that area. Unlike the center of gravity (G), which is fixed in position inside the hull, the center of buoyancy wanders around the boat as the boat changes its attitude with respect to the water surface.

When the boat is at rest, the forces of gravity and buoyancy are equal and opposite, buoyancy exerted upward and gravity downward. The center of gravity is fixed, so it is the center of buoyancy that moves until it finds the equilibrium and the boat settles into this position in the water, with the waterline remaining constant.

Two events can alter this state of equilibrium: either a movement of the center of gravity or a movement of the center of buoyancy. As noted, the center of gravity only moves if a weight is added, taken away, or changes position. If a weight is moved from one side of the boat to the other, the boat will respond by heeling over on the side with the new weight. This heeling changes the shape of the boat's underwater

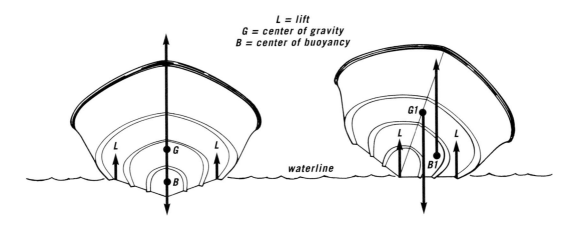

When a planing boat is at rest on an even keel (left) the lift factors balance each other to keep the boat upright. When a planing boat heels (right), the center of buoyancy moves in response to the boat's changing attitude in the water and the lift factor also increases, producing an additional righting force.

volume, so the center of buoyancy moves until it balances the center of gravity; equilibrium is again reached and the boat is stable in this position.

Now take the boat out into a seaway. The center of gravity will remain in the same place (unless a weight is moved). The center of buoyancy, however, will move around as the underwater portion of the hull changes shape in response to passing waves. As a wave passes the boat, the center of buoyancy moves toward where the wave is highest against the hull, exerting an upward force that causes the boat to lift at that point. Only as the wave passes under the boat and the center of buoyancy moves back toward its central position will the boat become level again, with equilibrium temporarily restored.

The corrective force of buoyancy works to restore both transverse (side-to-side) and longitudinal (fore-and-aft) stability. If the boat pitches into a wave, for instance, the center of buoyancy moves forward because of the increased underwater volume in the bow area. Movement of the center of buoyancy creates an upward force that lifts the bow over the wave. As the wave passes aft along the hull, the center of buoyancy also moves aft, balancing the hull.

A boat with a fine bow has reduced buoyancy forward, so the center of buoyancy will not rush forward in the same way that it would with a fuller bow shape. Less buoyancy is generated when a wave passes under this fine bow, and the force of buoyancy will be slower to react to the wave, generating less upward force. This means that the bow will tend to cut through the waves more than lift over them.

The distance that the center of buoyancy moves as a wave passes under the boat depends mainly on the shape of the hull. A full hull—such as a hard-chine hull, with its sharp angle between the bottom of the boat and its sides—produces a rapid change in underwater volume. This shift in the center of buoyancy causes a sudden movement of the boat as it tries to restore balance. A deep-V hull, with its more gentle transition from hull bottom to sides, responds more slowly to change and lifts farther before equilibrium is restored. A wide hull produces a quicker change than the more measured response of a narrow-beam hull. This slower response helps explain the cushioning effect of a narrow, deep-V hull compared with the harsher ride of a wide, hard-chine hull.

At sea there is a constant balancing act between gravity and buoyancy as waves pass by the boat. While the center of gravity doesn't move in normal circumstances, the center of buoyancy is constantly moving as it acts as an upward force to lift the boat, according to the movement of waves passing under and around it. After an initial lifting or heeling, depending upon where a wave affects the hull, the movement of the center of buoyancy creates a corrective force to return the boat upright.

We should also look here at the aspects of stability inherent in the cross-sectional shape of a hull. These apply to all hull types, fast and slow; they are relevant to fast boats, in terms of safety, when the boat is operating at slow speeds or stopped in rough seas. In this instance, the fast boat does not have the benefit of the dynamic lift it experiences while planing. Since there is no dynamic lift to give stability, the hull relies entirely on its inherent buoyancy for the required balance. For the shape of most fast monohulls, stability will probably rise as the hull heels over to around 60 degrees and then it will start to decline.

The critical factor affecting this reduction in stability occurs when the deck edge becomes immersed. Up to this point the stability, or righting moment, is increasing, but once the deck edge becomes immersed, stability decreases—probably reaching zero around the 80- to 90-degree mark. The hull has positive stability up to this point, but after that there is every chance that the hull will keep going over and capsize.

Dynamic Lift

We have looked at the forces of gravity and buoyancy and how they affect the movement of a boat in waves, but this is only the beginning. Other significant forces come into play when a boat is planing, and these also affect how the boat behaves at sea. The most significant of these forces is the dynamic lift created by the interaction of the hull's planing surfaces and the water. The angle between the planing surfaces and the water generates the upward force of lift, bringing a portion of the hull up and out of the water, thus reducing the underwater volume of the hull.

With the underwater volume of the hull reduced, the upward force of buoyancy is also reduced. When a hull is planing, there is a double effect in which the forces of buoyancy and dynamic lift combine to support the hull in the planing mode and also balance the force of gravity. Because the point of lift tends to be concentrated where the water surface meets the hull, this point moves around when the boat is operating in waves. Like the center of buoyancy, the center of lift moves forward when the boat encounters a wave and moves aft again as the wave passes. Thus the forces of buoyancy and lift tend to act in unison, although they are never fully in step with one another.

The dynamic lift of the hull is generated by the thrust from the propeller generated by engine power. This thrust acts at or near the transom, pushing the boat forward after it has overcome the resistance of the hull. Hull resistance comprises two elements: wave-making resistance and frictional resistance. Wave-making resistance occurs at displacement speeds up to around 10 knots, and it is caused by waves made by the hull

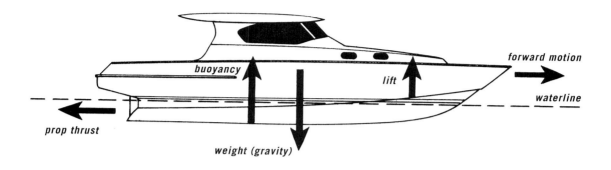

On a planing boat the weight of the hull balances the center of dynamic lift, and the boat trims at an angle to balance all the forces out.

as it passes through the water. As the boat comes onto a plane, the wave-making resistance becomes quite small, but the frictional resistance caused by the interaction between the hull and the water flowing past it becomes greater. As the boat picks up speed, the hull is lifted higher and frictional resistance decreases, because there is less surface area of the hull in contact with the water.

If the boat designer has done a good job, all these forces will play their complementary roles to give the boat a smooth and comfortable ride in waves. The constant change in all these fac-

tors occurs automatically without any human intervention, but various controls on the boat such as trim tabs (sometimes

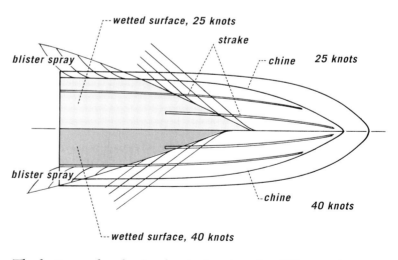

The bottom of a planing boat, showing the difference in wetted surface area at 25 knots and 40 knots. At 40 knots, less of the hull's surface is in contact with the water.

called tabs), power trim, and even the throttle can be used to moderate this constantly changing scenario. Using these controls, the helmsman has the ability to vary the boat's movements in response to changing conditions, effectively moving the centers of lift and buoyancy. This complex scenario is where the driver comes into play. Operation of a fast boat is really a partnership between the boat designer and you, the driver. Once you are at sea the designer's job is done, and then it's up to you.

Aerodynamics

At any speed over 30 knots, the wind passing over, around, and in some cases under the hull will affect performance. Wind has two effects on a fast boat: friction and lift.

Friction resulting from wind passing over the topsides of a boat slows it down. While this will hardly be noticeable at 30 knots, it can start to have a significant effect as speeds increase into the range of 50 to 70 knots. Unlike cars, which are shaped to minimize air friction, few boats are designed to reduce the frictional resistance of wind. Boat designers have a limited range of options to reduce air-friction drag, largely because the hull needs to have a specific shape to penetrate the water. That design element takes priority, while the top of the boat is usually shaped for style rather than for minimum aerodynamic resistance.

The second effect of the wind passing over the boat—lift—can be either negative or positive. The use of positive lift is seen in multihull designs—catamarans and trimarans—where air passing between the hulls strikes the underside of the cross-deck and generates lift. Some racing catamarans exploit this to the point of having the cross-deck shaped like an airfoil so that it acts like an aircraft wing to generate lift. Such catamarans can be faster upwind than downwind, despite the increased frictional resistance upwind.

In other, mainly racing designs, wings are fitted to struts at the stern. These can generate some lift at high speeds, although the turbulent air passing over a boat does not make such wings very effective, and the lift they generate is largely canceled out by the extra weight of the wings. These wings can improve hull stability, however; stabilizing wings of this type usually have a built-in dihedral (an angle at the center between each section of the wing) so that if the hull heels over, the main lift from the wing is on the lower side. Angled vertical fins are used for a similar purpose on monohulls.

Negative lift occurs when the wind passing over a boat strikes upward sloping surfaces of the superstructure, creating frictional resistance and generating a downward force that pushes the boat deeper into the water. This increases frictional resistance with the water and slows the boat. Virtually all fast boats, both leisure and commercial, have a superstructure that slopes up to the cockpit or the flybridge, and the wind striking this structure can significantly affect performance, particularly in headwinds where apparent wind speed can double.

The effect of wind is most apparent on fast monohulls when they are running speed trials on a measured mile. These trials are always run in two directions in order to, supposedly, cancel out the effects of wind and tide. This works fine on slower boats, but on faster boats, the loss through wind resistance when going upwind is not matched by a corresponding gain when going downwind. The boat will be faster downwind, but it cannot make up the losses incurred when going upwind. Measured-mile trials for fast boats are best conducted with the wind on the beam and speeds measured with a global positioning system (GPS) unit rather than with fixed shore marks.

Construction Methods and Materials for Fast Boats

The quality of the methods and materials used in fast-boat construction is more critically important than for ordinary craft, because fast boats operate under more severe conditions. The weight of the hull and superstructure must be kept to a minimum to optimize performance, but the hull experiences higher stress levels than on conventional craft. Hull pressures on the bottom of a racing boat when it is hitting waves can peak at around 100 pounds per square inch (three or four times the pressure in a car tire), requiring a very strong structure.

Two types of materials are generally used for fast-boat construction: composites and aluminum. In a third category are the materials employed in building the inflatable tubes for rigid inflatable boats (RIBs). Composites are the favorite for use in most leisure craft and racing boats. Aluminum is still used on some commercial craft, and it is also the basis for some RIB construction.

Weight is a critical factor in constructing a performance craft: the more weight, the more power needed and the more fuel. There are times when a heavier boat can be beneficial in fast-boat operations. In rough seas, when a boat is likely to fly off the waves, a light boat will be less stable than a heavy one. If the requirement is for a boat to make good progress in rough seas, then the heavier and hopefully stronger boat would be the one to choose, but the need to compensate with extra power has to be recognized. Lifeboats are a good example of boats that need to operate in rough conditions as well as maintain adequate speed in calmer water, and these craft are built to be both tough and relatively heavy.

Composites

Composites include a multitude of materials that are used for fast-boat construction. They have a common feature in that they are all composed of a reinforcement material combined with a resin. The most commonly used reinforcement material is glass fiber—very fine filaments of glass woven into a fabric-like material. Glass reinforcement is a good general-purpose material for use when light weight is not critical. Alternatives to glass are Kevlar fiber, which has a high tensile strength, capable of withstanding great longitudinal stress, and carbon fiber, which is strong in compression. Kevlar would tend to be used in a section of the hull structure that is being pulled apart (e.g., in the topsides), and carbon fiber where the structure is being pushed together (e.g., in the longitudinal stringers).

A designer may use two or more of these reinforcement materials in a boat, taking advantage of their differing characteristics to develop a hull with strength in all the right places. By using Kevlar and carbon fiber in high-stress areas, the weight of the hull structure can be considerably reduced without sacrificing strength. The design flexibility afforded by engineering a fast-boat hull using different materials, rather than more of the same material, has led to the widespread use of composites.

The resins used in composite construction are generally vinylester or epoxy. Vinylester is more commonly used, and it has adequate strength even for many high-performance structures. It is easier to use than epoxy resins, which tend to be chosen only for the strongest

structures. There are a number of molding systems in which the resins are introduced into the reinforcement under vacuum control rather than by the more normal hand layup. Vacuum infusion gives a better-quality composite and can be improved even further when the composites are baked at modest temperatures.

Some fast-boat composites are stiffened by means of a sandwich construction, whereby the laminate of resin-saturated reinforcement material is laid along each side of a balsa wood or foam core. The benefits are improved heat and sound insulation and improved rigidity, so that less internal support is required for the flat panels in the hull. Sandwich construction is generally used only for the top-

sides, deck, and superstructure of fast craft. Solid laminate tends to be used for the bottom sections of the boat, which are subject to high impact loading. Internal stiffening of these bottom panels is usually achieved by means of longitudinal stringers and transverse frames, which are created using foam cores over which the laminate is laid to create a girder-like structure. For very high-performance craft, the transverse frames will often be in the form of ring bulkheads in which a gap is left in the center for access.

A major advantage of using composites for fast-boat construction is the ability to mold the structure into complex shapes. This allows the designer to create the best hull shapes for the job and to incorporate com-

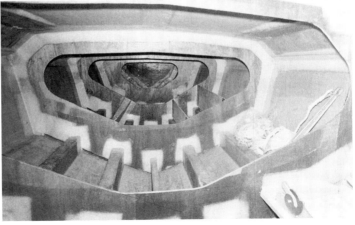

Deep ring plywood frames supporting the composite longitudinal stringers and hull laminate in a race boat hull.

plex curves. The only limiting factor for the designer is whether the final hull shape can be removed from the mold.

Aluminum

Aluminum is available in sheet form or as extrusions that have a defined cross section. Being metal, aluminum can only be shaped economically in certain ways, generally as a single (as opposed to compound) curve. It is possible to form complex shapes in aluminum, but it is expensive. When used for hull structures, the hull shape is usually developed so that the aluminum only has to be bent in one direction. For most fast-boat hull forms this is not a particular problem except, perhaps, in the case of cathedral hulls, where the use of aluminum would limit the creation of some of the complex shapes that are introduced into these hulls.

In aluminum boat construction the hull stiffening should always be by means of longitudinal stringers that support the hull plating, with these stringers in turn supported with transverse bulkheads or frames. The constant battering that a fast-boat hull undergoes at sea will eventually bend the hull plating between the support framing. With the plating supported by stringers, this minor buckling or

The complex structure in aluminum for a RIB hull. Shown are transverse frames that support longitudinal stringers that in turn will support the hull plating.

corrugation will be in a longitudinal (fore-and-aft) direction and should not affect the boat's performance.

The use of aluminum creates a hull that will almost certainly be heavier than a matching hull made from composites, but it has the benefit of being readily repairable in the field. Composites require controlled conditions for repair work, as well as repair materials not readily available in the field.

RIB Construction

The rigid section of the hull of a rigid inflatable boat (RIB) is constructed in a similar way to that of any fast boat, and the selection of materials is based on the

same criteria. The differences come in the requirements for tube attachment and in the materials used for the inflatable tubes (see chapter 2, "The RIB Concept"). An increasing range of materials is available for tube construction. Inflatable tubes are constructed of a woven fabric base, usually polyester, with Kevlar added for a combination of high strength and light weight as needed. The proofing material that covers the fabric base can be neoprene, hypalon, or polyvinyl chloride (PVC). Proofing materials are available in a variety of compositions and can be designed to meet specific boating requirements.

2

The RIB Concept

Rigid inflatable boats (RIBs) are becoming an important part of the fast-boat scene—particularly in Europe, with an increasing presence in the United States. While they have many of the characteristics of other fast boats, they also have features that make them stand apart, notably the variable geometry of the inflatable tube—that is, its ability to change shape under wave impact. RIB design has come a long way since the early days, and one of the major developments has been the increase in size of these boats. With greater size, their capabilities have increased. For example, RIBs are used as all-weather lifeboats by some organizations; the largest of these lifeboats so far is a massive 65-footer.

The RIB concept was first developed in the 1960s with the aim of producing something better than the pure inflatable. The

flat-bottomed inflatable was used widely in those days, even for rescue boats that were launched off beaches. The flat, fabric bottom gave a hard ride, even though the inflatable structure absorbed some of the shock. The inflatable design was not particularly seakindly and was also subject to high wear and tear. However, the flexible nature of the inflatable boat and its ability to absorb wave impacts were recognized, and the inflatable tube also made a good fender on rescue work at sea.

It was the wear and tear that led to the development of the RIB. The inflatables were being dragged across beaches where sand and gravel rapidly wore out their fabric bottoms. After several failed attempts by early RIB developers to introduce a rigid bottom, and ten prototypes later, the introduction of a deep V into the rigid section worked, and the RIB concept progressed to become a viable design for rescue boats.

But even today, structural stresses can be a problem with RIBs, particularly for high-speed craft that demand lightweight construction. These problems persist mainly because the rigid section of a RIB hull is extremely shallow compared with that of a conventional boat. There are no hull sides and deck to act as stiffeners for the hull structure, and all the strength must be built into the shallow rigid section, which is little more than the bottom section of a conventional deep-V hull. Consequently, deep girders and transverse frames have to be built inside the rigid section to give it the required longitudinal strength.

Design and Construction of RIBs

Modern RIB design still follows the basic concept developed in those early stages, with a deep-V hull connected to inflatable tubes that surround the hull. However, extensive design and development of additional details have significantly improved the concept, particularly in terms of durability. The modern RIB probably has the most seaworthy hull for its size of any boat afloat and can undertake the most arduous seagoing tasks. This results from the combination of the deep-V hull, the variable-geometry inflatable tube, and the novel

seating—known as saddle seating—that was introduced with the first RIBs.

The seating is particularly significant because, for the first time, it has been fully integrated into a boat design. The seating was designed for crew security, enabling crews to drive RIBs in a confident, agile manner that was well in advance of any other boats at the time—allowing driver and boat to "perform as one." We will look at this feature later in the chapter.

While the conventional RIB with its deep-V hull meets most requirements for leisure, commercial, and military users, there have been catamaran, landing craft, and a host of alternative RIB designs, most of them developed to meet specific customer requirements. These designs include the introduction of steps into the deep-V hull, alternative methods of attaching the tube to the rigid hull, and the construction of the tube itself. The way in which the hull interfaces with the tube has also seen several different approaches. On some RIBs the tube functions simply as an inflatable fender, while on others it is a fully integrated part of the boat.

Over the past decade, a new generation of RIBs has been developed with fully enclosed pilothouses or open pilot shelters that protect crew members from the elements, enabling them to undertake longer sea passages. In the leisure market, full-cabin RIBs have been developed with comfortable accommodations, and this concept

RIBs, with inflatable tubes offering hull protection, can explore coves that other boats cannot. (Courtesy Ocean Dynamics)

has also expanded into the military market to improve the crew facilities and allow longer patrols. Although the space taken up by the tube tends to restrict internal space, these cabin RIBs now extend up to 60 feet long, demonstrating just how far the RIB concept has advanced. With the wide variety of RIB styles, the designer has an even greater choice of alternatives than those available for ordinary fast boats.

How the Inflatable Tube Affects Performance

In order to drive a RIB capably, it is important to understand the function of the inflatable tube and how it affects performance. The inflatable tube plays a big role in three aspects of performance: stability, variable geometry, and fendering.

Stability

The inflatable tube extends the beam of the boat outward so that when the boat is at rest it produces a much more stable platform in comparison with a regular deep-V hull of the same dimensions. In most RIB designs, the tube is set either at or just above the waterline when the craft is at rest, so any heeling of the hull immediately brings the huge reserve buoyancy of the tube into play. This not only improves the boat's stability as soon as the tube is immersed, but it also introduces a considerable amount of reserve buoyancy if the boat should get flooded, a unique safety feature of the RIB.

At high speed, when the hull is lifted in the water as the boat comes onto the plane, the inflatable tube is clear of the water and does not add any resistance to the forward motion. Even when on the plane, the stability factor of the inflatable tube is still important because it can prevent the boat from heeling over too far when operating in waves or turning, thus promoting a more level ride.

The heavy-duty tubes fitted to RIBs used for patrol duty can add considerable weight to the boat. And because these tubes are mounted at the sides of the boat, their weight at the outer sides of the boat can reduce stability. The inertia of these tubes tends to exaggerate the movement of the boat, although it is generally balanced by the stabilizing effect of the tubes as they touch the water surface.

Tube Pressure

When you see a RIB exhibited in a boat show, the tube will look smooth and polished, without any wrinkles in the tube

A modern diesel-powered cruising RIB—this one a Revenger 34—showing the generous open space on board.

fabric. To get the tube to look like this it has to be pumped up very hard, often up to about 4 psi (pounds per square inch). At sea, however, tube pressure needs to be around 2 psi or less, or the hard tube will cause the boat to bounce rather than absorbing shock.

High pressure will make the tube behave rather like a tennis ball: it will bounce off the waves rather than absorbing the shock of impact. Instead of helping to stabilize the boat, excessively high pressure can exacerbate the motion of the boat as the tube responds to wave impact with a reflex bouncing action. In most cases, this bouncing will give the crew an uncomfortable ride. Overinflated tubes also make it hard to control the boat when coming up to a jetty or another craft because the RIB will bounce away instead of settling alongside.

Additionally, high tube pressure can cause the moving boat to bounce from side to side, bouncing first on one tube and then the other. In one instance, the driver of a racing RIB that was bouncing on hard, overinflated tubes tried to correct the situation by turning the wheel from side to side. But he only made the situation worse as the rudder movements tilted the hull, and eventually the boat bounced so hard that it capsized.

For maximum boat performance, you need to keep a watchful eye on tube pressure. Pressure in the tubes will vary depending on temperature. Tube pressure as a boat sits at rest on a hot, sunny day could easily rise to nearly double its normal pressure. Once the boat is under way, the pressure will decrease with the cooling effect of the seawater. It's easy to tell by feel whether the pressure is correct. If you hit the tube with your fist and you do not feel any bounce, it is probably close enough; it is better to have it too low than too high. If the pressure drops to around the 1 psi mark, the tube will start to lose shape, which will be clearly visible.

Variable Geometry

A unique feature of RIB design is that the shape of the inflatable tube, and thus the shape of the hull, changes under wave impact. If the bow buries into a wave, the inflatable tube will absorb some of the shock, changing its shape to match that of the wave and thus promoting a smoother ride. The same benefit can be found in beam seas or any other situation where the tubes hit the waves.

This benefit of the tubes is only realized if tube pressures are relatively low. Otherwise the tube will bounce instead of bend and, rather than absorbing the shocks, the tube will introduce sharp motions into the hull movement, which can make the ride harsh and uncomfortable.

It is not only the way the tube can mold to the shape of the wave that counts, but also the way the tube can move on its attachment to the rigid section of the hull. A RIB can be designed to permit the tube to roll over partially into the boat, giving a greater range of variable geometry. But the method of tube attachment has a considerable bearing on this variable geometry. RIBs give designers the ability to produce a boat that can change its shape automatically—as long as the various RIB features are correctly engineered. The benefit can be seen in a RIB's impressive ride in a seaway.

Fendering

The merits of surrounding the boat with inflatable tubes for fendering are self-evident and can be of particular benefit for rescue work or for a boat that has to go alongside another at sea. This explains why RIBs are widely used as yacht tenders. The fendering provided by the inflatable tube is also useful in harbor, and it avoids having to mess about with portable fenders.

This fendering feature is only viable if the tube does not encounter any sharp edges when going alongside a dock or other boat—edges that could puncture the tube. Most RIB tubes have doubling strips attached in vulnerable areas to reduce the risk of puncture. If punctured, however, the RIB can still operate because the tube is divided into sections, and usually only one section is punctured at a time.

This RIB feature of built-in fendering can make RIB drivers lazy, and you will often see them being overly casual about how they come alongside because the risk of damage is minimal. The inflatable tube will only function as a viable fender if tube pressure is relatively low; otherwise the boat will bounce off the jetty or adjacent boat, making it difficult to position itself alongside.

Alternative Tube Designs

A number of RIB designs use closed-cell foam within an outer casing as an alternative to inflatable tubes. This concept is used mainly on commercial RIBs operating in arduous conditions where abrasion and the risk of puncturing an inflatable tube is high. The foam collar is usually sheathed in polyurethane, which is highly abrasion resistant. Even if this outer casing is damaged, the foam still retains its shape, buoyancy, and fendering capabilities.

The foam-collar concept is moving into leisure RIB designs to eliminate the risk of puncturing and keep maintenance requirements low. However, many of the beneficial inflatable-tube features are lost with a foam-filled tube. These relatively rigid tubes deform only slightly upon wave impact, and as a result the variable-geometry aspect is lost; the ride will be harsh. A foam-tubed RIB performs more like a conventional boat than a RIB, with a hull shape something akin to a cathedral hull.

Hybrid tubes have been developed in an attempt to incorporate the benefits of both the inflatable and foam-collar tubes. In one concept the inflatable tube is retained around the bow, where it offers the benefits of variable geometry and shock absorption. This inflatable section then merges into foam tubing along the sides of the boat, where the fendering requirement is highest. This hybrid approach works reasonably well and increases reliability and ruggedness, but it loses some of the benefits of a purely inflatable tube.

Another concept uses a double-skin inflatable tube, with foam introduced in the space between the two tubes and with the inner tube fully inflated. The foam may be between 1 and 2 inches thick, which makes the tube somewhat rigid, but the inflated interior still allows the tube to change shape upon impact. This double-skin tube was developed primarily for use on larger RIBs where impacts can be especially severe.

Yet another hybrid tube has a thicker foam skin and an inflatable bladder inside which, when inflated, increases the tension throughout the entire tube. A further type has an empty space inside the foam tube in an attempt to add resilience to the design. Neither of these concepts allows much change in the tube shape under wave impact, however, so some of the benefits of the inflatable tube are lost.

Another concept that can improve puncture resistance while retaining tube flexibility is a conventional tube with a bladder inside. This is like the inner tube on old cars, with the outer casing absorbing the hard wear and tear and the inner tube doing the job of retaining the air. Access to the bladder is usually by means of an airtight zip fastener in the outer tube.

Interaction Between Tube and Hull

Just as there are many versions of the monohull fast boat, RIB designs offer many methods of matching the inflatable tube to the rigid deep-V hull to produce hulls with varying characteristics.

The deep-V rigid hull can incorporate a chine and then have the tube mounted above this chine, an arrangement that will tend to keep the tube well clear of the water when the boat is running at high speed. The tube will come into play only when the hull becomes immersed while passing through waves. This layout tends to keep the tube so high that it may not touch the water when the boat is at rest, so some stability may be lost.

Situating the tube so that it is at the waterline when the boat is at rest is probably the best arrangement, because then stability is maintained when the boat is stopped. This can be a great benefit if the boat is used for diving or for other activities when it stops in the open sea. For optimum seaworthiness, the tube should be attached to the hull so that the shape of the bottom of the tube follows the line of the V of the rigid hull. The tube, in effect, creates the

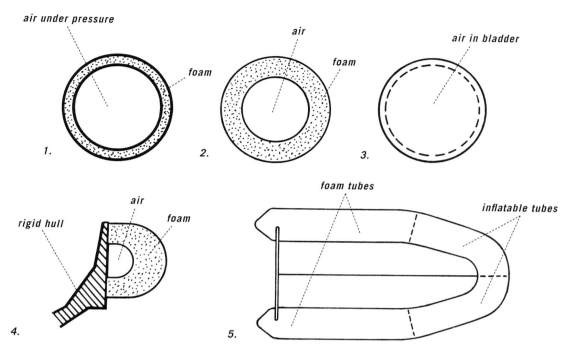

There are numerous variations in RIB tube design. (1) A double-skin tube with foam between the layers and air pressure inside. This was developed as a robust tube system for larger RIBs. (2) A tube formed from a thick outer layer of foam with a tough outside skin. The air inside is not under pressure. (3) A tube with an air-pressure bladder inside that allows the best abrasion-resistant material for the outer tube and the best air-holding material for the bladder. (4) A D-shaped foam tube that is tensioned in position by inflating an inner bladder. (5) This hybrid RIB has foam tubes along the sides where the tube is likely to encounter maximum wear, and an inflatable section around the bow to absorb wave impact.

chine. This arrangement will give a smooth flow of water away from the hull. In practice, the line is never perfect, but the inflatable tube has enough give in it to adapt to the required shape as water flows past.

In contrast, there are many RIB designs where the inflatable tube hangs down and away from the side so that an inverted V shape is created at the chine line. This makes the hull shape something like that of a cathedral hull, which will generate extra lift. This design could result in a harsher ride, however, unless the tube can roll inward to absorb the heavier shock loadings.

Tube Attachment

The interface between the inflatable tube and the hull that was originally developed

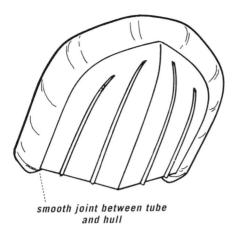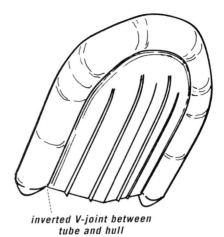

smooth joint between tube and hull

inverted V-joint between tube and hull

Optimum seaworthiness is maintained when the tube is attached to the hull so that the shape of the tube's bottom follows the line of the V of the rigid hull (left). On many RIB designs the tube edge meets the bottom in an inverted V-joint (right) that prevents smooth water flow outward, but generates more lift.

for RIBs was a narrow, curved landing above the chine of the rigid hull—a landing that matched the radius of the tube. The tube was glued to the rigid hull along this landing; with doubling strips to spread the attachment point, a permanent attachment for the tube was formed.

A further development was to widen this curved landing so that it was almost semicircular in cross section. This gave a much wider landing for the tube attachment, which helped to secure the tube toward its top as well as at the bottom, creating a more secure attachment. This secure attachment was important for RIBs that operate in extreme sea conditions.

One of the desirable features of the orig-

inal narrow, curved landing attachment was that it enabled the tube to absorb wave impact by rolling inboard, which in turn improved shock absorption when driving the boat hard and added to seaworthiness. The later development of the wider landing reduced this shock-absorbing feature, although the tube itself could still act as a shock absorber if it was at the proper pressure.

An alternative method of attaching the tube to the boat is to build a low bulwark around the open cockpit of the RIB and attach the tube to the outside. With the tube attached at the top and the bottom of the low bulwark, this system creates, in effect, a D-shaped tube. While providing greater usable space inside the boat, this method reduces the tube's ability to deform under wave impact and tends to reduce performance in rough seas. A benefit of this attachment method, however, is the added longitudinal strength provided by the raised bulwark.

In some RIB designs, this bulwark is only fitted in the bow, where stresses can be particularly high, especially when operating at high speed in following seas. There have been incidents in which the tube has come adrift at the bow and has peeled right back over the boat when the nose of the boat has buried into a wave at high speed. Straps are sometimes fitted over the tube to reduce the chance of this happening, and to supplement gluing or other methods of attachment in other areas of the boat.

With tubes that are glued to the rigid

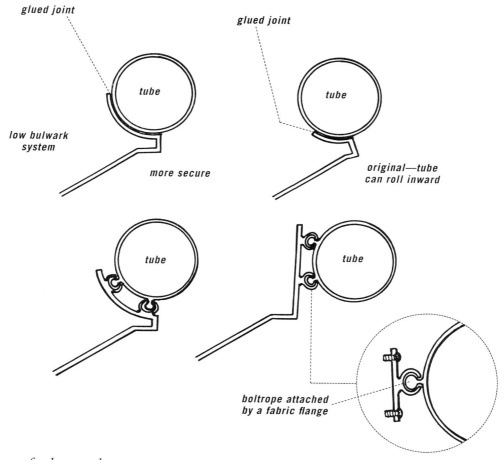

A range of tube attachment systems.

section of the hull, all repair work must be done with the tubes attached to the boat. This can make it difficult or even impossible to perform repairs in the field. While it is possible to remove a tube that is glued in place by gently peeling it away with the help of a hot-air blower, removing and replacing a glued tube is a specialist's job.

The alternative is to attach the tube so that it can be more easily removed, and there are two methods of doing this. One is to use flanges on the tube that can be bolted onto the rigid section of the hull. This provides a strong connection between tube and hull, but it can require a considerable amount of work when the tube has to be replaced, because of the large number of bolts needed for secure attachment.

The other method is to use a boltrope system, which is similar to the attachment of a sail to the mast of a sailboat. Two boltrope tracks are permanently bolted to the rigid section of the hull; the boltropes, affixed to the tube, are then passed through the tracks for a secure attachment. The security of the attachment is enhanced by inflating the tube. For removal, the tube is deflated and then it can be simply slid out of the boltrope channels, usually from the bow.

Bow Tubes

Especially strong tube attachments are required at the bow of a RIB if the tube is of full diameter. Another approach is to reduce the stresses at the bow by tapering the side tubes as they run forward, so that at the bow their diameter becomes half that of the main tubes. The smaller diameter reduces the impact of hitting waves, producing a finer, or sharper, entry into the water. This fine bow tube can significantly improve the performance of high-speed RIBs, where stresses around the bow can be particularly high; the smaller bow tube acts in similar fashion to the fine entry found on regular powerboats. Plus, these smaller tubes give the boat a much sleeker appearance.

In complete contrast, some RIB designs have a squared-off tube at the bow. These designs offer more space inside the boat and avoid the difficult construction of a pointed bow tube. They can be poor performers, however. The squared-off bow presents an abrupt resistance to waves if it becomes immersed, and at high speed this will likely occur in surf or in following seas. While such a tube generates a huge amount of buoyancy at the bow to help it lift to a wave, the resistance of the flat shape coming into contact with a wave can be enough to bring the boat to a stop. This can adversely affect the handling, especially when operating in a following sea, where the loss of speed could cause the boat to broach.

Water Drainage

With open RIBs, there is always a considerable risk of water running over the tubes and into the cockpit, particularly when operat-

A 30-foot RIB at speed. This RIB with its tapering tube and surface drive is typical of modern high-speed RIB designs.

ing in rough seas or launching off a beach. A big bonus of early RIB designs was the ability to position the deck high enough to make the cockpit self-draining. This feature, which allows water to drain straight out through the transom, has been used on most small- and medium-size RIBs ever since. To achieve self-draining, simple drainage holes may be cut in the transom, but a preferred design is to have *elephant trunks*—fabric tubes that fit over the transom drain holes. These can be lifted up to prevent water from coming back into the cockpit when drainage

is not required, such as when the boat is at a mooring or operating at slow speeds.

Outboard motors are usually mounted on a low or cutaway transom, with a second, higher inboard transom that is high enough to prevent water from coming in over the stern. Alternatively, outboards can be mounted on a transom extension, also called a Gill bracket, that positions the engine farther aft; this gives higher propulsion efficiency and increases the overall hull length as it affects performance. Gill brackets, which come in a variety of shapes and sizes, have the added benefit of creating more internal boat space.

With inboard engines, a coaming around the engine hatch needs to be raised at least up to the height of the inflatable tubes, so that water coming on board and into the cockpit does not find its way down into the engine compartment. This still leaves a requirement for the engine hatch to be sealed effectively so that water can't get in, and for air intakes to be high enough above the deck to keep water out. On many designs with inboard engines, the engine housing extends the full width of the boat from tube to tube—but this arrangement makes it harder to engineer an effective self-draining system.

With RIBs being virtually open boats that may have to operate in surf or heavy breaking wave conditions, the need for full watertight integrity above deck level is paramount. This need must be considered in all elements of the design, including stowages, machinery, and crew facilities. Many RIBs that operate in extreme conditions, such as those used for rescue and patrol duties, can continue to operate when filled with water because they are designed

A cruising RIB with good accommodation for two. With its deep-V hull, a RIB like this can cope with adverse seas.

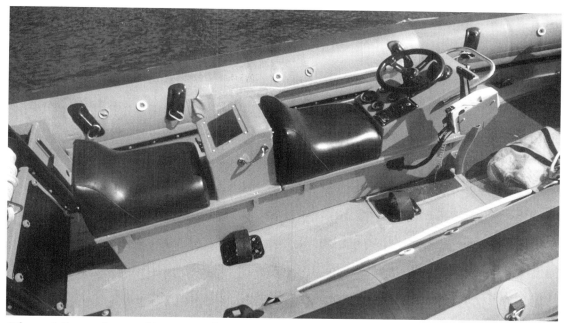

The saddle seating and low console typical of many smaller RIBs used for open sea work.

to clear the water quickly through self-draining systems.

Seating

Secure seating and handholds are vital on rigid inflatable boats if you want to enjoy the exciting ride and avoid getting tossed out. RIBs are safe and capable performers, but the ride will only be fun if you feel secure. Traveling in a small RIB is rather like riding a motorcycle, where you want to feel part of the machine.

A type of seating known as saddle seating was developed for RIBs. Because of their generally short height above waterline—low freeboard—RIBs often use this specialized seating to provide crew security. In saddle seating, the boater straddles a padded seat that faces forward and usually includes a backrest. The configuration helps secure the boater in both sideways and fore-and-aft directions.

Saddle seating uses foam padding to absorb the impacts between body and seat. The foam should be closed-cell so it won't absorb water. Dense foam is normally used because it does not bottom out under high shock loadings. A combination of dense and light foam can be an effective compromise, the light foam absorbing the initial shock, after which the dense foam takes over to prevent bottoming.

Saddle seating puts the crew relatively

The handholds and seating on this 16-foot RIB provide security for the crew.

high in the boat; this can add considerable weight high up in the boat, which will raise the center of gravity, causing a livelier ride. But for safety the seats need to be high enough so that boaters can use their legs to brace against the movement of the boat.

Backrests with saddle seating usually incorporate a handhold for the seat behind. Because of the narrow backrest, however, many of these handholds are barely wide enough for two hands, let alone for the grip needed for good lateral support. A flexible handhold is sometimes included at the front of the seat, but this is practically useless because you cannot push against it

when required, and it will quickly chafe your knuckles.

In many leisure RIBs the seating looks attractive but may be overly casual, to the point of being dangerous. A bench seat for two located behind the control console might look stylish and allow you to enjoy the ride with your partner, but the seat cushion will be situated just about level with the top of the tube; there is nothing to prevent you from sliding straight over the side in a sharp turn. At the very least, there should be armrests at the side as a precaution, as well as strong handholds.

Other examples of how some RIB designers get carried away with appearance at the expense of security include unsecured seats in the bow of the boat and the use of the tubes as additional seating. Boat design is all about compromises and balances, and some RIB designs have gone too far in the interest of fashion. The basic boat design needs to be seaworthy, and each individual detail and modification should match this standard.

Control consoles are widely used in RIBs and offer either a standing or sitting position, or sometimes both. As with everything to do with RIBs, careful design is needed for the console to work well, and this should include removing sharp edges around the screen, providing good handholds, and positioning the wheel in front of the driver rather than centrally, as is often seen on a two-person console.

3

Fast-Boat Features

Hull design is often looked on as the key to fast-boat performance, but equally important are the features provided for the driver and crew. A crew that is seated comfortably and able to operate the controls efficiently can contribute considerably to the performance of the boat and its safety. Remember what we said about fast powerboats being a partnership? Well, think about the interface between the boat and its crew around the helm and controls. Get this relationship right and you are a long way toward having the boat operate smoothly and safely. Get it wrong and difficulties and dangers are likely. Good seating, secure footrests and handholds, and, often, protection from the elements are paramount to fast-boat performance and efficient navigation.

Seating

Seating comfort is a relative term in fast powerboats: what is really required from a seating system is the ability to secure the crew members and to isolate them as much as possible from impacts, violent movements, and high acceleration forces. Crew members need their hands to operate the controls and instruments—but if hands have to be used for holding on to the boat at the same time, using the controls effectively takes a secondary role.

Saddle seating, an innovative concept from the first rigid inflatable boats, is still largely used only in RIBs (see chapter 2, "The RIB Concept"). Suffice it to say that saddle seating—the use of which is rather like riding in the saddle of a horse—was primarily designed for small powerboats.

Its main benefit is to allow crew members to secure themselves in the boat using mainly the body and the feet. Saddle seating provides a compact, relatively light-weight installation, making it good for smaller boats. Its popularity is limited by the fact that it lacks the visual appeal of the sculptured seating found in most leisure boats.

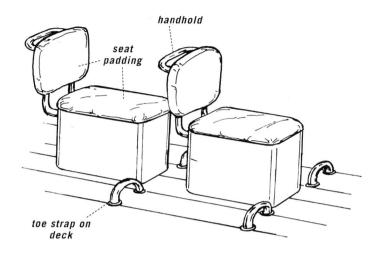

Heavy-duty bolster seats are commonly used in off-shore performance boats. These seats provide excellent

A typical saddle seating arrangement on a fast powerboat provides handholds for stability and toe straps for added stability.

lateral support because of their deep bolster padding, and they are often fitted with a bottom cushion that can be raised and lowered, offering the alternative of sitting or standing. In the seated position, the lateral support should extend up toward the shoulders; when standing, the hips should be supported.

These two-position bolsters work reasonably well, but unless they are carefully designed and positioned, the controls will not be in the right place for easy operation by the crew. When sitting in this type of seat, the full shock loading from the often violent movement of the boat has to be absorbed by the torso, whereas a saddle seat properly installed allows a degree of shock loading to be absorbed by the legs.

Special spring seating has been developed for fast-boat use, but to be effective it also needs a shock-absorbing element. Springs alone are not sufficient because the natural frequency of the springing will not always be in step with the natural movement of the boat: you could find yourself going up in the seat when you should be coming down, creating an effect that could be worse than having no spring action at all. A shock-absorbing element similar to that used on car suspensions will do the job.

Proper spring seating imposes a considerable weight penalty and so becomes viable only for larger boats. Another problem is that spring seats incorporate moving parts; with the constant action of the boat, they are subject to wear and tear, often in places that you cannot easily examine. Because of price considerations, I have seen truck seating used in fast boats, but this is rarely corrosion resistant and does not cope well with the higher shock loading found on a boat.

Any foam used in fast-boat seating is usually closed-cell so that it will not absorb water. It should also be of the non-springing type, allowing the seat to absorb shocks without creating a rebound. Springy foam is rather like having a RIB tube that is blown up too hard. Rather than absorbing the shock, the foam will cause the person in the seat to bounce. Dense foam is normally used so that it does not bottom out under high shock loadings. A combination of dense and light foam can be a good compromise, with the light foam absorbing the initial shocks and the dense foam taking over as needed to give a progressive shock absorption.

Standing Positions

You do not have to be seated in a fast powerboat; in most of the early racing boats, crews stood. But a standing position means you need at least one of your hands for holding on, leaving only one to effectively operate the controls. This can be difficult when you are trying to handle both the wheel and throttle. The wheel tends to become a handhold rather than a control, and you cannot master steering subtleties

this way. Your focus will be divided between personal comfort and the controls, and chances are that the controls will take a back seat.

Before the advent of enclosed safety capsules, the crews of offshore racing boats always adopted a standing position, believing that this was the best way to absorb the high shock loadings experienced at high speeds. Standing positions are widely used on other types of fast craft. With good lateral support from a bolster seat, standing remains viable, especially when a foam covering is used on the deck to absorb some of the impacts through the legs. Good angled footrests can help; handholds are also a requirement for optimum safety.

A standing position in a fast boat tends to raise the boat's center of gravity. The same is true of some seating systems in which both the weight of the seat and the weight of the crew can raise the center of gravity. This raised center of gravity can give the boat a livelier ride, increasing its motion and making it prone to heeling.

Footrests and Toe Straps

Secure placement for the crew in the boat requires toe straps or footrests so they can use their legs effectively for balance and shock absorption. Toe straps are often used in conjunction with saddle seating—rather like stirrups for horse riding. They allow you to help maintain balance by lifting a foot up against the toe strap as well as by pressing down against the deck. Toe straps should be located just below your body so that any attempt to take body weight on your legs acts directly upward.

Footrests, rather than toe straps, tend to be used with conventional seating. Angled footrests enable crew to brace with their feet while pushing their torsos against the backs of their seats, which can help seat them securely in the boat while leaving their hands free to operate controls or instruments. Footrests need to be strong and must be wide and long enough to receive the full foot.

If a fully standing position is used, some thick foam rubber on the deck can help with shock absorbtion and provide a nonskid surface. The foam should be closed-cell so it doesn't absorb water.

Handholds

Handholds are essential to the crew's security, and several features are required to make them effective. They need to be wide enough for both hands to be used simultaneously; if this is not possible, two handholds must be provided.

Handholds also need to be spaced widely apart so that a person can get good lateral support from them, and they need to be placed ahead of each seat so that a crew member can brace against them to prevent being thrown forward if the boat slows unexpectedly during wave impact.

Placing handholds in the right position is often difficult within the confines of a small boat; they tend to be mounted into the back of the seat in front, which gives very little scope for a wide spread. At the dashboard, handholds are usually located right on the dash, where they can be difficult to reach without bending forward and where they are rarely positioned for long-term comfort.

Handholds need to be rigid so that you

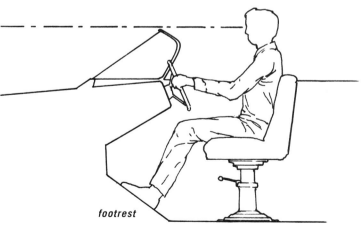

footrest

Footrests allow the driver to brace himself with his feet—here at an open steering station—leaving the hands free for the controls.

can both press and pull against them, depending on the movement of the boat. They also need to be strong because they must, at times, support the whole weight of the body.

Good handholds can be difficult to engineer and tend to be fitted as an afterthought rather than considered at the early design stage. They can be particularly important in smaller craft, where boat movements can be quicker and more intense. On larger fast boats, handholds need to be situated at strategic positions around the boat for security as crew members move around. They do not always look good on a boat that is designed for leisure, so the designer may try to ignore them altogether.

Seat Belts

Seat belts are required in cars for safety reasons but are rarely seen in fast boats. There is no apparent safety reason for using them in fast boats because the chance of collision is small—but if you go aground at high speed or if the boat stops suddenly, perhaps because it hit floating debris, a seat belt could save your life.

Seat belts are mandatory in offshore powerboat racing because if you are strapped into your seat and the boat gets into trouble, you can let the boat take the punishment and hopefully walk away from the accident. If you have experienced using a seat belt in a powerboat that is being driven hard, you will know they bring an enormous feeling of security and comfort.

To be effective, seat belts need to be fitted to seating that is designed for the job. They cannot be easily fitted to saddle seating. A seat belt

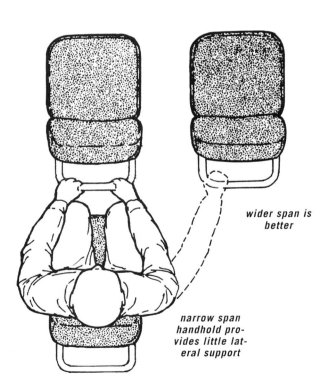

wider span is better

narrow span handhold provides little lateral support

Handholds should be widely spaced to provide good lateral support.

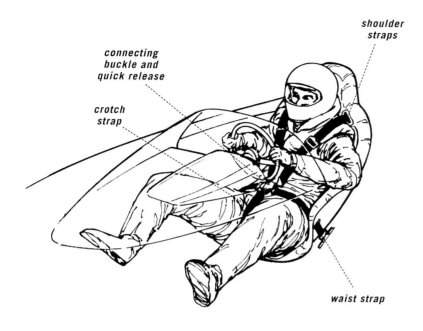

connecting
buckle and
quick release

shoulder
straps

crotch
strap

waist strap

A well-padded five-point harness holds the fast power-boater in the seat in all directions of movement and allows him to concentrate on driving.

could be fitted to a bolster seat, but this likely would eliminate the option of standing.

The belts need to be well padded because, unlike in a car, the boat goes up and down and this movement can chafe your shoulders. A five-point harness will hold you firmly in the seat against all directions of movement.

A seat belt allows you to relax to a degree, and should leave you with both hands free for operating controls. You can use the steering wheel for steering rather than partly as a handhold, and the throttles can

be used more effectively. With a seat belt, you really become part of the boat.

The arguments against seat belts include the fact that they do not allow for quick and easy exit from the seat and they restrict your movement in the boat. They take time to secure, and they require seating designed specifically for the job. They also require a dashboard with controls that can all be reached without moving from the seat. Seat belts are not yet generally accepted, but in the future we are likely to see them in wider use. From my experience, they are well worth trying if you are serious about fast boating.

Windshields (Windscreens)

A windshield positioned in front of the crew can make a great difference in comfort and safety at high speeds by deflecting the wind away. Being battered by wind and perhaps rain is not conducive to keeping the driver alert to changing circumstances. Rain or spray hitting you at high speed can be painful. If the boat has no windshield, at the very least you will need goggles.

A windshield must be strong enough to withstand the impact of any solid water that comes down the deck and hits it. If you have had a windscreen disintegrate in front of you, you will know what I mean. The material used needs to be high strength: Lexan is one of the best. Race boat canopies are often made of Lexan, adapted from fighter aircraft canopies.

Windshields add weight in a high position on the boat and they can also create considerable wind resistance that could affect high-speed performance. A windshield with a V-shape (rather than flat or rounded) sheds water better and offers less wind resistance.

Windshields tend to be reflective, a particular problem at night when lights from the dash can reflect on the glass and reduce visibility. It can also be a problem in daylight when the sun shines on areas below the windshield. If possible, areas around the dash and below the windshield should be painted a matte black to reduce reflection. Tinted windshields should be avoided, as the darker glass tends to be more reflective.

Rather than using a windshield that the driver looks through, some fast boats incorporate a wind deflector, in which the deck is simply curved up as it approaches the cockpit. The deflector allows the driver to look over the top, avoiding the visual distortion that can sometimes be caused by a windshield.

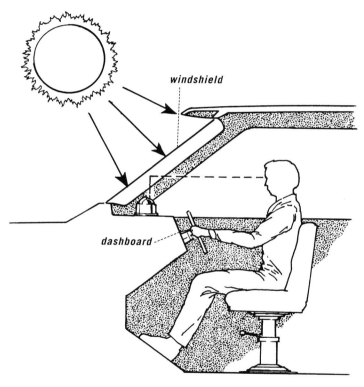

The sun shining on the windshield can cause reflections from the dash. The dotted line shows the area that the helmsman sees reflected on the windshield, reducing the view ahead. At night, lights from the dash can also be reflected on the windshield. A forward-sloping windshield can solve the problem for an enclosed cockpit but is infeasible for an open helm station.

A well-designed wind deflector creates a current of air rising over the heads of the crew and deflects most of the wind and water coming on board. Where there is a choice of standing or sitting, as is the case on most larger fast boats, you may be able to look through a windshield when sitting and over it when standing. With this arrangement, you can choose the way to operate depending on sea and weather conditions.

Helm Station

Designing the helm station for safety and comfort can make a huge difference to the way you drive a boat. As we have said, the wheel and throttles are for driving the boat, not for use as handholds. The controls need to be carefully located in relation to the seating or bolsters for proper boat control. An adjustable steering wheel is a good idea because it allows the angle to be varied in relation to the driver; life at the wheel can be a lot more comfortable if you have the option of sitting or standing at the helm.

Many fast boats use a vertical wheel, which works reasonably well if you are standing up, but it is not the best solution. Even an angle like that of the steering wheel in a car may not be the best for boat use. A flatter angle, like that seen in larger trucks, can be most comfortable to use. A lot will depend on the effort required to turn the wheel: if it turns easily, then the wheel can be set at an angle that feels most suitable for comfort; but if the steering is heavier, the flatter angle is best because you can pull the wheel toward you with either hand rather than trying to push it up or down.

Fast boats come with an array of dials, switches, and displays in front of the driver. These are often laid out to impress rather than to impart practical information, and many could be dispensed with. Often there is too much information for the driver to take in at any given moment.

Most switches can be removed from the dashboard to a separate electrical panel, leaving just the windshield wiper switches, which are the only ones that you will need immediate access to. The autopilot control box will need to be mounted close to the helm for easy use, and you will want the VHF radio close by.

Depending on the size of your fast boat, you may be left with the radar and the electronic chart as the main display screens, and these might be offset so that a person alongside the driver could operate them as well. These displays need to be close enough so that the controls to adjust the picture can be reached easily, but far enough away for easy viewing. This can be a difficult balance to find, and the possibility of a control panel separated from the radar or display might be worth considering. Some form of joystick control in the arm of the helm seat is one option here.

Mounting displays where you can actually see them is also important. Reflections from the screens and dials can make them impossible to read in sunlight. This can be a severe problem on open boats, but you will find the same problem in an enclosed helm with the light coming through the windshield. The easy solution is to recess the displays so that there is an eyebrow above them that creates a shadow, and to mount them close to vertical. You also need to consider the reverse reflections that can occur at night, when the display lighting is reflected onto a windshield.

The area around the helm should be finished in a matte black where practical, to reduce reflections on the windscreen and also to make it more comfortable on the eyes in bright sunlight. With most boats you will have to take what you are offered by the boatbuilder, but with a little thought and modification, the helm can be made a lot more user-friendly.

A careful design of the dashboard and wheelhouse is needed to avoid reflections on the instruments and enable easy access to controls.

Antennas

The radar antenna is usually mounted on the arch mast that is a feature of most fast-boat designs. This takes it up clear of the deck area and gives it the best possible view around the horizon. However, the low arch masts fitted to some boats in the interests of sleek styling can cause a problem. Anything that gets in the way of the radar beam—and this includes the crew—will blank out the picture in that direction. People standing on the flybridge can block the radar if its antenna is too low. A low radar may also be blocked by the bow of the boat as the boat picks up speed and the bow rises, cutting off the vital forward section of the radar picture.

Other antenna are usually mounted on the arch mast as well. It pays to keep the VHF radio antenna and the radar antenna as far away as possible from the GPS antenna. Transmission signals from the radar and VHF antennas can disturb the sensitive reception required for good GPS operation.

4

Engines and Propulsion

The engine(s) and propulsion system are the lifeblood of a fast boat. This is what makes the boat work, creating both the speed and the control. If you are going to be a better fast-boat driver, you need to understand how engines and propulsion systems work and what they do. It's not just engine basics that need to be understood—most people know these from driving a car—but also the advanced aspects critical to fast-boat performance.

The type of engine(s) and propulsion system fitted to a boat have a significant effect on the way the boat has to be driven. They affect the response to the throttles and the way the boat performs on the water. Understanding the engines, the systems that support them, and the propulsion method that transmits power to the water will enable you to detect problems and work on them. This understanding will also enable you to drive a fast boat by feel. It's rather like riding a horse: understand the animal and its character and you will be able to make it go where you want it to go and do what you want it to do.

Engines

In this section we will look at the basic types of engines that power fast boats and at the cooling, fuel, and electrical systems that support them.

Engine Types

Four basic types of engines are used in fast boats: the inboard gas engine, the diesel engine, the gas turbine, and the outboard gas engine.

Engine Comparison Chart for Fast Boats

TYPE	WEIGHT	POWER	FUEL CONSUMPTION	RESPONSE
INBOARD GAS	LOW	GOOD	MOD/HIGH	GOOD
INBOARD DIESEL	MOD/HEAVY	MODERATE	LOW	MODERATE
OUTBOARD	LOW	GOOD	HIGH	GOOD
GAS TURBINE	LOW	GOOD	HIGH	POOR
ELECTRONIC ENGINES	MODERATE	GOOD	MODERATE	MODERATE

Inboard Gas Engines

Inboard gasoline engines for fast boats are mainly derived from automobile engines. The manufacturers take a powerful car engine, usually a straight-6 or a V-6 or V-8, and add the seawater pumps and the special exhausts and electrical components required for marine use. The main difference between car and marine use lies in the cooling system: marine engines utilize a circulating-seawater cooling system rather than the radiator found in cars. Seawater sent through this system is ejected through the exhaust, making the exhaust very different from that on a car. Another difference is seen in the starter and the alternator, both of which are spark-free and sealed to resist corrosion.

Some of the more powerful engines used in fast boats have fuel injection in place of carburetors and may have superchargers or turbochargers to increase power. A lot of high-performance tweaking goes on at the top end of the power range to produce engines for the fastest boats. This is a very specialized sector of the market for inboard gas engines. Lower down the performance scale, inboard gas engines used in smaller boats are usually combined with a stern-drive propulsion system.

When you open the throttle on a fast boat with an inboard gas engine, the response is almost immediate, which is what you want when operating a boat in waves. But the response will depend to a degree on the way in which the engine is tuned. A good marine gas engine combines strong low-speed torque with high top-end power. The torque, which is the turning force or power that the engine develops at lower speeds, is required to get the boat onto a plane, while the top-end power is needed for high-speed performance. Good throttle response should continue throughout the boat's speed range, but of course near the top end the response will start to slow as the engine reaches its peak output.

Another feature of the inboard gas engine is its relatively light weight compared with a diesel engine. Equally important is the low weight of individual engine components. This low component weight helps to give the engine good acceleration because all the working parts can move quickly, providing a fast response to throttle opening. Again, in a modern gas engine the response is nearly immediate, particularly when the engine is fitted to a lightweight boat.

The downside of gasoline engines is the flammability of the fuel and the high level of maintenance needed to ensure reliability. Fuel systems are so well-engineered these days that there should be no problem—provided you follow the safety rules. Gas engines rely on the boat's electrical system to keep running—but with the increasing use of electronic engine controls on diesels, this has become true of most marine engines.

Diesel Engines

Most of the modern diesel engines that are used in fast boats are also derived from automobile or truck units. Because diesels use compression ignition and internal pressures are much higher than in a gas engine, stresses on the engine are also higher. Therefore the internal components need to be stronger, which in turn increases the weight of the moving components.

With heavier components, there is more inertia to overcome and this can slow the throttle response as the engine accelerates. In a fast boat fitted with diesel engines, do not expect the same throttle response you would find in a gas engine boat. However, as diesels improve in design, the gap is narrowing; modern diesels operate at high rpm (revolutions per minute), which allows for a smaller engine for a given power output and thus a smaller component weight.

There is a weight penalty with diesel engines, which weigh more than comparable gas engines, but there is some compensation in the better fuel efficiency of the diesels, which means you can reduce the amount of fuel carried for the same range.

Most modern marine diesels use electronic injectors, fuel pumps, and governors to improve engine and fuel-burning efficiency. This helps to increase engine power output, cut fuel consumption, and reduce exhaust emissions. But these electronic components do make the engine reliant on the electrical system to keep running.

To further increase the efficiency of diesel engines in fast boats, they are generally fitted with turbochargers and intercooling systems. Turbochargers are small turbines that are incorporated into the air intake system and are powered by the hot exhaust gases leaving the engine. These turbines or blowers force the intake air into the cylinders under pressure to increase engine efficiency.

With intercooling, the intake air passes through a heat exchanger that is fed with cold water from the engine seawater intake. This means that the air going into the cylinders is cooler and thus denser, which in turn means that more can be fed into the cylinders. Fuel under high pressure is in-

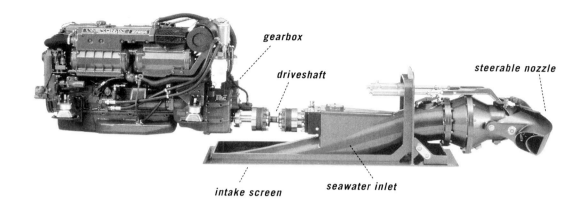

A propulsion system comprising a diesel engine coupled to a water jet via a gearbox and short shaft.

jected into this air in the cylinder, which then ignites when compressed by the ascending piston.

One additional factor should be noted about electronic controls on diesels. When engine designers get their hands on this level of control over the parameters that affect engine operation, they want to exploit its capabilities to the fullest, both to enhance engine efficiency and to protect their beloved engines. Quick acceleration is not conducive to long engine life, so engineers strive for an acceleration that is slow and gentle to help reduce stress on the engine. To achieve this, there is a general tendency to build in an electronic time lag between the opening of the throttle and the engine response.

This is fine on larger diesels, where response time is relatively slow anyway. But for smaller, high-speed engines, this artificial time lag reduces the ability of the boat to accelerate: it can change it from an exciting boat to drive into a sluggish, unresponsive machine. Fast boats with such electronic diesel engines can achieve good speeds, but they exhibit disappointing throttle response that can also degrade handling in rough seas.

Gas Turbines

Despite their promise of high power and low weight, gas turbines are still rare in fast boats. This is mainly because of the high cost of these units and the lack of people to service them. The steep cost is mainly a product of the high-quality components needed to withstand the engine's extreme temperatures and the close engineering tolerances required to make the turbine efficient. The gas turbines that have been installed in fast boats are often secondhand helicopter units, purchased at prices lower than new.

Turbines have the drawback of slower acceleration and throttle response compared with diesel engines and standard gas engines. Turbines develop tremendous torque, so there is no problem getting a turbine boat onto the plane—but fuel consumption is higher than that of a diesel and they are only really fuel efficient when operating at full power. Turbines are also sensitive to the ambient air temperature: power can fall off considerably in warm climates.

Gas turbines have two main components: the compressor and the power turbine. The compressor draws air into the engine, compresses it, and feeds it into the ignition chamber. Fuel is injected into the ignition chamber, and when this burns, the hot gases expand and are fed into the power turbine to generate the power.

Light weight is a big attraction of the gas turbine—but in considering the weight, you must take into account the complete installation. This includes the gearbox, air filters, specialized exhausts, and other components which can add up to a lot of weight.

Outboard Gas Engines

Outboard motors are a complete engine and propulsion package; as such, there is compatibility between all components including the propeller(s), and they are fully tested as a unit. Outboard engines tend to look quite fragile, but they produce a lot of power from a relatively compact, lightweight package. Even though they incorporate advanced engineering with finely engineered components, their reliability tends to be excellent provided they are maintained well.

Not so many years ago all outboards were two-stroke (also known as two-cycle) engines, unique designs developed exclusively for marine use. Four-stroke out-

One of the gas turbines in a twin-engine installation in a performance catamaran.

boards are now much more widely used than before, many of them developed from motorcycle engines. The two-stroke engines are smaller and lighter than comparable four-stroke models, but they tend to be fuel hungry—thus more fuel has to be carried for a given range, offsetting gains from the lighter engine. Four-stroke outboards are smoother running, particularly at idle. They are available in sizes to match those of two-stroke outboards, making them a viable alternative to power fast boats.

Advances in technology have made two-stroke engines more fuel efficient, but this has only been achieved at the cost of increased engine complexity. The latest two-stroke outboards feature fuel injection and electronic control systems. The multicylinder units used for high performance have almost watchlike components, but the full integration of the engines and their housings ensures good reliability. Rather than requiring the mixing within the fuel tank of lubricating oil and gasoline, many modern two-stroke outboards have a separate oil tank; the oil is then mixed with the gas as it flows into the engine.

The throttle response of outboards is excellent, largely because of the small size of their internal components. In driving an outboard-powered fast boat, you will become aware that engine weight is located relatively high. This placement raises the boat's center of gravity and can make the movement of the boat in a seaway more lively than would be the case with an inboard engine—movement that could complicate the handling of the craft.

Because an outboard simply bolts to the boat's transom, it can easily be removed for maintenance or replacement. On some outboard boats, the engine is mounted on a bracket some two or three feet behind the transom. This effectively extends the waterline length of the boat and allows the outboard propeller to operate in cleaner water, thus improving efficiency. In this type of installation, however, the engine is likely to be higher and therefore the boat's center of gravity will be higher too.

In a boat that is using a single powerful outboard, there can be a considerable pull to one side while steering. Trim fins built into the engine leg can counteract this pull by creating a steering force that counteracts the propeller torque.

Outboards are the engine of choice on many small powerboats because of their simple installation and integrated design. And because the engine is on the stern, there's typically more usable space within the boat.

Engine Throttle Response

The throttle is the main control on the boat, and what happens after you open or close the throttle depends a great deal on the responsiveness of the engine. Because the propulsion system and the weight of the boat also affect response to the throttle, these have to be considered when talking about engine responsiveness to throttle commands.

A quick throttle response is important when you are operating a fast boat in waves. This throttle response is largely related to the weight of the engine. Lighter-weight gas inboard and outboard engines on lightweight boats have an almost instant response to throttle commands—mainly because the internal moving parts are light weight and can thus accelerate more quickly.

You will find that throttle response is also related to the speed (in rpm) at which the engine is operating. Toward the top end of the engine speed range, the power curve of the engine usually levels off and there is not a lot of power left for a quick response. You may find that with a highly tuned gas engine, most of the power comes in near the top of the range; this is where it might get the best throttle response. However, a good marine engine will have a power curve that rises steadily throughout the engine speed range so that there is a good response all the way up to the maximum.

It pays to take a look at the power curve for your engine, because it will enable you to see any flat points in the curve where throttle response might not be what you are expecting. In general, engine designers go to great lengths to get an even power curve. You will find illustrations of these curves in the manual for your engine.

With diesel engines, the response to

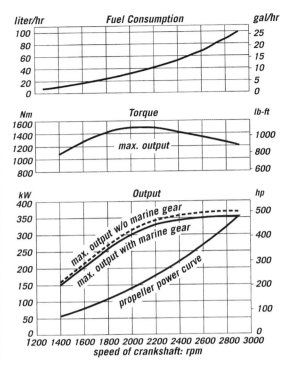

Perfomance curves for the 500 hp Yanmar engine.

throttle opening is more complicated. The internal components in a diesel are heavier than those in a gas engine, so they will be slower to respond, but with modern, high-speed diesels there should not be a great deal of discernible difference. However, when an engine is fitted with a turbocharger, as is the case with all high-speed diesels, things get more complicated. This turbocharger is powered by the exhaust gases, and its speed is governed by the speed of these gases—but the exhaust gases will only speed up as the engine speeds up. This means that there can be a noticeable delay between opening the throttle and the turbocharger responding to allow the engine to accelerate—a phenomenon called turbo lag.

Turbo lag can be accentuated at low speeds when the turbocharger is not contributing to engine performance at all because it is running too slowly. Most turbochargers begin to be effective only at engine speeds of around 1,500 rpm, and when the turbocharger kicks in, there will be a noticeable increase in engine power. Below this threshold the engine response will be slower, and this fact needs to be considered when powering the boat onto a plane and when operating in waves. Where possible, the engine should be kept at a speed at which the turbocharger is operating and is effective so that increased power will come on quickly.

Most engine manufacturers recognize this problem and work hard to ensure that there is little or no lag in engine response. They may fit twin turbochargers that come into operation progressively, or they may provide controls in the exhaust system that dictate when the turbochargers cut in. Some designs use a belt-driven supercharger at lower rpm and a turbocharger at higher speeds. When you open the throttle on a diesel boat, you will often be able to hear the whine when the turbo cuts in, and this will indicate that power levels are climbing. Also bear in mind that the engine designers may have built an artificial time lag into the electronic controls.

There are factors outside the control of engine manufacturers that have to be taken into account, and these relate mainly to the propulsion system. A small propeller will cavitate—create harmful air bubbles in the water—at low speeds and have a lot of slip that will allow the engine to accelerate before the prop can bite the water and start to absorb engine power. The engine thus reaches higher rpm before it is required to produce significant power. A large propeller will have the opposite effect, slowing things down because the engine is overloaded. But if the engine and propulsion are carefully matched, you will get the good response you want.

Heavier and more powerful diesels, such as those producing over 1,000 hp or so, have a slower response time simply because they must overcome the inertia of the engine's greater weight. For fast boats, when high power is required, it can be a better solution to have three or four smaller diesels with a quick response rather than two larger engines that are slow to accelerate. Surprisingly, you may find that these smaller engines can be cheaper to buy and operate for the same amount of power output.

With gas turbines, throttle response is slow. The power turbine, which is designed to rotate very fast, takes some time to build up speed when the throttle is opened; there is a similar lag when the throttle is closed. This means that a fast response is out of the question. You cannot drive a turbine boat and expect the quick throttle response of a gas engine or even a diesel.

Engine Support Systems

Engines have a tough time on fast boats because of the rapid motions of the boat and the heavy impact and acceleration forces associated with speed and waves. The engines themselves tend to survive, however. Engines that stop often do so because of faults in the various systems that support the engine: the cooling, fuel, and electrical systems.

It's essential to keep these systems in good order. The fast-boat environment is one of the most demanding for engine systems and you, the driver, will need to be very conscious of this. Try to imagine what the various engine components and systems are going through as the boat bounces across the waves. And it's not just the boat movement but also the highly corrosive, salt-laden atmosphere that can do damage.

Because of the vital role these systems play in keeping the engine running, it's a good idea to understand them and check them regularly. In an ideal world you would check the boat as soon as you get into port from a trip. That first beer is probably higher on your list of priorities than a boring engine and systems check. However, if you don't do it then, you may not get around to it before you go to sea again. This leads to taking unnecessary chances. Fast boats can be a lot of fun, but they also bring added responsibilities.

Cooling System

There are two types of engine cooling systems: direct cooling and indirect cooling. With direct cooling, seawater is pumped around the engine block to cool it directly, and the water is then injected into the exhaust to cool that before being ejected out with the exhaust gases. Indirect cooling systems are more complex, with the seawater passing through a heat exchanger where it cools the freshwater circulating system that does the actual engine cooling. This fresh water is contained in a closed system that reduces the possibility of engine corrosion and gives much more effective engine temperature control. In a diesel engine, the seawater will also be used in the intercooler for directly cooling the air going into the engine before the water is injected into the exhaust pipe and then goes overboard.

In either type of cooling system, the seawater poses two potential threats. First, any failure in any part of the seawater system will allow water into the boat, with the potential for flooding and sinking. Second, seawater is very corrosive, so the seawater system needs to be closely monitored for corrosion. The seawater system can be required to work under considerable pressure as water is forced into the intake when the boat moves up and down in the water at high speeds.

Every hose and fitting in the seawater

Engine Care Checklist

ON RETURN FROM SEA

Check fuel remaining and refuel if necessary
Check fuel filters for contamination and clear if necessary
Perform a visual check for fuel leaks
Perform a visual check for water leaks
Check for any signs of wear on water pipes and hoses and electrical wires
Check for any signs of metal wear (indicated by a cocoa-like rust powder)
Check bilges for water and check bilge pump operation
Check security of batteries and their connections
Check water pump for leaks and drive belt for tension
Check engine and gearbox oil levels after the engine has cooled down

BEFORE GOING TO SEA

The same as above (this works as a double check), and after start-up do the following:
Check that seawater cooling is coming out of the exhaust
Check that the battery charge is OK
Check that the engine and gearbox oil pressures are OK

system is critical to security and vital to prevent the boat from flooding. Closing the seacock on the intake can isolate any failure, but because this is likely to be underwater if flooding occurs, its position needs to be clearly identified.

One of the biggest difficulties with a failure in the seawater system is that there is unlikely to be any immediate indication that it has occurred. The engine water temperature will not rise immediately and the extra weight of water in the boat will not become apparent until the situation is quite serious. The first sign of trouble may be when the water flows over the batteries and the engine and all your other systems come to a halt.

This could mean that the bilge pump might stop working so you would be unable to get the water out, and the radio might stop working so you couldn't call for help. Failure of the seawater system also brings a serious concern involving the exhaust. Most fast boats use what is called a wet exhaust system, in which a flexible rubber hose takes the exhaust gases away from the engine and out through the transom. Such a system relies on the seawater from engine cooling being injected into the exhaust to cool the hot gases. A failure in the seawater system would stop this water injection, and without it the hot exhaust gases could melt or even set fire to the rubber exhaust hoses. Even if you have beautiful water-jacketed exhaust risers,

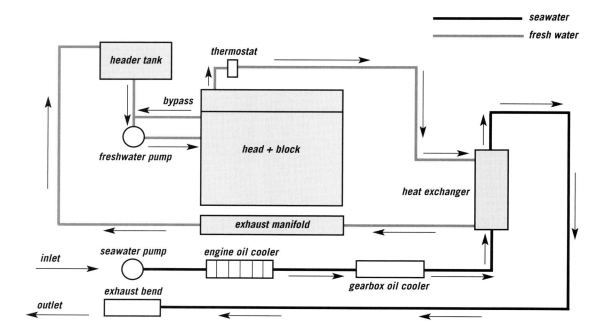

seawater

fresh water

header tank

thermostat

bypass

freshwater pump

head + block

heat exchanger

exhaust manifold

inlet

seawater pump

engine oil cooler

gearbox oil cooler

exhaust bend

outlet

The indirect cooling system of a gas or diesel engine.

as found on very high-performance boats, these could glow red-hot without the water-cooling system in operation.

This exhaust problem may be a worst-case scenario, but it's an important demonstration of the way in which the failure of one component can lead to an escalating disaster. One minute you are bouncing along quite happily at high speed, and in the next minute the boat could be sinking or on fire. The seawater system is probably the most vulnerable of the onboard systems, and any failure can have far-reaching effects. Clearly, there is no room for compromise in the quality of fast-boat systems.

Only the best will do, and they will stay that way only if you check them regularly.

Fuel System

All engines—gas, diesel, and turbine—require a clean, uninterrupted fuel supply. The fuel system is designed to provide this. On multiengine boats the fuel supply for each engine should be fully independent, but with interconnecting pipes and valves that allow either engine to be operated from either fuel tank. With a common tank and pipework this independence can be lost; on some newer vessels, multiple engines run off one large tank.

Onboard fuel is normally cleaned via two filters—one fitted to the boat and designed to remove coarse sediment and water, and a fine filter on the engine itself to ensure near-perfect cleanliness. Diesel engines, with their finely tuned injection systems, need the cleanest possible fuel and can be very susceptible to any dirt in the system. Modern outboards with their delicate components are similarly sensitive.

The filters need regular servicing. The filters will stop dirt and water, but these contaminants have to be removed from the filters on a regular basis in order for them to function properly. It is also a good idea to identify and know what the various valves in the system do, so that if there is a problem such as air, water, or dirt in the system, alternative fuel supplies can be switched in without delay.

Fast boats consume considerable quantities of fuel. You need to keep an eye on what is being used and, perhaps more importantly, how much is left and how far you can travel with it. Running out of fuel is probably the most common reason for fast boats stopping out at sea: in the excitement of fast boating it can be easy to forget to check fuel levels. Consumption varies with speed and with time under way. If the gas tank has a fuel gauge, you can see how much fuel remains. Without a gauge, you will have to calculate the fuel supply by assessing the time elapsed and the speed of the boat to determine how much fuel has been used. The fuel consumption curve for your engine, similar to the power curve discussed earlier, will illustrate the basic information you can use for this determination.

One bonus of modern electronically

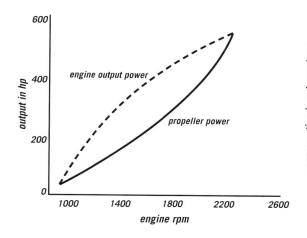
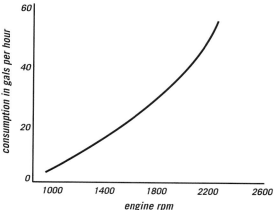

If your propeller is correctly matched to the boat and engine, the engine power curve will meet the propeller power-absorption curve at maximum engine rpm. Note how much fuel is consumed by reducing engine speed a few rpm.

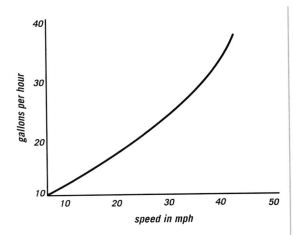

Typical fuel consumption curve as a function of boat speed.

controlled engines is that they can give a constant readout of fuel consumption; more sophisticated systems that are linked to a GPS unit can tell you how many more miles you may travel before fuel supplies are exhausted—assuming of course that you told the system how much was in the tank at the start of the trip.

Electrical System

The electrical system provides power for engine starting, engine running, electronics, and navigation. The electrical system is typically divided into segments or circuits to ensure that a failure in one section does not affect the rest of the system. Each circuit is protected by a fuse or a contact breaker that will isolate a faulty segment.

Assuming that the original installation was done to a high standard—and there is no room for compromise here—there are two main problems that can affect the working of the electrical system on a fast boat: corrosion and chafing. The connections in the electrical system are the main places where corrosion is likely to occur when seawater comes into contact with their metal components. The connections can be protected with special aerosol sprays or compounds, but better yet is to have all connections in sealed units so that water cannot come into contact with any part of them.

Chafing can be caused by wires moving slightly because of the often violent movements of the boat. The heavy hull impacts that are common in fast-boat operations can put the electrical system under considerable stress. Wires and equipment need to be firmly secured to prevent their movement. Wiring tends to be hidden away behind panels and under the deck, and this can lead to an attitude of "out of sight, out of mind." Regular inspection of the electrical system should be a standard part of any fast-boat maintenance program. Even then it can be difficult to detect cracking or chafing of the insulation around electrical wiring because, as luck would have it, this usually occurs in the hidden, least accessible places, where wiring touches sharp edges of the internal structure of the boat. The only real solution is to make sure a good job of electrical installation is done in the first place.

The battery is a vital part of the electrical system and needs to be firmly secured so there is no possibility of movement, even under extreme impact. The heavy-duty cables taking power from the battery typically carry a high electrical current, and any loose connections could lead to sparks or fire. A boat can catch fire even if just one of the battery cables comes loose.

On outboard motor installations, battery cables have to be flexible to accommodate the steering and tilting movements of the engine or engines. These cables and all engine connections need careful and regular inspection.

Propulsion

The engine may be the heart of a fast boat, but the propulsion system is what actually powers it along. The engine is connected to a propulsion system that can comprise a conventional shaft and propeller or any one of a number of proprietary alternatives. The choice of propulsion systems is becoming vast as new drive systems enter the market and some boatbuilders develop their own drives to avoid the high prices of the proprietary ones.

Many proprietary systems are supplied as part of a combined engine and propulsion

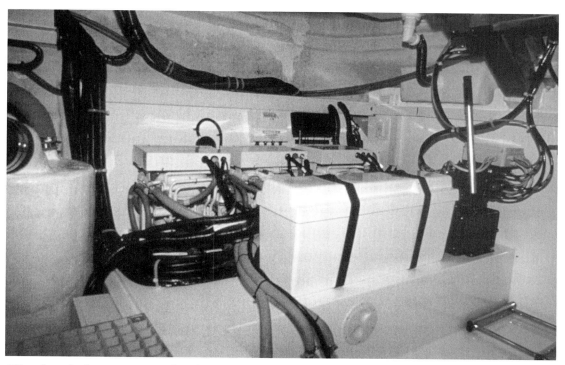

The electrical system on a fast-boat installation with everything well secured.

Electrical System Checklist

Check all visible connections for security and corrosion
Perform a visual-and-touch check of wiring for wear and cracking of the insulation, paying particular
    attention to places where wires touch hard spots on the hull or the engine
Check security of batteries and all connections
Check the adjustment of the alternator drive belt
Check external lights and fittings for watertightness

package. There is a lot to be said for this approach. Because these integrated engine and drive packages are built and tested as complete units, the reliability is typically better than with separate components. The integrated units avoid the problems that can come from trying to match differently manufactured parts.

These packages also incorporate the steering, either by directing the propeller thrust through an articulated drive, such as with a stern-drive unit, or by means of a separate rudder. Everything needed for the control of the boat is thus contained in one package. These packages are common to outboard and stern-drive systems but tend to be capable of handling only a limited power output: outboards up to 300 hp, stern-drive diesel engines up to 350 hp, and stern-drive gas engines topping out at 600 hp or more in some specialized applications. Additional packaged systems will be coming onto the market that can handle higher power outputs, particularly with diesel engines.

Propulsion systems can be categorized into several principal types: outboards; stern drives; conventional shaft-and-pro-

peller drives; surface propulsion units; and water jets. We will look at each of these in the following sections. Since outboard and stern-drive propulsion systems have a lot in common, they will be discussed together.

Outboards and Stern Drives

Outboards and stern drives are the two most popular types of combined propulsion packages. Outboard propulsion is simply a component of an independent outboard motor; stern-drive propulsion is powered by either an inboard gas or inboard diesel engine. With both outboards and stern drives, the lower unit that includes the propeller turns to alter boat direction. Both outboards and stern drives alter the direction of the drive shaft through 90 degrees in a hub in front of the propeller.

With outboards, the drive shaft is taken directly from the vertical engine crankshaft and then redirected through a 90-degree gearing to the horizontal propeller shaft at the bottom of the lower unit. Because the entire outboard engine turns to direct the propeller thrust for steering, there is no need for a universal joint in the drive train. This arrangement helps to simplify the system; everything is contained in the one package except the battery and the fuel tank. However, the need to make the transmission components as compact and light as possible means that, relatively speaking, outboards are delicate units. Although they may operate under high stress, however, the reliability of modern outboards is generally good.

With stern-drive propulsion, the drive shaft has to pass through two 90-degree changes of angle between the engine and the propeller shaft. To allow steering and trim movement, a universal joint is also required in the transmission; this is incorporated into the head of the stern drive, in line with the steering swivel. The gearbox, which allows forward, neutral, and astern movements, is also usually incorporated into the head of the unit. Combining all these requirements makes the stern drive a complex piece of equipment, but the concept is well proven and reliable.

Both in outboards and in stern drives, the 90-degree gearbox at the bottom end of the drive is the weak point. Here the designers have to fit the bevel gears that take the

drive through a 90-degree angle. These gears have to handle high torque loadings—the turning or twisting power applied to a shaft or gear—and also be as compact as possible so the water flow around the gearbox housing will not interfere with the smooth flow of water into the propeller. One solution to this weakness is to deliver the engine output power through two vertical shafts, each of which has its own helical gear to link to the horizontal propeller shaft.

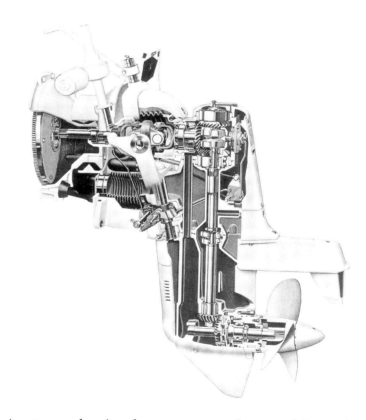

A cutaway showing the components of a stern drive as the power is taken through two right angles.

Diesel engines usually operate at lower engine speeds (lower rpm) than comparable inboard gas engines. This lower speed imposes a higher torque on shafts and gears and creates an upper limit on how much engine power a diesel stern drive can handle. The 350 hp limit for diesel-engine stern drives is adequate for many smaller powerboats. However, many such boats might be better suited to gas-engine stern drive, which can handle up to about 600 hp from the cheaper and faster-accelerating inboard gas engine.

The lower unit of an outboard or stern drive is fitted with the propeller and is the lowest part of the boat. A skeg, fitted at the bottom of the lower unit and in front of the propeller, offers some protection to the prop in the event of a grounding or running over debris. The skeg also gives a degree of steering effect at lower speeds, acting like a rudder when the propeller is stopped; but when the propeller is running, the skeg can interfere with water flow to the lower blades.

The outboard or stern-drive leg or lower

A cutaway of a performance stern drive showing how the drive is split between two vertical shafts in order to allow small gears where the drive changes to the horizontal at the bottom.

unit is designed to kick up automatically under serious impact that might damage the leg. While this feature can help to reduce possible lower-unit damage, there will still remain a high risk of propeller damage in this situation.

Both stern drives and outboards are fitted with trim and tilt functions. Trim can be operated under full power and is used mainly to optimize the propeller angle in relation to the hull for maximum running efficiency. We will talk about this later in a section on power trim (see chapter 5, "Fast-Boat Controls"). Tilt is used to lift the lower unit clear of the bottom of the boat when putting the boat on a trailer. In situations where the boat is operating in known shallow water, the outboard or stern drive can also be tilted to reduce the boat's draft and

to protect the propeller, but only minimal throttle should be used with the leg in this position because it is no longer fully supported by its mounting bracket.

With a twin-engine outboard or stern-drive installation, the two drive legs are linked by a tie bar and steering connections so that both units move together. When twin units are tilted, it is important that both are tilted at the same time in order to avoid undue stress on the tie bar or other connections. Individual trimming of the legs can be done if necessary to adjust the trim of the boat, but anything more than about 10 degrees of angle variation between the drives will strain the linkage above the trim angle when the tilt is being used. The geometry of the steering will not normally allow the legs to be moved individually.

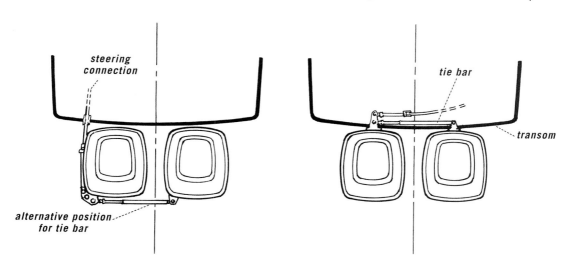

A bird's-eye view of alternate positions for a tie bar linking two outboards so they move in unison.

Whether outboard or stern drive, twin-engine units are usually angled slightly in toward each other to improve propulsion efficiency. The amount of toe-in, as this angle is called, is usually judged by the wake from the propellers. When the toe-in is correct, the two wakes will meet at a point between one and two boat lengths astern of the propellers. The toe-in can be altered by adjusting the tie bar that links the two units.

Some multiple-engine outboard installations on high-performance boats include a height adjustment, made possible by mounting the engines on a bracket that can be moved up and down under hydraulic power. This adjustment, which is in addition to trim control, permits the propellers to be moved into surface-piercing mode at high speed. This feature can improve performance at the top end, though it represents yet one more control that the driver has to cope with.

Conventional Shaft-and-Propeller Drives

Conventional shaft-and-propeller systems are still the favored option for powering fast boats—provided that speed requirements do not exceed 40 knots. Conventional pro-

A quadruple outboard installation showing the tie bar that links the steering movement of the engines together.

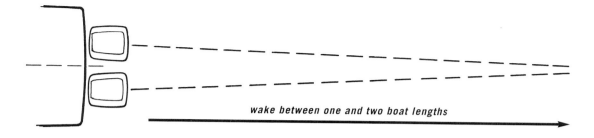

wake between one and two boat lengths

When the toe-in of multiple engines is correct, the two wakes meet at a point between one and two boat lengths astern of the propellers.

pellers can operate above this speed, but they are far from ideal for this purpose. At higher speeds, the more efficient surface propulsion systems do a better job; these will be discussed in the next section.

The main reason for the reduced efficiency of a shaft-and-propeller system as speed rises is that drag through the water from the exposed propeller shaft and its supports increases with speed. With higher speeds, water flow to the propeller becomes more turbulent and the propeller is prone to the effects of cavitation, in which air bubbles are drawn into the prop, reducing its efficiency and, in extreme cases, causing pitting or erosion of the blades. Combine these factors and you need more and more power to get a significant increase in speed.

Another factor reducing the efficiency of shaft-and-propeller systems is that the shaft has to be angled downward as it passes through the hull in order to get sufficient clearance between hull and prop. Because of this angle, thrust from the propeller is partly directed toward trying to lift the stern instead of pushing the boat forward.

It is now common on fast boats that use twin shaft-and-propeller systems for the propellers to be located in semi-tunnels that are molded into the deep V of the hull on each side. These semi-tunnels or ducts allow the propellers to be tucked up under the hull, reducing the shaft angle by half as well as offering reduced draft and better protection for the propellers. The semi-tunnels have little negative effect on the performance of the boat, and the rudders can also be tucked up under the hull behind the propellers to make a compact installation.

When a single propeller is used to drive a boat, there is a torque reaction between the propeller and the hull: when the propeller turns in one direction, it creates an equal and opposite torque against the direction of propeller turning. This reaction tends to cause the hull to heel—to tilt away from the direction in which the propeller

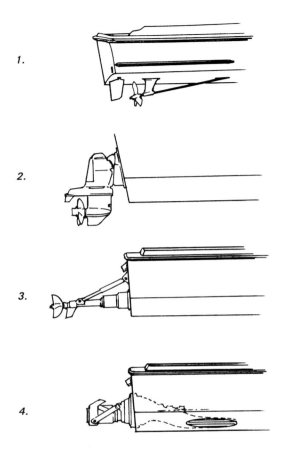

The four main types of final drive: (1) conventional inboard engine with submerged propeller, propeller shaft, and rudder; (2) an outboard or stern-drive engine where the drive unit can be turned, eliminating the need for a rudder; (3) a trimmable surface drive; and (4) a water jet.

is turning. This can be counteracted and balanced by using a trim tab to keep the hull level. On twin-screw boats where the propellers turn in opposite directions, the torque from each propeller cancels out.

Surface Propulsion

Surface propulsion also makes use of a shaft and a propeller, but the system differs markedly from conventional shaft-and-propeller design. The theory behind surface propellers is that if you have only the bottom blades of the propeller in the water doing the work, there will be no drag from the shaft and its supports, which remain above water.

A conventional fully submerged propeller has to deal with drag from the propeller shaft and its supporting brackets, which can impede the flow of water to the propeller. By having only the bottom blades in the water, the system will be more efficient. Surface propellers certainly work and produce extra top speed, though there can be a penalty to pay at lower speeds.

To give an idea of just how much more efficient a surface propulsion system can be at speeds over 30 knots, consider the following experiment involving two identical 60-foot boats with the same engines. Under the same conditions, the boat with a conventional shaft-and-propeller system produced 35 knots; the boat with surface propulsion recorded 43 knots.

In surface propulsion, the propeller op-

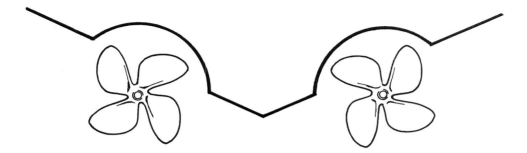

Twin propellers recessed into semi-tunnels produce less draft with conventional running gear.

erates with the surface of the water approximately at the hub of the propeller when the boat is planing, so that only the bottom blades are in the water. There is nothing to interfere with a smooth flow of water from the transom to the propeller. In calm water this enables the propeller to get a clean bite on the water and it can operate at maximum efficiency.

It took a long time to get surface propellers to work reliably and effectively. The first ones were used more than a century ago on a Mississippi steamboat; the first high-speed models were developed in the mid-1930s. When the concept was reintroduced in the 1970s, there were major problems with propeller strength and propellers tending to lose a

blade. The blades of a surface propeller are subject to very high stresses. Because the blades only come under a load when they are underwater, they will be loading and unloading perhaps a thousand times per minute as they enter and leave the water.

The early surface propulsion systems used short shafts that emerged from the

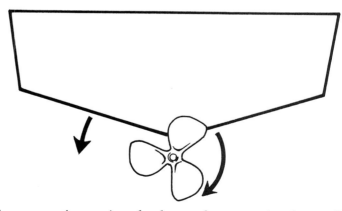

Torque reaction against the thrust of a conventional propeller will cause the hull to heel in the direction opposite of the propeller's motion.

bottom of the transom, with the propeller mounted close against the transom. This allowed only the bottom blades to be in the water flow under the boat, which was fine for high-speed work once the boat was on the plane. These installations only started to generate good thrust once the boat was planing. But getting onto a plane was difficult, and they produced very little thrust in reverse. Thus, they were not good for general boat handling. Modern surface propulsion systems extend the shaft well behind the transom to overcome these problems.

With improved metals and special propeller designs, surface propulsion now works well. Surface propellers—sometimes called cleaver propellers—have thicker blade sections than conventional propellers and a thick trailing edge that improves performance and reliability. The propellers also tend to have sharp, knifelike leading edges to improve efficiency; they need to be handled with care. When the boat is out of the water, the propellers should be covered along this edge to prevent injury. It's a sensible precaution to wear gloves when you change propellers.

Cleaver propellers are not subject to the cavitation problems that can occur with conventional (cruising) propellers when air bubbles are drawn down to them. Because the surface-propulsion blades are entering and leaving the water all the time, air flow into the propeller is encouraged.

Surface propellers operate more effectively with an odd number of blades, allowing a smoother transition between opposite blades entering and leaving the water. With

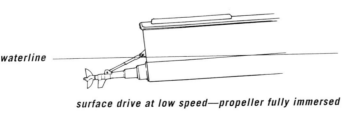

surface drive at low speed—propeller fully immersed

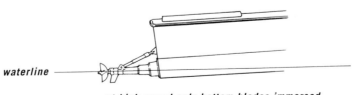

at high speed only bottom blades immersed

Surface propulsion systems are much more efficient at high speeds because of the reduced appendage drag.

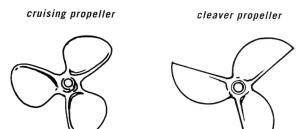

cruising propeller   **cleaver propeller**

Surface propellers (also called cleaver propellers) have thicker blade sections than cruising propellers and various other design features that make them more efficient with surface propulsion systems.

an even number of blades, one blade will be leaving the water as the opposite blade enters, which can set up unwanted vibrations at high speed. Five-bladed and even seven-bladed propellers are common where high power is being transmitted.

There are two principal types of surface propulsion systems. Fixed surface drives have a fixed propeller shaft so that the position of the propeller in relation to the transom is unchanging. Trimmable surface drives incorporate a universal joint in the shaft at the transom, allowing the drive to be trimmed up and down and, in some cases, to be used for steering.

Fixed Surface Drives

Fixed-shaft surface drives have the propeller height fixed in relation to the water coming away from the transom. In this type of drive the height of the propeller has to be a com-

promise, set at an average height between the conflicting requirements of calm water and rough seas and the conflicting needs of high speed and moderate speed. It's easy to visualize that the level of the water surface coming away from the transom will vary according to speed and will also change as a boat pitches in waves.

Despite this compromised setting, the benefits of the fixed system are its simplicity and robustness. The fixed shaft is strong, and the boat driver has no trim controls to worry about. It's just a matter of opening the throttle and going. With a fixed drive, a rudder is used for steering. You will not get the best efficiency with a fixed-drive system, but in practice it works well.

You will need powerful engines to help get the boat onto a plane. When the boat is going slowly, the propeller is fully immersed, so the engine will be overloaded until the top blades can break free from the water to reduce the load. Using trim tabs to lift the stern will help, but good low-speed engine torque is the best solution for powering the boat up onto a plane.

Many fixed-drive systems now feature an angled horizontal plate running from the bottom of the transom to a point above the propeller. When the drive is operating in reverse, this plate directs the reversed water flow down and under the hull to give good thrust astern, but it does not affect high-speed running.

Another feature of these fixed drives is the way in which the exhaust from the engine is directed to an exit point just in front of the top blades of the propeller. The exhaust gases help the top blades break out of the water as the throttle is opened. An air duct can be used for the same job, with the propeller sucking air down into the top blades. When building the 65-foot *Virgin Atlantic*

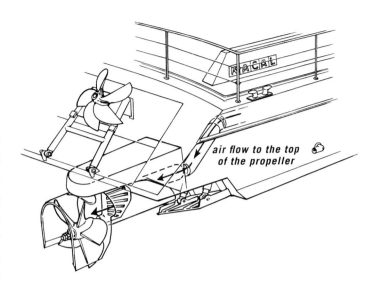

Ventilation to the upper blades of the propeller (here shown on Virgin Atlantic Challenger II*) helps the water break away in a fixed drive unit.*

Challenger catamaran back in 1985, we used an early fixed-surface drive, and on the first trials it would do only 8 knots. Ducting air down to the propellers allowed the top blades to break free, and the boat roared off to a top speed of 54 knots.

Trimmable Surface Drives

While fixed surface drives feature both proprietary and boatyard-developed designs, the trimmable drives are all proprietary units, reflecting their added complexity. Of these, the Arneson drive is the best known and most widely used and has become almost a generic name for trimmable surface drives. The Arneson was the first to

make these drives a practical proposition for fast-boat use.

With a trimmable drive unit, the height of the propeller or the angle of the shaft in relation to the transom can be varied under the control of a hydraulic cylinder. Propeller height can be fine-tuned to match operating conditions. A universal joint built into the propeller shaft, usually at the point where it emerges from the transom, allows the shaft to be swung from side to side as well as up and down so that the drive unit can also incorporate steering. With its ability to trim the propeller up and down, the Arneson drive provided a solution for operating at different speeds. Part of the early

Fixed surface drives matched to balanced spade rudders on a fast boat.

A fast boat with its trimmable surface drives trimmed too high, creating an impressive rooster tail.

success of the Arneson drive was due to the fact that boatbuilders loved it because installation was simple and you had everything you needed for high performance contained in one unit.

At slow speeds, before the water has broken away from the transom, a surface-drive propeller is fully immersed, which means that it is overloaded. This is not a problem for moving around a harbor at low speeds, when the engine is lightly loaded, but when the throttle is opened to get the boat onto a plane, the overloaded propeller will not allow the engine to accelerate easily. With diesel engines this acceleration can be made more difficult because power from the engine will only start to develop once the engine rpm can rise to the point where the turbocharger can cut in and start to produce more power. This all means that a surface-drive boat may have difficulty getting onto a plane, and this applies to both fixed and trimmable drives.

In order to improve the situation, you need to reduce the load on the propeller at modest speeds so that it can rotate more freely and absorb more engine power as engine speed increases. This can be accomplished in two ways, depending on the type of drive.

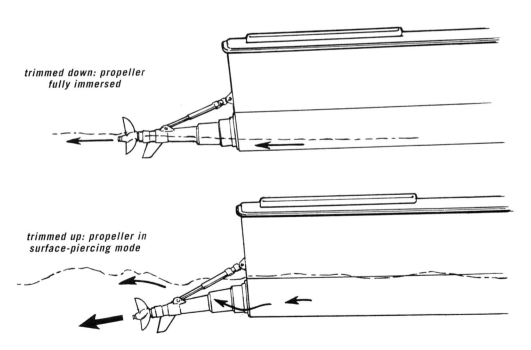

trimmed down: propeller fully immersed

trimmed up: propeller in surface-piercing mode

The operating mode of a trimmable surface drive at speed (top) and at slow speed or when getting onto plane (bottom).

With a trimmable drive, the propeller can simply be adjusted higher so that it comes closer to the water surface. This will reduce the loading on the top blades and allow the propeller to rotate at a faster speed. With a fixed drive, air or exhaust gases can be introduced immediately in front of the top blades to reduce propeller loading and allow higher rpm to be developed, as mentioned above.

The hydraulic cylinders that allow the drive to be trimmed up and down and moved side to side for steering are clearly visible on this trimmable surface drive.

Introduction of air on a fixed drive is automatic, but with the trimmable drive system, the trim adjustment has to be initiated and controlled by the driver. This driver control of the trim is both a good and a bad feature. It is good because the driver is in control of the operation; by monitoring engine rpm, boat speed, and trim gauges, he can see what is going on and make adjustments to get maximum efficiency from the drive. The bad aspect is that it takes an experienced driver to understand what is happening. I've seen many boats fitted with trimmable drive units running with the propeller too deeply immersed or too near the surface, both of which could cause the engine to overheat.

A characteristic of surface drives is the rooster tail thrown out from the transom, which is mainly generated by the propeller operating at the surface of the water. This rooster tail will be at its maximum and most spectacular as the boat begins planing, but should flatten out as the boat gains speed. If the rooster tail persists as a high torrent of water, it might look spectacular but it indicates that the drive is probably set too high. With a properly adjusted surface drive, the rooster tail should be quite visible as the propeller goes into full surface-piercing mode and diminish as speed increases.

Rough-Sea Operation

The weakest point of most surface-drive systems is their performance in rough seas.

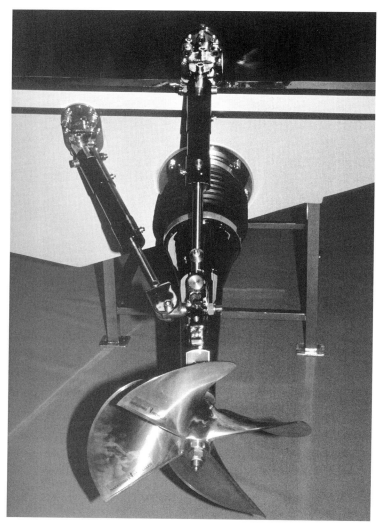

A trimmable surface drive that combines steering with trim adjustment.

ond the propeller could be fully immersed; the next it could be running with only half of each bottom blade in the water.

The surface-drive propeller likes to run in controlled conditions, with a fixed water flow from the transom. In rough seas this will not happen, although at planing speeds of around 40 knots, the propeller will probably cope with an average flow and absorb the ups and downs that come from pitching. Once you have to reduce speed in rough seas, the problems start. For diesels especially, not only will the pitching of the boat take place at a slower rate but the engine will also be approaching the rpm range where the turbocharger may start to cut out, hurting overall performance.

As the boat slows in the rough seas, it will approach the critical point where it can quickly drop off the plane. You can picture the scenario: a boat trying to climb over a wave, with the bow pointing to the sky. This puts the propeller into the fully immersed position— just at the time the engine needs all its

Inevitably you will want to slow down in these conditions and run the boat at moderate speeds, perhaps in the 20- to 30-knot range. As the boat pitches and rolls, the position of the propeller in relation to the water surface will constantly change. One sec-

power to drive the boat up and over the wave. Even if the throttle is opened, there may not be enough response to increase boat speed and, with the engine overloaded, the boat will drop off the plane.

This scenario can happen with both fixed and trimmable surface drives. You could find yourself in the dilemma of having to either come down off the plane or increase speed beyond what seems safe. With a trimmable surface drive, you could, in theory, trim the drive up and down to match the changing seas, but the wave changes happen too quickly for this to be effective. In my experience, no surface-drive system runs comfortably for any length of time at speeds between 15 and 25 knots—a "dead area" somewhere between slow travel and planing. This problem with surface drives can be a real handicap when operating in rough conditions.

Water Jets

For pure speed nothing beats a surface propulsion system. However, water jets are also a viable propulsion system for fast boats. A water jet is basically a pump that sucks in water through an intake under the boat, accelerates it as it passes through a rotor, and then expels it through a nozzle to generate thrust. The controlled flow conditions inside the body of the jet, with no air being sucked in, means that the flow is less prone to cavitation, and this is one of the reasons a water jet can operate over a wide speed range efficiently. Water-jet systems also incorporate steering and reverse movement, so they are fully self-contained propulsion units. Unlike most other propulsion systems, water jets are not simple bolt-on units except in very small sizes. They require the hull to be modified to create the water inlets.

The water-jet nozzle is moved from side to side to give steering control, while a deflector can be swung over the nozzle to divert the thrust forward under the hull to provide a powerful reverse. A gearbox is usually installed in the transmission—not as a reverse gear but so that the water jet can be back-flushed to clear debris and also to provide a positive neutral during engine starting and at other times when no thrust is required. It is possible to find a neutral by balancing the position of the deflector, and even in this neutral position with the boat stationary, steering control is still available. The control that is possible with water-jet propulsion is quite startling to someone accustomed to maneuvering with propellers. With water jets, it is possible to, quite literally, make the boat travel sideways.

With a twin water-jet installation, you can control the movement of the boat in all directions when operating at slow speed. This is achieved by operating the jets independently, something that is not normally available on a straightforward water-jet installation because the steering control on the two jets is linked. It can be complicated

Water-jet propulsion at high speed showing the twin water flows coming out of the jets.

trying to operate the controls manually to get this full maneuvering effect, but a computer, controlled by a joystick, can do the trick. A number of fast boats with water-jet propulsion have this computer operation at slow speed; you have full control by simply pointing the joystick in the direction you want the boat to move. At high speeds the controls revert to conventional use with the wheel and throttle.

For maximum efficiency, the hull of the boat has to be suitable for water jets. Lifting strakes should be terminated well forward so that they do not produce stray flows of water or air into the jet intake. The hull shape should offer a clean run aft. It is important for hull designers and builders to heed the advice of the jet manufacturers when the intakes are designed, because the manufacturers know best how to achieve a smooth flow of water.

Water jets are not widely used on sports boats, except for some small designs, and they are used only on a few larger designs in the leisure market. These systems are expensive. But it is mainly the unusual driving skills required with jets that keep them out of popular favor. However, in many workboats, military craft, and RIBs, water jets are the preferred form of propulsion.

Following are some of the pluses and minuses of water jets. First the advantages:

- A water jet can absorb the full power of the engine even at low speed, and will have good acceleration and get onto a plane easily even when heavily loaded.

- The propulsion unit, contained within the depth of the hull, is fully protected for shallow-water operations.

- There is excellent maneuverability, stopping power, and flexibility in operating at different speeds.

- It is safe for operation close to people in the water.

- There is no propeller to be fouled with fishing gear or lobster trap lines.

And some disadvantages:

- The weight of the water contained in the jet becomes part of the weight of the boat, thus increasing overall weight.

- If the water-jet intake comes clear of the water when operating in waves, there can be slow pickup until any air is cleared from the jet.

- It may be necessary to add fins to the bottom of the boat aft to help give good directional stability. This can be the case on a shallow-V hull, which has a poor grip on the water.

- If the boat is not used for some time, weeds and barnacles can grow inside the water jet, greatly reducing its efficiency.

- Water jets have unconventional controls with unconventional handling characteristics.

- The costs of buying, operating, and maintaining a water-jet engine are high.

Gearboxes

The standard gearbox in the transmission between the engine and the propulsion offers forward, neutral, and reverse gears controlled by dashboard levers. You will use the gearbox a lot in harbors and ports but rarely at sea, where the forward gear will remain firmly engaged. For harbor work, many boat drivers just set the throttles to a speed somewhere above idle and maneuver the boat on the gear levers alone. With modern electronically operated gearboxes, electrical switches can replace the gear levers.

The gearbox can also provide a reduction gear. With diesel engines, engine speed may be quite close to that required for the propulsion unit. But with higher-speed gas engines, a reduction gear may be needed to reduce engine speed to that required for the propeller. Modern gearboxes with their multiplate clutches normally change gear smoothly and easily, and single-lever controls automatically reduce engine speed as the gear is changed. Where separate throttle and gear levers are used, you need to throttle back before operating the gear selector lever.

With both types of control levers it's necessary to pause momentarily in neutral before moving from ahead to reverse. Electronically controlled gearboxes take some of the decision-making away from the driver by determining the speed of change automatically, and a delay may be built into the gearbox to reduce the chance of damage. This can come as a surprise when you are maneuvering in harbor if you are not familiar with the boat.

Gearboxes are normally operated hydraulically, using the oil pressure from the gearbox lubricating system. A gearbox oil pressure gauge on the dashboard shows whether the oil pressure system is working satisfactorily. The gearbox requires little adjustment or maintenance.

Two-Speed Gearboxes

Two-speed gearboxes are a relatively new thing for leisure boats, and they make such a difference to the performance of a fast boat that it is surprising they have not been offered before. It is rather like using a gearbox in a car, selecting a lower gear for takeoff and then moving into a higher gear for cruising.

Race boats use gearboxes with up to five gears in order to match the engine speed to the speed of the boat for optimum performance in different conditions. We are not likely to see these complex multispeed gearboxes in leisure boats, but the two-speed box can do the job in a less sophisticated way. They are mainly used in conjunction with surface-drive propulsion systems and can overcome many of the problems inherent in these systems.

The low gear in a two-speed gearbox offers a number of advantages. The low gear permits engine speed to rise in relation to propeller speed to produce a higher thrust when getting onto a plane. It helps in reducing maneuvering speeds, and it provides better acceleration. The high gear permits higher top speeds.

The ratio between the two gears is usually around 1:1.2, which is not a lot, but it can make a huge difference to the performance of a boat. On a lightweight boat using the lower gear, it might be possible to get onto a plane with just a single engine running.

You will keep the engine in low gear much of the time. You could consider this to be the normal gear; you can switch into the overdrive high gear once you get up to fast cruising speeds. The low gear permits more delicate harbor maneuvering and takes away some of the fierceness found when using surface drives at low speeds.

The big bonus of using a two-speed gearbox with surface drives comes when getting the boat onto a plane. Because the engine in low gear is running at a higher speed in relation to the propeller, the acceleration will be better and the boat should simply power onto a plane with no hesitation.

You will probably keep the engine in low gear in rough seas, where throttle response and good acceleration are more important than top speed. The problems with surface drives in rough seas, when speed has to be reduced and thrust is lost, can be partially overcome by use of the low gear. When high speed is wanted, you simply flick the switch; the boat suddenly gets long legs and you power away.

Gear selection is usually made through a dashboard switch marked with high and low. When changing from low to high gear under acceleration, ease the throttle slightly to reduce stress on the gearbox. It is not good practice to constantly change gears; you should need to do this only a few times when cruising.

Systems that change gear up or down automatically at preset engine speeds are available, but these are for the lazy driver. Most fast-boat drivers will want to make changes manually, particularly when operating in waves.

Slow-Speed Maneuvering

It can take a lot of the fun out of boating if you have to struggle to operate your boat at low speed. Fast boats spend a surprising amount of their time operating at low speeds when traveling in or out of harbors, and a boat that is comfortable at low speeds

is a lot more user-friendly. We have seen how a two-speed gearbox can improve low-speed performance; an additional option is to have the gearbox fitted with what is called a trolling valve. This valve allows a certain amount of slip in the gearbox clutches so that the propeller turns at a slower speed relative to the engine, producing an effect similar to a lower gear in the gearbox.

Surface drives can be quite brutal in operation, and at minimum power the boat can still be running at 6 or 7 knots when not using a two-speed gearbox. This can force you to operate on just one engine when you want low speeds in harbor channels—and this means lessened straight-line control. Overall, water jets have the edge here because you can adjust the jet's reversing bucket to get any speed you want, from zero to fast idling. Water jets give the best control for harbor maneuvering of any type of propulsion; combine them with computer operation through joysticks and you have even better control.

A bow thruster—a propeller that operates sideways from a tunnel in the bow—can be a useful addition to any fast boat, making boat handling in harbor much easier. They are particularly helpful in keeping things under control in strong winds. The bow thruster can also serve as an alternative steering system if the main system breaks down. Bow thrusters typically work only when the boat is moving slowly, because the bow lifts out of the water as speed rises.

Stern thrusters are also available, but they can only be fitted when the boat has conventional shaft-and-propeller drive because there is little transom space to spare with stern or surface drives. Both types of thrusters add weight to the boat, which will handicap performance, but the benefits of improved harbor handling outweigh this disadvantage except on very high performance boats.

5

Fast-Boat Controls

In the partnership between a fast boat and its driver, the control system is the main link. This is where the driver connects with the boat to vary its speed, direction, and attitude. Understanding and operating the controls is the key to fast-boat driving. Through the controls, the driver can influence the way the boat performs, improve the ride and comfort, and ensure safety.

The main controls are the throttles and the steering. These dictate speed and direction, but like most controls on a fast boat, they also have secondary effects. Moving the steering wheel not only changes the direction in which the boat is heading but also causes the boat to heel to one side or the other. Moving the throttle not only changes the speed but can also affect the trim, causing the bow to rise or fall. It is the same with trim tabs and power trim. These

change the trim of the boat, but they can also affect the steering, and the power trim can affect speed.

Fast-boat controls are complex. What you are looking to accomplish is to get the right balance among the controls—to optimize the balance for the conditions in which the boat is operating.

Throttle

On a fast boat the throttle is the single most important control. It is used to manage the speed of the boat, but more significant is its use in controlling acceleration and deceleration, notably when operating in waves. Even within what appears to be a regular wave pattern, there can be considerable variation in wave shape and size. The throttle allows the driver to accelerate and

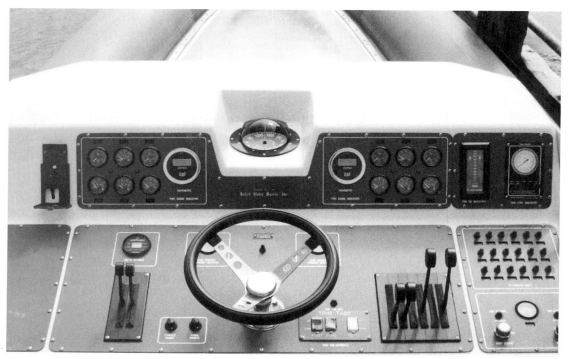

A fast-RIB twin-engine helm station with separate throttles and gears on the right, trim tab switches close by the wheel, and ballast tank lever on the left. The two small switches close by the wheel on the left are for the two-speed gearboxes.

decelerate in response to these changing waves. The throttle is the only control that gives this type of immediate response.

The faster the boat, the more vital the throttle control for both progress and safety. At really high speeds, as in offshore racing, the essential role of the throttle can be seen in the fact that the steering and throttle are operated by different crew members. At these speeds, a single person cannot provide the level of concentration needed to operate both. On slower craft, a single person can operate both steering and throttle, but only by paying the closest attention to the task.

Response to the Throttle

The boat's quick response to the throttle is vital to the effective driving of a fast boat. Response will tend to be best once a boat is fully onto a plane and running smoothly, which for many boats is around the 25- to 30-knot mark. Below this speed, expect a slower response because the boat may not be fully planing and will have a higher resistance.

When a boat is running close to top speed, there may be little acceleration left, because the engine power usually peaks just below peak rpm. There will be little or no throttle response for the last few knots, and the boat will only slowly climb to top speed.

Much will depend on the top speed of the boat, but when you drive in waves, a throttle opening of around two thirds of maximum should provide a margin of speed that will allow a good throttle response, both up and down. You will then have the necessary flexibility to adapt your speed to changing wave conditions.

The quickness of a boat's response to the throttle depends on several factors, including throttle location, the type of control levers, engine characteristics, the propulsion system, and the weight of the boat.

Throttle Location

The ability of the driver to move the throttle lever quickly depends on the position of the throttle in the boat and the reaction time of the driver. You can produce a fast response only if you keep your hand on the throttle lever, ready to act. Thus the lever must be in a comfortable position next to the wheel. It helps to have an armrest immediately behind the throttle to give your throttle hand a place to rest.

Control Lever

Boats are outfitted with either a combined throttle and gear lever or separate levers for the two functions. The standard engine controls used on fast boats are single-lever designs that combine both throttle and gear change. Many high-performance boats, however, use separate levers.

An option on smaller fast boats is a foot throttle. This is just like a car accelerator and it can certainly produce a fast, instinctive response—though you may find yourself looking for the brake pedal when you want to slow down. You have to be sitting

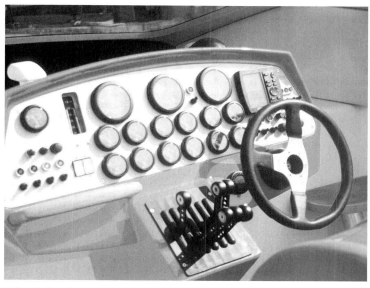

The helm layout on a multiengine fast boat with the throttles and gear controls separated out.

to use a foot throttle, which can make life difficult when you're trying to maneuver in rough seas or in a harbor.

Combined Throttle and Gear Controls.
The combination throttle and gear lever provides a logical means of controlling the boat. Initial movement of the single lever puts the engine into gear; continuing movement of the lever progressively opens the throttle. This approach ensures that the engine is at low rpm before a gear change is made.

However, because the single lever has to accommodate both the forward and the reverse throttle range, as well as a neutral band, within its total scope of movement, there is only a limited amount of throttle range available for the forward-gear section of the throttle. And this forward section is the most vital part of the movement for good fast-boat control. Given the limited throttle range in a single-lever installation, it's not always possible to get the sensitive control necessary for fast-boat operation.

This limited movement results in a tendency for the throttle to be either wide open or closed; it is not easy to find com-

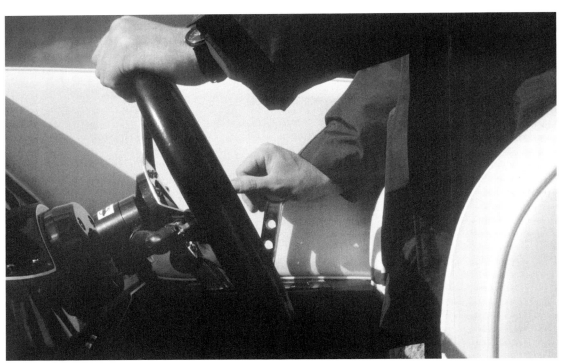

The typical position for your hands when driving a fast boat: one hand on the wheel and one on the throttles.

fortable intermediate speeds. This problem can be made worse by the considerable resistance often found in single-lever controls, a factor that can slow the boat's response to the throttle. This is particularly true in boats fitted with twin engines, where resistance to throttle movement can be considerable. Outboard-motor throttle controls can also be stiff and difficult to operate smoothly.

At the same time, the lever needs a degree of resistance to help prevent inadvertent throttle operation. It's easy for your throttle hand to accidentally change the lever if it moves too easily. With some resistance in the lever, you should be able to rest your hand against the lever, ready to act—but without actually changing the setting. The balance between too free and too stiff can be a delicate one. Some throttle controls allow the stiffness to be adjusted.

The lever control box should be positioned so that it is angled downward at the rear to permit the ahead/forward section of the throttle movement to be in the upright position when the lever is set at around half throttle. This allows maximum control from the lever and improves response time.

Modern electronic engine controls offer little or no resistance to movement of the throttles. Designers of the controls make the levers short in the interests of a compact design, and these short levers are less sensitive. For fast boats, where the

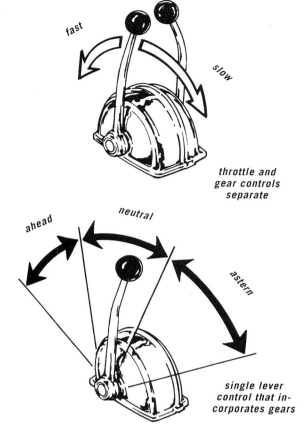

throttle and gear controls separate

single lever control that incorporates gears

A wide throttle range is available on fast powerboats where the gear and throttle controls are separate (top). When a single lever controls both gear and throttle there is a shorter throttle range available (bottom).

throttle may be in constant play and require sensitive adjustment, these electronic levers are not generally suited to the task.

Separate Throttle and Gear Controls.
High-performance fast boats can benefit from use of separate controls for the throt-

tle and the gears. This gives the separate throttle lever a wider range of movement to provide sensitive control for operating in waves, where the throttle can be in constant use. This leaves the gear controls mainly for use in harbor maneuvering.

Another advantage of a separate throttle lever is that it eliminates one problem of combined levers: that a rapid lever movement can accidentally take the engine out of gear.

With a separate throttle lever, as with a combined throttle and gear lever, the control box should be mounted so the lever is upright in the half-ahead position.

Engine Characteristics

Outboard motors respond quickly to the throttle, thanks to the small, lightweight moving parts inside the engine. Inboard gas engines usually respond faster than diesel engines, mainly because of the lighter weight of the components inside a gas engine.

Diesel engines fitted with a turbocharger can hesitate in pickup. Good acceleration only comes when the turbocharger is fully operational, which is usually above 1,500 rpm—although this turbo lag is a thing of the past in most modern electronic diesels. Diesel engines

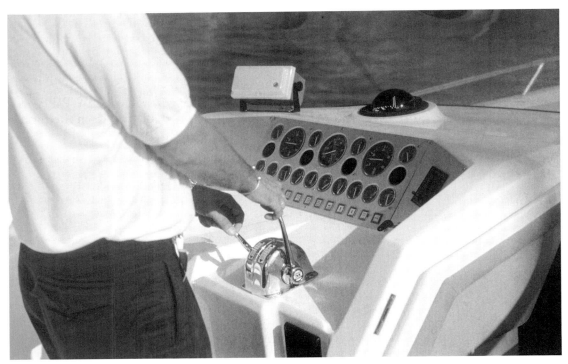

Using the gear levers for controlling a boat in harbor maneuvering.

that operate up to 3,000 rpm or more provide good acceleration; slower-speed engines will not accelerate quickly.

Some electronic diesels demonstrate poor throttle response because of a built-in delay through the electronic control system. This is done in the interests of prolonging engine life, but it detracts from boat handling at upper speeds and does not allow the level of control that is desirable. See also the section "Engine Throttle Response" in chapter 4, "Engines and Propulsion."

Propulsion System

The pace of a boat's acceleration depends a great deal on the way in which the propulsion system absorbs power. In conventional shaft-and-propeller systems, a propeller that is small in pitch and diameter will provide better acceleration than a large propeller. The large propeller has a better grip on the water and will thus have less slip, so the engine will struggle to overcome this, slowing down the rate of acceleration. The smaller propeller allows the engine to speed up rapidly and, while it may slip in the early stages of acceleration, the rate at which it speeds up will be faster, allowing engine power to be more quickly absorbed.

Boat designers aim for a propeller size that is a combination of the small size needed for fast acceleration and quick throttle response and the larger size needed to maximize the top speed. For boat buyers, top speed is usually a more significant fac-

tor and the one that the designer will probably focus on—to the detriment of good throttle response.

With surface propulsion drives, correct propeller sizing is even more critical because of the heavy loading on the propeller when it is fully immersed during the early stages of acceleration. Quick acceleration occurs only after the top half of the propeller is clear of the water and the propeller is operating in the surface-piercing mode, which comes at around 15 knots on most boats.

Fast opening of the throttle with a fully submerged propeller can lead to cavitation or excessive slip on initial acceleration, but modern propeller design has largely overcome this problem. However, it can still manifest itself with outboards and stern drives if the steering is off-center when you open the throttle, causing the propeller thrust to be directed away from the direction the boat is heading.

With both submerged and surface-piercing propellers, a two-speed gearbox can maximize throttle response at both high and low speeds by allowing a better match between engine rpm and propeller speeds at different boat speeds. See chapter 4, "Engines and Propulsion" for more detail.

Most of the throttle response problems associated with propulsion systems occur only at speeds up to 25 knots or so. Once the boat is up and fully planing, the response will be much better. The designer will usually aim to get the propeller size right for a good response at planing speeds, where you need it most.

Water-jet propulsion is one of the best systems for throttle response because the jet absorbs full engine power even at low boat speeds. Water jets are notable for smooth and powerful throttle response throughout the speed range. The only hesitation occurs if the intake for the jet comes clear of the water, which can happen if the boat leaps free of the water or heels sharply under heavy turning.

Weight of the Boat

The heavier the boat, the slower the acceleration and throttle response. The slow response of a heavy boat can produce propeller cavitation if the throttle is opened quickly, though this type of boat usually has larger propellers that are less likely to cavitate. On many sport cruisers and fast motor cruisers, particularly those powered by diesels, the weight of the boat and its slow throttle response will mean that that there is little point in trying to use acceleration as a handling feature in waves, because the response will be too slow to be effective.

The same can apply to larger power-boats, mainly those over 50 feet in length. The size and weight of these craft and the slower-speed diesels usually fitted to them simply do not provide a fast enough throttle response for it to be an effective handling tool.

Throttle Control of Trim

Throttle response tends to be considered in terms of the boat going faster or slower, or accelerating or decelerating, as these are the immediate effects that are felt. But there is also a more subtle response to the throttle that can be used to control the boat's trim.

When the throttle is opened, the bow of the boat rises; when the throttle is closed, the bow falls. This bow response can be put to good use when driving a fast boat in waves. You can force the bow up to meet an approaching wave by a quick opening of the throttle, thus helping to ease the boat over the wave; and you can close the throttle to make the bow drop.

The opening or closing of the throttle produces an immediate change in boat trim. In the initial stages, this change takes place before there is any difference in the speed of the boat. You will start to feel the acceleration or deceleration as the throttle is moved, but by that time the trim will have changed. This means that a change in trim can be achieved with virtually no change in the speed of the boat. Try this technique in calm water, and you will see how much the trim can be changed while the boat is still making fast progress.

To achieve this sort of trim reaction, you must open and close the throttle very quickly. Driving a fast boat in waves can often consist of a series of quick openings and closings of the throttle as you read the approaching wave and try to produce a matching response from the boat via the throttle control. You want the bow to lift as the boat approaches the wave, but to be dropping slightly as the bow passes through the crest. This method of driving will not be effective on slower, heavier boats: the change of trim will still occur, but the reaction will be slower.

The adjustment of trim by using the throttle occurs because the change in engine power alters the thrust of the propellers. Increasing or reducing propeller thrust will, in turn, change the position through which the center of lift is effective—and it is this change in the center of lift that creates the instant change in trim (see the section "Dynamic Lift" in chapter 1, "Fast-Boat Design"). The force that is effective through this center of lift will also fluctuate, increasing as the throttle is opened and decreasing when it is closed.

Trim tabs and power trim, which we will discuss in the following sections, also produce a change in trim, but the response to these controls is slow. The change is not fast enough to be used in adjusting trim to approaching waves. These controls are used for longer-term adjustments.

Trim Tabs

Powerboats use trim tabs to adjust both fore-and-aft and side-to-side (transverse) trim. These two hinged plates, one mounted at each side of the transom's bottom edge, are also called flaps to differentiate them from the power trim (discussed later in this chapter).

Trim tabs are usually operated by hydraulic cylinders that allow them to be raised or lowered at the hinges on the transom. In the raised position they are flush with the bottom of the boat, and usually set to match the V of the hull. They can be lowered to an angle of as much as 10 to 15 degrees using dashboard switches.

A dashboard angle indicator is often provided to show the position of the tabs; often this takes the form of a column of LED lights that switch on progressively as the flap lowers. In order to have confidence in the dashboard reading, you should periodically check the relative positions of the tabs and the indicator while you are in port. Without such an indicator you have to bring the tabs to their full up position and then lower them, estimating how far down they are by the change in trim of the boat or by how long the switch has been operating.

The response to a trim tab adjustment is relatively slow; it takes three or four seconds to lower the flaps from their up position to the maximum down position. This means the trim tabs tend to be adjusted to a set position that matches the general requirements for the prevailing sea conditions rather than being continually adjusted.

Lowering both trim tabs will push the bow of the boat down; raising both tabs

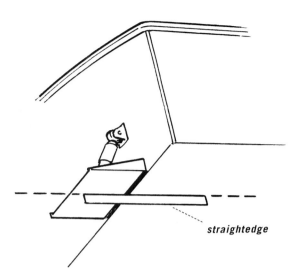

straightedge

Check the trim tab with a straightedge: you want the tab to be aligned with the hull when the indicator dial on the dash reads zero.

from their down position will allow the bow to lift. In the horizontal raised position the tabs have virtually no effect on performance. From the raised position, the tabs can be used only to push the bow down; they can be used to lift the bow only if they are already in a down position. To adjust the transverse trim of the hull—its heeling—the trim tabs are used individually.

When to Use Trim Tabs

Trim tabs are used both to trim a boat and to improve its performance. Lowering the tabs in order to drop the bow might be done with the intention of operating the boat at a more efficient angle of trim to achieve higher speeds—but this is not usu-

ally effective. Lowering the tabs adds drag to the hull, which tends to cancel out any speed gained by the improved angle of trim.

Trim tabs can be used to help get a heavy boat onto a plane, and in this situation the tabs are lowered before opening the throttles; the additional lift generated toward the stern by the steeper angle of attack of the tabs helps to get the boat up and planing.

The main use of trim tabs on a fast boat, however, comes when the boat is operating at high speed in a head sea. Lowering the tabs will help to keep the bow down and reduce the chance of the boat flying off the top of a wave. Trimmed down with the tabs in this position, the boat is much more likely to remain in contact with the water, and this can allow higher speeds to be maintained in rough conditions—but this requires delicate adjustment to achieve the optimum setting.

The difference that well-adjusted trim tabs can make is surprising; you may have the feeling that the hull is glued to the water, rather than the skittish feeling you can otherwise get. Even on slower boats—perhaps running at 30 knots—using the tabs in this way can be beneficial, with the pitch-

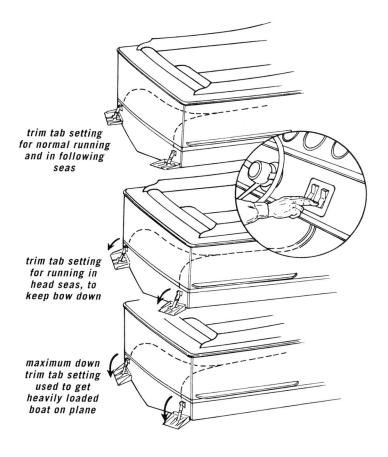

trim tab setting for normal running and in following seas

trim tab setting for running in head seas, to keep bow down

maximum down trim tab setting used to get heavily loaded boat on plane

Trim tabs settings vary depending on sea conditions. For running in moderate conditions they would normally be kept level. Their main use is in head seas to help keep the bow down.

ing of the boat in head seas considerably reduced. There will be a penalty to pay in terms of increased resistance and there could be a noticeable increase in spray, but the end result of a more comfortable ride is well worth it.

Tabs are used individually to adjust the transverse trim of the boat. If the port tab is lowered, the port side of the boat will lift; lowering the starboard tab lifts the starboard side of the boat. Tabs are used this way to keep the boat on an even keel—particularly important on a deep-V hull, which needs to stay upright to gain full advantage of the cushioning effect of its hull shape. If the boat is heeled, waves will hit the flatter surface of this low side of the V and produce a much rougher ride.

Using the tabs as separate units can be particularly beneficial when operating in a beam wind, where the hull tends to lean into the wind. Lowering the trim tab on the weather, or lower, side will bring the hull upright and make the ride more comfortable.

Lowering a single tab affects the steering by creating drag on the side on which it is lowered, thus tending to pull the boat around toward that side. To counteract this, the steering has to be biased in the opposite direction. When you adjust the transverse trim by using the tabs individually, it might take two or three attempts

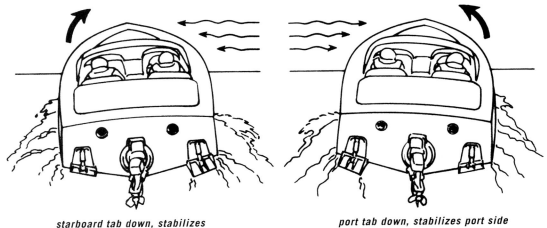

*starboard tab down, stabilizes
starboard side*

port tab down, stabilizes port side

Trim tabs can be adjusted individually to help keep a fast powerboat on an even keel, counteracting the tendency to lean into a strong beam wind (as here) or to heel in response to the torque of a single propeller.

to find the correct balance between the steering and the tabs. Use of just a single tab also has a slight effect on the fore-and-aft trim, tending to push the bow down a little. You'll need to do a bit of experimenting to find the right balance among all these factors.

Balancing a Boat with Trim Tabs

A boat's hull shape is fixed, established by the designer as a compromise among the requirements for different operating conditions. But by using tabs, you can vary the constructed characteristics of the hull to a limited extent, making it better balanced for a particular sea condition.

As a general rule, tabs will be down while operating in head seas, when the bow needs to be kept down. And they will be raised completely to the horizontal position while operating in following seas, when the bow needs to be kept up.

The effects of the tabs on trim are proportional to the speed of the boat. At high speeds only minimal adjustment may be required to get the desired change of trim. During low-speed operation, likely in rough seas, you may need to set the tabs at their lowest positions.

Interceptors

Interceptors, a relatively new development, are used in much the same way as tabs, but they operate much more quickly and control the attitude of the hull more effectively. The quick reaction available with interceptors allows them to be used as the basis for ride-control systems that automatically adjust trim to reduce both pitching and rolling.

Instead of being hinged tabs attached to the transom, interceptors are metal plates that can be lowered vertically so that they project just below the transom on both sides. Here they intercept the water flowing under the hull, and this interruption of flow generates lift at the stern—lift that is more effective than that generated by trim tabs. At maximum setting, the interceptors project only an inch or so below the bottom of the boat; added resistance is probably less than that generated by tabs.

Interceptors were first introduced on fast monohull ferries for which tabs would be too large and heavy to be practical. The compact interceptors are well proven on

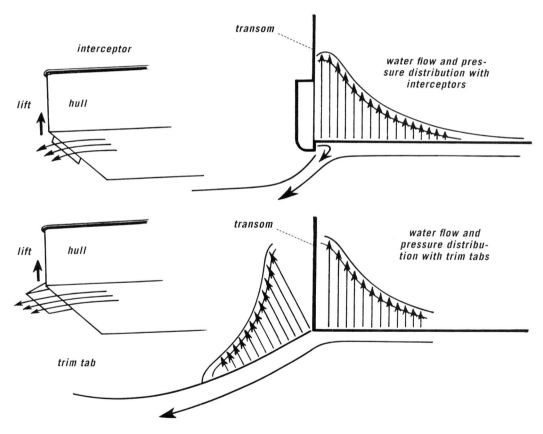

Interceptors (top) generate lift more efficiently at the stern because the interuption of the water flow is concentrated at the transom. Trim tabs (bottom) generate lift but also add to the wetted surface, creating more drag.

these ferries, and interceptors are now available for fitting to smaller high-speed craft.

Three types of interceptors are available for fast boats. One, as mentioned above, is the metal plate that moves vertically up and down, with its bottom edge parallel to the bottom of the transom.

A second type also consists of a metal plate fitted just behind the transom, but this plate is hinged at one end, near the centerline of the boat, and the outer end is lowered and raised under hydraulic control. This system is particularly effective in controlling the transverse trim, or heeling, of a vessel because the main trimming effect is at the outer edge of the transom.

The third system, using rotary interceptors instead of a plate type, can give more subtle control of trim. This interceptor is hook-shaped in cross section; the rotary action under hydraulic control brings the tip of the hook down so that it intercepts the water flowing away from the transom. This gives the same effect as a plate interceptor, but the rotating action provides smoother operation.

The fast action of interceptors gives the driver an effective way to reduce the inclination of the bow off the top of a wave. If

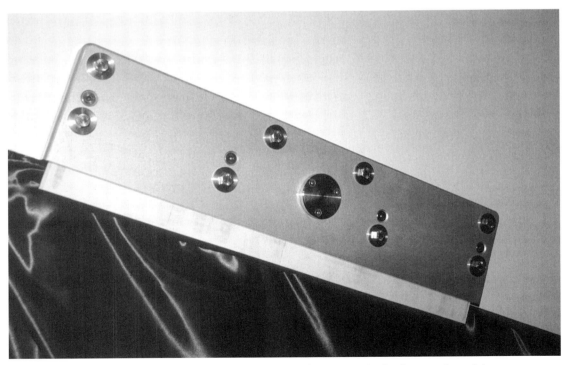

A transom-mounted interceptor of the vertical plate type, in its lowered position.

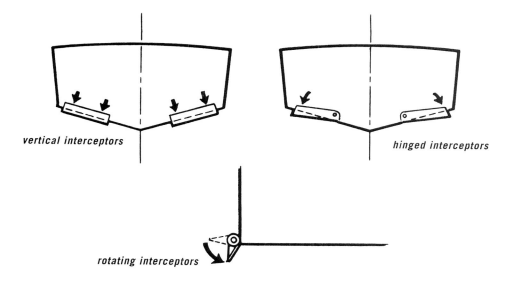

vertical interceptors

hinged interceptors

rotating interceptors

Three types of interceptors are available for fast powerboats, offering different methods of connection and control.

the control of the interceptor is by lever rather than push button, a flick of the lever brings the bow down quickly and effectively within a second; then another flick of the lever brings the bow up again. I tried this method of driving a boat using a newly designed Swedish lifeboat, and found it to be effective.

Using the interceptor control in this way is similar to using throttles to control a boat's trim, but probably even more effective. The problem is that the driver cannot operate throttles and interceptors at the same time. This is an area in which computer control may eventually be able to take over some of the work. The use of interceptors for boat control is still in its infancy, but shows considerable promise for the future.

Another technique that, in some ways, offers the same rapid response as an interceptor is water-jet propulsion. Water jets offer a powerful reverse when the reversing bucket or deflector is lowered. The effect is so powerful that the boat will stop almost within its own length, causing the bow to drop rapidly. I have seen this reversing used with great results on a patrol boat operating in difficult head seas. Every so often there would be a larger than normal wave and, on this heavy boat, the response to the throttle was too slow to prevent the boat from crashing down into the trough on the other side. But by using the reverse on the water jet, the speed was slowed in time to ease the boat into the trough without hard banging and crashing.

It required concentration, but the ride

was much more comfortable when using this technique. The penalty for this method came in the slower progress that was made, with the boat almost coming to a stop when the reverse was used. This is another case of balancing the requirements of fast progress with the comfort and security of the crew.

Power Trim

Power trim is a feature of most powerful outboards, stern-drive legs, and some surface-drive systems. The basic prerequisite is the ability to alter the vertical angle of the propeller shaft, which in turn alters the angle of the propeller thrust. Since propeller thrust is an important component of the forces that act on the hull of a fast boat, it is obvious that this will affect the balance of the boat.

There are two basic power-trim systems, and they can have different effects. One is used on outboards and stern-drive propulsion units; the other on surface propulsion drives.

When power trim is used on outboards and stern-drive units, adjusting the trim moves the propeller in toward or out from the transom under hydraulic power, altering the angle of the drive leg in relation to the transom. The propeller depth changes only slightly through this operation, but the direction of propeller thrust alters by as much as 10 degrees when trimmed all the way out or in. When the drive unit is trimmed out (away from the transom), the propeller's thrust is directed downward, depressing the stern and lifting the bow. When the drive is trimmed in, the stern rises and the bow drops.

The power trim on a trimmable surface drive acts much more in the vertical plane, so that the propeller is lifted up and down rather than angled forward or back. This adjustment has a lesser effect on the boat's trim because the alteration in the angle of propeller thrust is quite small, probably no more than 5 degrees.

In the following sections we will look more closely at stern drives and outboards separately, since there are some differences in their power trim operation, and then at surface drives.

The Effect of Power Trim: Stern Drives

Jacking out the drive leg under power trim to alter the angle of propeller thrust results in lifting the boat's bow slightly, which enables the hull to operate at a better angle of trim, reduces its wetted surface, and promotes more efficient propulsion. With a stern drive, optimal efficiency is achieved when the drive is trimmed slightly out and the hull is running level and true as it would in calm or slight seas. Generally the drive is trimmed out for higher-speed operation.

In rougher waters there can be a need to keep the bow down and the propeller fully immersed as the boat pitches in waves: the

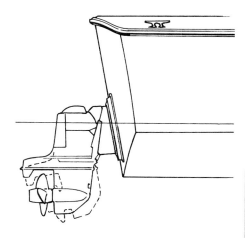

The adjustable tilt angle of a stern drive can be used to make a boat trim flatter. When the drive is angled out from the transom, the resultant propeller thrust angle will depress the stern and lift the bow. Trimming the drive in toward the transom lifts the stern and drops the bow.

drive would then be trimmed in toward the transom. The drive should also be trimmed in when the boat is executing turns to reduce the possibility of drawing air into the water circulating around the propeller, causing cavitation. When good acceleration is required, the drive is trimmed in.

With stern drives, the amount that the drive has been trimmed out is usually shown on a dashboard indicator. With experience, you can determine the best setting for particular conditions. Finding this optimum setting is, at first, a matter of watching the engine rpm gauges as the drive is trimmed out to ensure that the engines are not overspeeding, and then observing the wake of the boat emerging from the propeller. A flat, smooth flow of water from the propeller is an indication that the drive is set at optimum power trim. Too much trim out will introduce cavitation, which you will see and hear; too little trim out will cause a distorted flow pattern away from the propellers.

To find the best setting for high-speed operation, take the boat out in calm conditions and adjust the power trim until the boat attains maximum speed. Note the setting on the trim indicator dial so that it can be used as a guide in open-sea operation.

If you take the power trim out too far, you may find that your boat is porpoising—the bow is bouncing up and down. This is normally caused by having the hull trimmed with the bow up too high. Trimmed this way, the hull is supported mainly at the stern and can have difficulty finding a state of equilibrium. The porpoising, which usually occurs only in calm water, can be stopped by trimming the drive in a shade or possibly by lowering the trim tabs a touch. You can experience porpoising on outboard boats as well; it is less likely with surface drives because there is less change in hull angle when these are trimmed up.

The Effect of Power Trim: Outboards

The power trim on outboards operates in much the same way as it does on stern drives. The assessment of the position for

TRIM TAB POSITIONS	STERN-DRIVE POSITION
1. Zeroing in:	To create a reference point, use a straightedge such as a yardstick to line up the tabs and drive so they are parallel with the bottom.
2. Getting on plane:	To get on plane faster, use the drive and tabs to raise the stern and keep the bow down.
3. 25–30 knots: (smooth water)	The tabs are now aligned with the bottom, and the drive is up.
4. 50 knots or more: (smooth water)	The tabs are lifted out of the water stream and the drive is trimmed up to a point just before the prop ventilates.
5. 50 knots or more: (rough water)	To keep more of the boat in contact with the water for a smoother ride, bring the drive down from its maximum position and lower the tabs slightly.

Tandem use of drive and trim tab positions to control the trim of a stern-drive boat.

optimum trim is the same, but there may be no dashboard gauges to show the trim angle. You can look astern and watch the outboard moving under the power trim control, and with experience you can see the right setting just as clearly as you could by viewing a dashboard gauge. You can also look astern at the wake pattern to see the effect of trim, as you can with a stern drive.

With outboards, the optimum setting for the trim is best determined in calm water or slight seas, using the same technique as described under stern drives. Once this setting is established, it's easy to set the power trim angle as the boat comes up onto a plane. Coming off the plane it's normal to bring the outboards right back into their minimum setting on the power trim, as would be the case when turning or operating in waves. For all slow-speed operations the outboards should remain trimmed right in against the transom.

There is an additional trim system available for outboards. In this system the outboard is mounted in a frame—sometimes called a transom jack—on the transom, and the frame allows the engine to be moved up and down. The main effect is to raise the propeller so that it can operate in the surface-piercing mode for greater efficiency.

On some performance craft without this vertical adjustment frame, the outboard is fixed at a height at which the propeller can operate in surface-piercing mode during planing. But such a fixed setting comes with a penalty: it makes it more difficult to get the boat onto a plane. The transom frame system overcomes this problem by making it possible to adjust propeller height according to performance requirements.

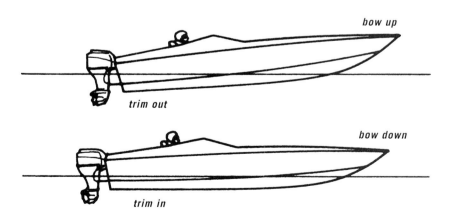

Power trim on an outboard produces the same results as with a stern drive. The drive is trimmed out for high performance and trimmed in for slower speeds and when turning.

The Effect of Power Trim: Surface Drives

With a trimmable surface drive, the power trim has the effect of lifting the propeller up or down, rather than in or out as with a stern drive or outboard. This will still have some small effect on hull trim. When the drive is up in surface-piercing mode, propeller thrust is angled more downward, which raises the bow of the boat.

However, the main function of power trim on a surface drive is to allow the driver to fine-tune the position of the propeller in relation to the surface of the water. The optimum position is with the hub of the propeller just above the surface so that only the bottom blades are in the water. This setting eliminates drag from the hub, propeller shaft, and supports.

Of course you cannot see the propeller when you are trying to trim it, so you have to watch for the effects of trimming the drive. You will have one eye on the rpm gauge and the other on the wake of the boat. With surface-piercing propellers there is a very clear indication when the top blades of the propeller break free from the water: the characteristic rooster tail will appear. As boat speed increases and the propeller starts to operate at top efficiency, the rooster tail will flatten out, indicating the drive is trimmed close to its optimum setting. This is when the bottom blades of the propeller are doing all the work.

Steering

Two distinct types of steering are used on fast boats: passive steering, with a rudder, and dynamic steering, which uses propeller thrust to steer the boat. There are significant differences between these two types of steering in terms of boat handling at high speed, and it is important to understand the mechanics of each.

Passive Steering

In passive steering, the rudder acts by diverting the flow of water, creating a sideways thrust at the stern to alter the boat's heading. Because the rudder usually lies in the propeller slipstream, the system can be very effective in providing smooth steering at high speeds. At low speeds, while maneuvering in a harbor for example, rudder steering is more effective if short bursts of power are given. This helps the boat angle into a berth with very little forward movement. With a rudder, the steering effect increases as boat speed increases. At high speed, minimal movement of the wheel will be enough to keep a boat on course.

On a planing boat the rudder size has to be a compromise. For slow-speed work the rudder should be as large as possible so that it has maximum steering effect, but at high speed, such a rudder would create considerable resistance and would be much too sensitive. At high speed you want the minimum amount of rudder in the water in order to reduce resistance, and the speed allows effective steering with a tiny rudder.

In part this compromise can be achieved by designing the rudder so that as the boat lifts in the water to get on a plane, the area of rudder blade actually in the water decreases. With a fixed surface drive, only the portion of the rudder that is behind the lower blades of the propeller will likely be in the water when traveling at speed.

On a twin-screw boat, twin rudders are normally used—one behind each propeller. With the rudders directly behind the propellers, the steering effect is optimized because the water flowing away from the propeller is moving faster than the water simply flowing past the hull of the boat.

High-speed boat rudders are invariably of the balanced type that has part of the blade forward of the vertical pivot. This balanced rudder considerably reduces the force needed to turn the rudder, because the area of blade in front of the pivot point is actually helping to turn the rudder against the resistance of the area behind the pivot. The distribution of blade area might be 40 percent in front of the vertical pivot and 60 percent behind, helping to make the steering light and responsive. Fast-boat steering with

a rudder is not normally self-centering, so the driver needs to turn the wheel to bring the steering back to the centerline.

Dynamic Steering

Dynamic steering is used on every outboard, stern drive, water jet, and most trimmable surface propulsion systems. In dynamic steering, the propeller shaft is moved from side to side to give a steering effect—except in the case of water jets, in which a nozzle is turned.

Propeller thrust creates a much stronger steering effect than rudder steering does. Of course this steering is only effective when the propeller is turning. When you take the engine out of gear, there is virtually no steering effect. Therefore you need a different handling technique when bringing craft

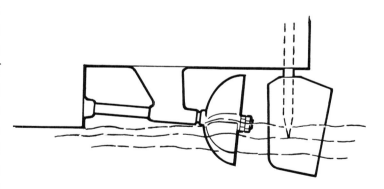

A balanced rudder working with a surface propeller. When the water flow is only through the bottom blades of the propeller, the effective area of the rudder is reduced. The balanced rudder has part of its blade forward of the pivot point to reduce the load required when turning.

of this type alongside a dock or into a slip. The answer is to keep the engine in gear right to the last moment in order to preserve steering control.

The stronger steering effect generated by dynamic steering is not usually noticeable on a straight-line course, but it can make a significant difference when you execute sharp turns. The turning circle of a boat with dynamic steering can be half that of the same boat with rudder steering. Care needs to be taken when turning sharply with outboards and stern-drive propulsion systems because cavitation could occur, with air bubbles around the propeller reducing its efficiency. Once cavitation sets in, it can normally be eliminated only by slowing the boat down rapidly, centering the steering, and then opening the throttle again to regain full steering control.

Outboard and stern-drive steering is normally self-centering, which does not create any problems on a twin-screw boat, where the side thrust or torque from the two propellers cancels out and gives balanced steering. With a single engine, however, there is a sideways component to the engine thrust generated as a reaction to the propeller turning. If you let go of the steering wheel this side thrust could cause the boat to spin around sharply. Some types of steering are designed to eliminate this "feedback" or side-thrust effect; such steering can be a good safety precaution that will

prevent the boat spinning out if the driver lets go of the wheel.

On high-speed boats there can be dangers in using dynamic steering when the boat leaves the water as it flies off the top of a wave. With the propeller out of the water, the steering effect is temporarily lost and is only regained as the propeller reenters the water. The first part of the boat to reenter the water will normally be the propeller. If the steering was turned or was off-center just as the boat became airborne, there will be a steering thrust that has nothing to act against for a very short period of time—until the boat reenters the water. Then the boat will act on this steering thrust with possibly disastrous consequences. Such a scenario is believed to be one of the primary causes of spinout, in which a boat turns sharply in one direction or the other at high speed, sometimes turning 180 degrees or end for end.

This type of spinout is only likely to occur in very high speed boats—and even then, only when the steering is turned sharply just as the boat leaves the water. But it does happen. The driver may turn the helm farther than normal because there was no reaction to the smaller steering corrections that were attempted just before the boat went airborne. The proper driver reaction, however, is to keep the helm amidships if the boat leaves the water. (For details on other types of spinout, see the section "Spinout" in chapter 7, "Driving a Fast Boat.")

In theory, spinout could also occur with rudder steering. But because the steering effect from the rudder is less, the chances of this happening are small.

The Effect of Steering on Trim

Turn the wheel on a fast boat when it is traveling at high speed and you will feel the boat heel over into the turn in a reassuring manner. It feels comfortable for the boat to heel in this way, the heeling tending to counteract the centrifugal force that wants to fling the boat outward from the turn. The same effect happens on a smaller scale when small adjustments are made to the boat's course. Each movement of the steering wheel will have a small effect on transverse trim, causing the boat to heel in the direction in which the wheel is turned.

This effect increases with speed. In boats traveling at 50 or 60 knots, the boat heels from side to side as each steering correction is made. This occurs at all planing speeds, but it is magnified at higher speeds because as speed increases, the amount of hull in the water is reduced, with a consequent reduction in dynamic stability. This reduces the ability of the hull to counteract the trim effect created by turning the steering wheel.

With the hull heeling over from side to side, there is a much greater possibility that the flat sides of the V of the hull, rather than the keel, will impact the waves. And such impacts make for a harsh ride.

To avoid this phenomenon, only very small corrections should be made to the steering when running at moderate to high speed. It should require no more than a degree or two of rudder to maintain course on a fast boat, and these corrections should be made gently to avoid unnecessary heeling.

It can be hard to use this lighter touch when steering at high speeds because the normal reaction is to grip the wheel tightly in order to feel in control. A light touch on the steering can only be achieved if the driver is stationed so securely at the helm that it's not necessary to use the wheel as a handhold or brace. There's always the danger that the driver will hold the wheel tightly, which can result in larger course corrections that cause the hull to swing from side to side; these swinging movements produce a rougher ride, and this makes the driver hold on even tighter, causing the ride to become even harsher. In extreme situations, wrestling with the wheel in this way can lead to a boat capsizing. The situation can be amplified on a RIB if its tubes are inflated hard, because they can bounce as the boat heels, starting the boat into a violent swinging motion.

Another situation where you can find a boat heeling is when the wind is on the beam. It's a characteristic of deep-V hulls that they heel into the wind. The beam wind will blow the bow off course, and the driver will instinctively correct this by using counter helm, which of course makes the boat heel into the wind.

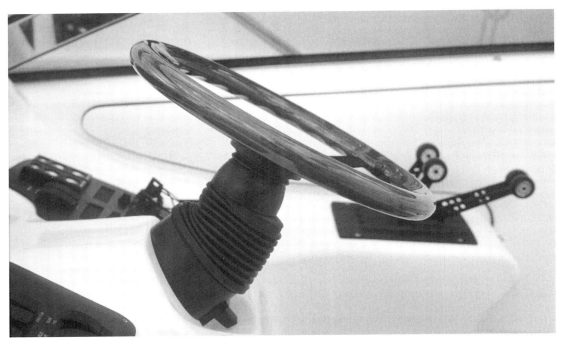

An adjustable wheel improves steering control.

This heeling can be corrected by dropping the windward trim tab to bring the hull upright. Lowering this tab also adds resistance on the windward side, which helps counteract the effect of the wind blowing on the bow, so that it should be possible to restore balance to the boat. The lowered tab also will bring the bow down a little.

Control of Directional Stability

A hull is directionally stable if it is able to maintain a steady course with little or no steering correction. One purpose of the controls on a fast boat is to help provide this stability, which makes the steering much easier and can also help to give a smoother ride.

With a deep-V hull, directional stability is normally achieved by having a cutaway forefoot to reduce the amount of the forward part of the hull in the water, and also by introducing lifting strakes into the hull shape, which help keep the boat on a straight course. You will find that a hull with a deeper V—with a deadrise of around 20 degrees or more—will tend to have better directional stability than one with a moderate or shallow V.

You may be able to improve directional stability by using the power trim—trimming the drive unit out, which will lift the bow. Too much power trim can have a negative effect, however. As with most things on a fast boat, it's a question of finding a compromise, a balance.

Hulls fitted with conventional shaft-and-propeller propulsion tend to have good directional stability because the propellers give the hull some bite on the water. With surface drives this bite is reduced; with water-jet propulsion, it virtually disappears. Water-jet boats have poor directional stability also because the lifting strakes on the hulls are usually stopped well short of the stern in order to avoid disrupting the smooth flow of water to the jet intakes. Fins are often added at the stern to improve directional stability.

In fine-tuning the directional stability with adjustments to the trim of the boat, the overall balance of the vessel can be quite critical. These experiments need to be carried out in calm water so that the effects of waves are taken out of the equation.

Gears

Two-speed gearboxes, providing both a low and high range for forward travel, provide considerable performance benefits for a fast boat and make it more user-friendly (see the section "Two-Speed Gearboxes" in chapter 4, "Engines and Propulsion"). These

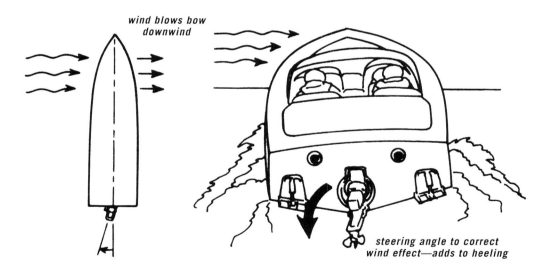

Moving a propeller shaft from side to side for steering—known as dynamic steering—also contributes to the heel of a fast powerboat when the wind is on the beam. In this situation the bow tends to blow off course, and the helmsman's instinctive correction with the steerable propeller increases the heel.

gearboxes contribute to directional stability by permitting better throttle response.

In any situation where the speed of the engine is being varied—maneuvering in harbor, getting the boat onto a plane, turning, operating in rough seas—a two-speed gearbox in low gear aids performance tremendously. Low gear improves the acceleration characteristics of the boat and gives a more sensitive response to the throttle, a wider movement to the throttle producing smaller increases and decreases in speed than with the single forward gear of a standard gearbox.

High gear is usually used when the boat is operating at or near top speed. High-gear operation produces maximum boat speed, but there will be a penalty in decreased acceleration and throttle response. It would be natural to tune the propeller to be at its most efficient for this high-speed operation in high gear in order to generate the most speed. However, the propeller choice has to be balanced against the need for lower-speed operation in low gear and, like all propeller choices, there has to be some compromise between the requirements of different speeds. A two-speed gearbox makes these compromises easier to accommodate.

Ballast Systems

By changing the location of weight on a boat, you change the center of gravity and thus alter the trim of the boat and its sta-bility. Most racing boats are fitted with a ballast tank in the bow. The main purpose of the tank, when filled with water, is to keep the bow down in challenging head seas.

Trim tabs and power trim offer ways to adjust the longitudinal trim of a fast boat, within certain limits, by bringing the bow down. A ballast tank also offers this capability, but because the ballast adds weight to the boat, trimming by means of ballast is not normally used during high-speed operation in good conditions. The benefit of using ballast comes in rough seas, where the additional weight not only trims the boat down by the bow but also helps to keep the boat on the water, reducing the chances of flying off the top of a wave.

There are two ways of using ballast to trim a boat, and both require that specific systems be installed. One system has a ballast tank built into the bow that can be filled with water or emptied anytime through controls on the dashboard. A typical ballast tank adds 200 to 300 pounds at the bow, moving the center of gravity of the boat farther forward when the tank is filled.

The second system, which can complement the first, uses fuel transfer as a means of varying weight distribution in the boat. Fuel tanks are normally located around the center of gravity of the boat so that variations in fuel weight do not affect the trim. But with a fuel-transfer ballast system, the

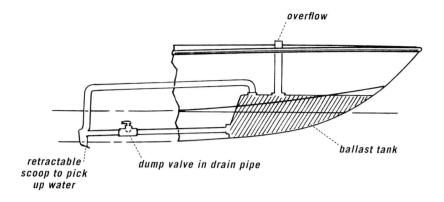

One method of filling and emptying bow ballast tanks with water. The ballast tank should be empty when running downwind.

fuel tanks need to be as widely separated as possible, one in the stern and one near the bow. Fuel lines connect the two tanks, and a pump moves fuel from one tank to the other.

The fuel-transfer system can be used to trim the bow of the boat either up or down. In head seas, the driver can transfer fuel to the bow tank to help keep the bow down. In following seas, fuel can be transferred to the stern tank to help raise the bow. An independent bow water-ballast tank, on the other hand, is useful only in bringing the bow down.

The fuel-transfer system is effective only when there is some free space in the tanks—when they are neither full nor nearly empty. If the tanks are full, of course it won't be possible to move fuel between them. If the tanks are close to empty, there will be too lit-

tle fuel weight to have any helpful effect.

Overall, a fuel-transfer ballast system may be better suited to a fast cruising boat, where ultimate performance is not as important as comfort, than to a racing boat. A fuel-transfer system can make cruising more comfortable by shifting the center of gravity for a smoother ride as prevailing conditions change.

Another form of ballasting involves shifting the crew around in the boat. However, no crew member should ever go forward of the steering position in head seas. This important safety prohibition greatly limits the possibility of crew movements having any major effect on trim. The main use of crew shifting comes during operations in following seas, when any movable weight should be concentrated as far aft as possible in order to permit maximum lift at the bow.

Balance

We started off this chapter talking about the various controls available to fast boats and about the need for a balance among them. The objective for the driver is to find a balance in the performance of the boat that enables it to perform well under the prevailing conditions.

A wide range of controls is available to a fast-boat driver. You will not find all of them on every fast boat, and you may be limited to just the throttles, steering, trim tabs, and power trim. Even the power trim will be absent from boats with conventional shaft-and-propeller systems or fixed surface drives, so there will be limits to the level of control you have.

There is a school of thought that says the fewer the controls the better, because in a fast-boat environment, it's not always easy to adjust the multiple controls required to keep the boat operating at its best. You can do this in calm water, where you can take your eyes off the water and where you don't need to keep one hand on the throttle at all times, but in rough seas you have all you can do to handle the throttles and steering. You have little or no time to think about, not to mention operate, the trim and other controls.

With many cruising boats operating in the 30- to 40-knot range, your options for controlling the boat are likely to be limited anyway. Any response to the throttle may be too slow to be immediately effective, so you will tend to set the throttles for a comfortable speed, with some reserve in hand, and just deal with the steering. You may even let the autopilot do the steering in order to concentrate on navigating and keeping a lookout. Tabs might be your only convenient option for trimming the boat for the best balance in a particular prevailing condition.

No matter what controls you have available, you will not always be able to get the balance completely right, because there are some sea conditions in which a boat simply will not be able to get into step with the waves. However, as you've now learned, there is a surprising amount you can do with the controls to improve performance. You'll discover that there are almost magical times when you get it just right and the boat is "on song."

You'll recognize when this happens. The boat will be going faster than you ever thought possible for the conditions; the trim will be giving you a comfortable ride, with the boat remaining almost at the same attitude all the time. This is when the adrenaline flows and powerboating becomes pure poetry. It can take courage to get the boat to this level of performance, and there may be some hard bangs along the way, but the result is more than worth it.

6

Wind and Waves

When you take your fast powerboat out on the water you will be operating in one of the most complex arenas you can imagine. On the interface between the atmosphere and the sea, the two can mix together to create great turbulence. It's mainly wind energy that starts the commotion. The waves born of this turbulence have a dramatic effect on fast-boat performance.

If you understand what happens when wind and waves mix, you will have a much better understanding of the environment in which your boat is operating. In this chapter we will discuss wind and waves, learning how waves form and how they behave. But the best way to learn about waves is to watch them. Watch them from the beach, from a ship, and from a boat; watch them in all conditions. The more you watch the sea the more you become aware of its complex-

ity and its constant changes. Then you will understand it better and get better performance out of your boat.

A flat calm or perhaps a light chop presents the ideal conditions for a fast boat, allowing it to operate at its best. Here there is minimum turbulence, the running conditions for the boat remain constant, and the forces acting on the boat are in equilibrium. But everything changes when the wind starts to generate waves. The boat's center of buoyancy and distribution of dynamic lift are in constant motion as it struggles to retain an equilibrium with passing waves. Any equilibrium is transient, immediately shattered by the combined movements of boat and waves.

If the waves are regular, the adjustment between boat and waves takes place in a predictable and repetitive manner as the waves pass. But perfectly regular waves are no more likely than the chances of finding a perfect flat calm. Even waves generated by a steady wind will rarely be regular. And when the effects of previous, decaying wave trains, transient changes in wind direction, surface currents and tides, shallow water, underwater topography and shoreline configuration are taken into account, the sea can—and usually does—present a very irregular surface. This is a far cry from that ideal environment for operating a fast boat, but it is there and we can't change it. It's up to us to learn how to operate our fast boats safely and efficiently under the conditions that exist.

How the Wind Generates Waves

Imagine still water and still air. There is no interaction between them. But once the air has energy—usually generated by heat differences in the atmosphere—it starts to move. This interaction between two fluids, air and water, has two results. First, the air starts to drag the surface water along with it because of the friction between air and water. This is what is mainly responsible for oceanic currents, and it occurs when the wind tends to blow in a constant direction most of the time.

The second result is that the friction generates turbulence in the air. This starts as local turbulence on a tiny scale, and it creates small areas of low and high pressure in the air close to the surface of the sea. These high and low pressure areas start to make the water surface uneven. Now ripples start to form, which in turn increase the irregularity of the surface, which leads to an increase in the friction between air and water, and so the process continues.

Given a steady horizontal movement over the water surface, this airflow will exert pressure on the windward slopes of ripples and create a partial vacuum on their leeward sides. This pressure difference causes the ripples to be driven along in the direction of the wind, and as long as the wind is moving more rapidly than the ripples it is generating, these ripples will grow into waves that will increase in size until a state of equilibrium is reached.

Wave Basics

Let's begin by defining what we are talking about. A *wavelength* is the distance from the crest of one wave to the crest of the next wave. *Wave height* is the height from the bottom of the trough between two crests to the top of the adjacent crest. Wave *period* is the time it takes for two successive wave crests to pass a fixed point, and is thus an indication of wave speed. Wave *gradient* is the angle of the wave slope to the horizontal, a measure of how steep the wave is. There are close relationships among all these factors, and they affect the shapes of waves and the ways they behave.

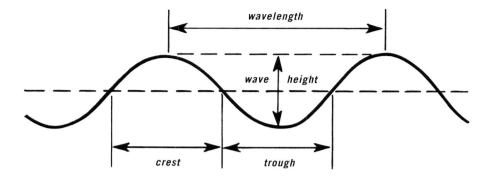

Terms associated with waves.

In practice, the relationship between the size and shape of waves means that the larger or higher the wave, the faster it will travel. This is because wavelength is directly related to wave height, assuming a constant gradient, and wave speed is directly related to wavelength: the greater its length, the faster a wave will travel.

A typical 80-foot wavelength that might be found in open coastal waters in a moderate breeze will consist of waves that travel at just over 12 knots. Out in the open sea, where wavelengths will be longer, a wave with a length of 150 feet will travel at 18 knots. Very long ocean swells can travel at speeds of several hundred knots, but the low height of these waves makes them barely perceptible; they do not present any danger until they meet shallow water.

The differences in wavelength, and hence wave speed, of different sea conditions are particularly relevant when a boat is operating in following seas. In these conditions you need enough speed to be able to overtake the waves. A considerably higher speed will be required for this in open waters, where wavelengths and wave speeds are greater, than for inshore waters, though wave height will also be a consideration. The speed of waves also can be affected by external influences such as tides, currents, and shallow water that can lengthen or shorten the wavelength, as we'll see later in the chapter.

An important factor in assessing waves for fast-boat operations is the wave gradient, or steepness. Most waves have a gentle gradient, generally only 10 to 15 degrees from the horizontal, but the slope may feel a lot steeper than this when you are operating your boat. A wave at sea tends to have a variable gradient: shallow near the bottom of the wave and steeper near its crest. This is particularly true on the lee side of a wave, since the pressure of the wind on the windward side helps to create a concave slope to leeward.

When looking at a wave from a fast boat, it is the steeper part of the wave, rather than the average gradient, that gets your attention as you head into it. This steeper part could have a gradient of 15 to 18 degrees or even more, certainly steep enough to make a significant difference for fast-boat operations.

It is the combination of wave height and wavelength that determines steepness. A 20-foot-high wave with a wavelength of 2,000 feet will have a very gentle gradient, even though the wave can look high. Such a wave is likely to be a swell, the smooth leftover sea that emanates far from a gale after the wind has stopped blowing.

A more common length for this height of wave under the influence of a strong wind would be 250 to 300 feet in the open ocean, making a much steeper and more dangerous gradient. It's generally recognized that a critical gradient for a wave is 18 degrees: above this steepness, the wave becomes unstable. Then the wave generally can no longer support its own weight, and it will likely break at the crest in order to restore stability.

Types of Waves

You will encounter a variety of wave types as a fast-boat driver, each having a different effect on your boat. Among the varieties you'll see are ripples, oscillation waves, pressure waves, breaking waves, and clapotic waves. Except for pressure waves, these waves are generated primarily by the wind. Some of them are transformed by contact with features such as shallow water, tidal currents, or land.

Ripples are disturbances in the water that form in very light winds; they grow into small wavelets and then recognizable waves as wind strength increases. *Oscillation waves* are those typically found in the open sea—waves in which each parcel of water oscillates up and down and backward and forward but returns nearly to its prior position after the wave passes. *Pressure waves* are generated when a ship passes through the water. *Breaking waves* are also known as translation waves, the name deriving from the wave's translation from an oscillating wave to one in which there is a release of energy in the form of a forward rush of breaking water. *Clapotic waves* are particularly chaotic waves formed by intersecting or colliding wave trains; they form most commonly near shore and can produce some of the more dangerous and unpredictable of boating conditions.

Oscillation Waves

In an ideal waveform, each of the water particles within a wave describes a circular orbit, perpendicular to the crest of the wave returning to its starting point when the wave passes. These are oscillation waves. You can see the effect of this motion if you watch waves in a harbor when there is some light debris lying on the surface. The debris tends to bob backward and forward and up and down as the waves pass; the debris is simply following part of the circular motion of the water particles, though its buoyancy prevents it from describing a full circle.

Thus in an oscillation wave the waveform travels, but the water particles do not—this is the ideal wave. The oscillations of water particles are confined relatively close to the surface. At a depth equivalent to one wavelength, water movement related to the wave is virtually damped out, and the water is largely undisturbed.

There is a direct relationship between wind strength and wave height. Under the influence of wind—assuming a wind of sufficient duration blowing over a sufficient distance, or fetch, of open water (see later in chapter)—waves will continue to build until a state of equilibrium is reached. An oscillation wave has to be supported by a cer-

tain amount of energy from the wind or it will simply collapse, but this energy requirement is quite small, because although the wave appears to be moving bodily forward, the circular orbits of the particles within the wave mean that the water is actually almost stationary.

In theory the shape of an oscillation wave should follow the tidy pattern of a regular curve. The wind should produce a regular series of waves of similar height and shape. In practice, however, waves vary considerably in height and shape. The wind itself modifies the shape of the wave simply because of the pressure it exerts on one side and the partial vacuum this creates on the other side. This means the wave is likely to be more convex on the windward side and more concave on the leeward side, particularly near the top of the wave where the influence of the wind is greatest. This change in shape of the wave can become more extreme as wind strength increases, which is why there is a

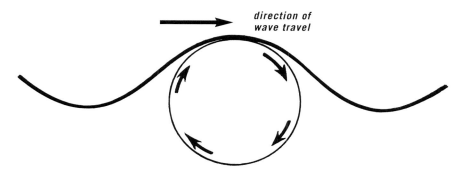

The particles in a wave follow a circular path.

greater tendency for waves to break in stronger winds.

Breaking Waves

With wind pressure on one side of a wave crest and a partial vacuum on the other, quite a force develops that aims to topple the wave—especially if the wave is higher than average in a wave train and thus more exposed to wind. Wind pressure toward the top of the wave also means the top wants to move faster to leeward than the bottom does. The result is a steepening wave face and an instability that is alleviated only after the very top of the wave breaks to leeward.

These breaking waves, in which only the crest breaks, creating a foaming mass of broken white water that runs forward, are known as "white horses" or whitecaps. They appear when wind speeds start to reach about 15 knots (force 4).

These initial white horses are not partic-ularly dangerous to fast boats, because only the very tops of the waves topple, and there is not much strength or volume in the breaking water. This comparatively minor breaking of the crest temporarily relieves the pressure differences around the wave, and the wave quickly stabilizes again once the gradient angle (steepness) has been reduced. As soon as the wind decreases, the white horses disappear.

In stronger winds, however, white horses can become potentially dangerous because of the additional weight and volume of water in the breaking crest. Usually around a wind speed of 30 to 40 knots (force 7 to 8 on the Beaufort Scale), instability from the increase in wave gradient means the white horses tend to lose their random behavior and become much more frequent and more powerful.

The formation of breaking waves in shallow water will be covered later in this chapter, in the section on inshore waves.

Typical wave cross section with steeper face leeward.

Swell and Cross-Seas

Once a train of waves has been started by the action of the wind, it might keep going forever were it not for the internal friction created by the movement of the water particles and the surface tension of the water. Both of these act to gradually reduce wave size and increase wavelength after the wind has stopped imparting energy to them. The cross section of the wave becomes a more flowing, balanced curve.

These residual waves are called swells. The fact that wave trains can persist as swell for a long time after the wind has changed or dropped is one of the factors that complicates the forecasting of wave heights and directions and can also contribute to the formation of rogue waves.

When the wind dies away it will rarely freshen again from the same direction. When a new wind blows in, it sets up a wave train from the new direction. This pattern interacts with the decaying swell from the previous wind, and the result can be a confusing sea that produces difficult conditions for a fast boat.

At this point there will be a significant cross-sea—and where two wave crests coincide, the height of the resulting wave will be the combined heights of the two individual waves. Likewise, two troughs can combine to create a deeper trough. (When a trough and a crest coincide, the depth of the trough will be subtracted from the height of the crest to reduce wave height.)

When wind-generated waves 4 feet high cross a swell that is 2 feet high, there could be transient 6-foot peaks where crests of the intersecting wave trains coincide. If the wind and swell do not cross but instead happen to travel in roughly the same direction at different speeds, the waves resulting from the two wave trains combining could have longer, higher crests. Either of these

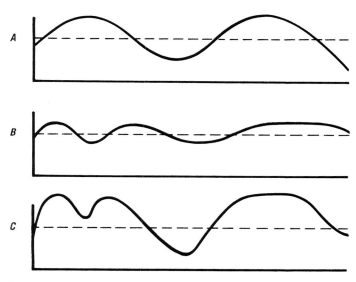

The combination of wave trains A and B produces the wave pattern shown in C. Interactions like this account for the irregular wave patterns often found at sea.

types of transient waves can create problems for a fast boat.

More difficult to cope with are the deeper troughs that can result when two troughs combine. While it might be possible to see and anticipate a higher than normal wave, you will not see a deeper trough until you come over the leading wave. At this point you are committed, in terms of speed and trim, and a deeper trough, or "hole," can be a nasty experience. I've encountered such holes in shallow water, and you think you can almost see the seabed. It's not so much coping with the boat falling *into* the hole that can be tough, but rather the possibility of the boat being overwhelmed as it tries to climb back *out.*

The severe form of cross-seas that results in dangerous clapotic waves will be discussed later in this chapter, in the section on inshore cross-seas.

Inshore Waves

In the open ocean, the size and behavior of waves are directly related to wind strength and direction, but closer to shore, additional factors influence waves. Shallow water, tides, currents, and the topography of the land both above and below the low-tide

The sort of breaking seas that can occur in shallow water or with strong tides and current. They tend to be localized, as can be seen from the calmer conditions farther out to sea. (Pim Korver)

mark all cause changes in sea conditions. With the exception of currents, these forces have little influence on the open sea. But because you will probably be operating your fast boat in coastal waters most of the time, an understanding of these forces is essential.

Tides and other near-shore features can all be forecast with some accuracy. A study of navigational charts and tide tables can guide you in avoiding or coping with tides, currents, shallow waters, and other potentially troublesome variables. These factors can produce local wave changes, especially when their influences combine, but learning what these changes are will help you deal with them. Keep in mind that larger than normal waves can arrive without warning, and caution is always needed to cope with such unpredictable conditions.

The following sections will take a close look at the factors that influence inshore waves. Shallow waters have a dramatic effect on wave behavior, as anyone will know who has watched waves breaking on a beach. Currents cause a whole body of water to move, and this can affect wave shape and gradient, particularly when the current is moving against the wind. Tides (tidal currents) have a similar effect, but the consequences can be more dramatic because the direction of flow usually changes four times every 24 hours or so. The topography of the land and seabed also produce significant changes, including the phenomena known as wave reflection and wave refraction that can result in cross-seas, clapotic waves, and other challenges for a fast boat.

Shallow Water and Breaking Waves

When a wave becomes unstable, either through increasing wind pressure or other factors, it changes from the regular shape of the oscillation wave, in which water particles simply orbit around and around, into a breaking wave (translation wave).

An obvious place for a wave to break is on a beach. The wave is slowed down as it approaches the beach because of resistance from the shoaling seabed. This causes the wavelength—the distance from one wave crest to the next—to become shorter, because the waves behind are catching up with the slower-moving waves ahead of them. Thus the waves get steeper, which in turn makes them unstable. These unstable waves will then tend to break over a long front and expend their energy as they crash onto the beach.

For a better idea of how this works, consider that you see only the top portion of a wave on the surface, but the circular movement of water particles in the wave can extend some distance down. When these moving water particles start to touch the seabed, they are slowed down, while the top of the wave continues its normal progress toward shore. It is thought that the influence of the seabed on the behavior of a wave can be found at considerably greater

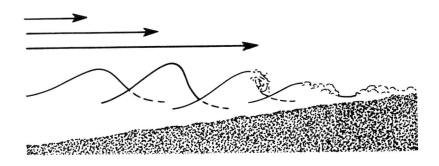

A breaking wave in shallow water. Here the whole wave rears up and breaks heavily with considerable violence.

depths than double the wave height. This helps explain why ocean swells, with their long wavelengths, can start to be affected by contact with the seabed a long way from shore.

In shallow water the top of the wave still travels forward at close to its original speed, overrunning the bottom. Meanwhile the slowing down of the bottom of the wave results in a reduction in wavelength and an increase in steepness. Around shoals and along the shore, these effects accumulate to the point where the wave becomes unstable and breaks.

A beach area with breaking waves is not a place a fast boat would operate by choice, but you can get similar breaking-wave effects over and around shoals, even though the water might be deep enough for navigation. The possibility of waves breaking in shallow water like this increases as the waves get higher. What might be a perfectly acceptable stretch of shallow water to cross

in calm or moderate conditions could produce dangerous breaking seas when stronger winds and larger waves rule the day.

In shoal water and on beaches, a wave breaks differently from the way it breaks in the open sea. At sea the crest tends to run down the face of a wave gradually, since it is only being influenced by the wind. In shallow water, the wind effect may still be there, but because the wave is also slowed by contact with the seabed, the wave in effect trips over itself, and a near-vertical wall of water is formed before the crest falls violently forward into the trough. The energy of the wave is then translated into a strong horizontal rush of water onto the beach. Over a shoal there may not be so much of this forward movement, but the breaking of the wave can still be quite violent.

In shallow water it is the depth of the water and the size of the waves that determine whether waves break or not. Even if the waves don't actually break, it is often possible to feel the influence of shallow water by a discernible shortening of the wavelength and a steepening of the gradient. These changes can generate nasty sea conditions, and they should serve as a warning to fast boats to seek deeper water.

The depth of water at which a wave will start to shorten and steepen is roughly equal to the wavelength itself. A typical wavelength for waves in inshore waters might be 60 feet, so you can see that it's readily possible to experience this shallow-water effect in waters that are perfectly viable for navigation. However, the shorter wavelength and steepening of the waves won't be clearly noticeable until the depth of water is about half the original wavelength, in this case 30 feet—still a normally safe depth for navigation. At this stage the gradient of the wave is unlikely to approach the critical 18-degree angle for breaking. That will occur when the wave is in comparatively shallow water, perhaps around 15 to 20 feet.

It's now obvious that in more severe sea conditions it pays to give areas of shallow water a wider berth than normal. Think of "shallow" in its relative sense. Breaking waves can be found in any area wherever there is a significant change from deeper to shallower water, and therefore it should be possible to anticipate their formation from a study of a navigational chart. The wavelength is the significant factor to look at when trying to anticipate where oscillation waves will be transformed into breaking waves.

Pressure Waves

Pressure waves are a specialized phenomenon encountered, most commonly, with the passage of a large ship on inshore waters. All hulls must overcome their own wave-making resistance, and the energy they expend in doing so creates the familiar bow and stern waves that run outward from a boat or ship. Because they are generated by a one-time input of energy from the ship, such waves decay fairly rapidly and are unlikely to be felt more than a mile or so from their point of origin.

In calm or near-calm conditions, it's quite easy to see these waves approaching (at least in daylight). Yet they can present a hazard to fast boats, and in moderate seas they can be difficult to identify among regular wave patterns.

Pressure waves can be particularly dangerous at night, when it is not possible to see and assess their size. However, you may have warning of the possibility of these waves from seeing shipping in the vicinity. You can anticipate the approach of pressure waves by knowing the heading of the ship and figuring that the waves will emanate from its bow and the stern at an angle of about 20 to 30 degrees from its centerline. These pressure waves could cause dangerous local conditions if they arrive on top of an already rough sea; the mixing of the two wave trains could lead to high crests and breaking waves.

Another danger comes from pressure waves created by the new generation of ferries that can operate at speeds up to 40 knots. While these ferries tend to have long, slender hulls that minimize wave-making, they can generate considerable waves when they are operating at intermediate speeds, between 15 and 35 knots. This occurs when they are speeding up or slowing down as they enter or leave a harbor, and at this point they could be close to shallow water. This combination can create dangerous waves. In one incident involving a fast ferry, a fishing boat encountered a 15-foot breaking wave in what were otherwise moderate seas.

Currents and Tides

Currents and tidal currents can have a significant influence on both wavelength and wave height, and consequently on the gradient of waves. Prevailing currents are mainly wind generated, while tidal currents are generated by differences in sea level due the varying gravitational attractions of the sun and moon.

Currents

On moving water, wavelengths will be shortened if the wind is blowing against the current and lengthened when wind and current are flowing in the same direction.

In general, currents flow continuously in one direction, and because the current is caused by wind, chances are it will be flowing with the prevailing wind.

With wind and current flowing the same way and increasing the wavelengths, there will be a consequent reduction in the gradient of the waves, and sea conditions are likely to be moderate. But if the wind blows in the opposite direction, or even across the current, watch out. The shortened wavelengths mean steeper, more aggressive waves that can make life uncomfortable for fast boats. It's important to keep an eye on currents in areas where they run strongly. Conditions can deteriorate quickly—most notably when the wind changes direction and starts blowing against the current.

Difficult currents occur principally in near-shore areas. Open-sea currents rarely flow at more than 1 knot, so their general effect on sea conditions will be fairly minimal. But there are exceptions: winds blowing against the current in the Gulf Stream can cause nasty seas.

Tides

Tidal currents can have a much more pronounced effect on sea conditions than wind-generated currents. This is partly because the tidal flow changes direction every six hours or so, but also because the speeds of tidal currents can be higher, in extreme circumstances up to 10 knots. This combination can have a profound effect on waves,

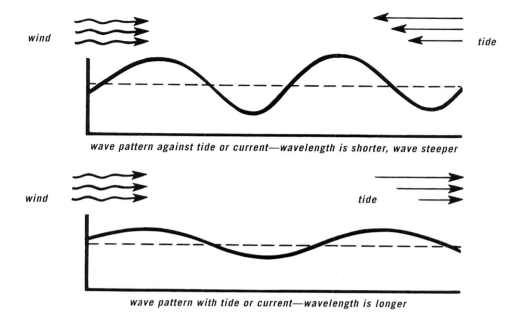

wave pattern against tide or current—wavelength is shorter, wave steeper

wave pattern with tide or current—wavelength is longer

Wave profiles are modified under the influence of currents or tide.

creating some of the most dangerous sea conditions in the world.

It's one thing when tidal flow and wind travel in the same direction, but quite another when they move in opposition. When the wind blows against the tide, two effects are evident. First, there is an apparent increase in wind strength as far as the waves are concerned, resulting from wind and tide working in opposition. Second, the progress of the waves to leeward is slowed by the water flow upwind. These two factors combine to cause wavelengths to shorten considerably. Shortening the wavelength while maintaining the wave height increases the gradient, imposing a far higher risk of breaking waves.

Wind-against-tide conditions are characterized by a wickedly short, steep sea. Even in relatively light winds the sea can become quite uncomfortable. Because the crests arrive in quick succession, it's easy for a comparatively small boat to get out of step with the waves, failing to fully recover from one before the next is upon it. In stronger winds or tides, when these steep seas break, conditions for smaller fast boats can get difficult and dangerous.

Conditions within a tidal current can deteriorate suddenly. The switch from a strong tide running with the wind to a tide that has turned and is running strongly in the opposite direction can take place within an hour. From a comparatively benign sea with wind and tide running together, the change of tide can create short, steep waves that result initially in a mass of the breaking waves known as white horses, with white water spilling forward from the very crests of the waves. As the tide gains strength, and the wind perhaps also increases, these white horses can rapidly develop into heavy breaking seas of the type that are often described on the chart as overfalls. These dangerous seas are commonly limited in extent and it should be possible find a way around them, often by keeping inshore, where the tide has less strength.

When winds approach gale force, any wind-against-tide situation is apt to produce severe seas even when the tidal flow is moderate. Fortunately, these are not likely to be the conditions in which you will choose to go to sea.

Effect of Land Features on Tides and Currents

Where a current or tidal stream is interrupted by a headland or is forced into a channel between an island and the mainland, the speed of the flow will usually increase. This accelerated movement can generate steeper, possibly breaking waves, particularly when the wind is against the flow.

Breaking waves are more likely to be encountered at the entrance or exit of narrow channels or on either side of a prominent headland, places where the flow meets currents that are moving more slowly or in different directions, creating so-called tidal races.

Conditions can become more severe if an eddy forms behind a particularly prominent headland, with this eddy turning back to meet the main tidal or current flow. Shallow water also can make things worse, compressing and accelerating and possibly diverting the current. This can create breaking waves.

The wind also tends to be stronger around headlands and in narrow channels, where it is accelerated by the land features in something called the venturi effect; this factor, too, will generate rougher conditions. Adding to the challenge, the wind tends to follow a channel or coastline, so you may not find sheltered waters where you expected them based on prevailing winds.

Narrow channels, shallow waters, and known tidal races are shown on navigational charts. You can study your chart and the flow of currents and tidal streams in the area for clues to where difficult sea conditions might be expected, although this picture has to be developed with the present wind conditions in mind.

Inshore Cross-Seas

Difficult seas in which two wave trains cross each other and form high, pyramid-shaped waves are more commonly encountered in near-shore waters than out at sea. Cross-seas do form at sea, such as when wind-

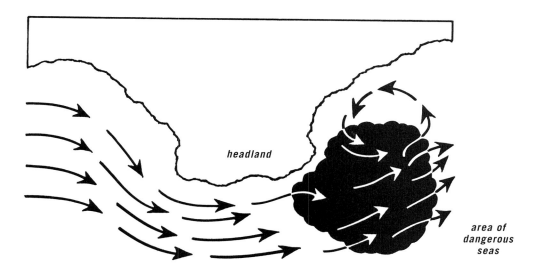

Tidal current flow around a pronounced headland creates an area of rough seas.

headland

area of
dangerous
seas

Severe surf conditions as waves encounter shallow water at the entrance to an inlet.

generated waves cross through a swell traveling in a different direction, creating a confusing wave combination (see the earlier section "Swell and Cross-Seas" in this chapter). But there is less chance of finding steep pyramid waves in the open sea because changes tend to occur more slowly there, without the landforms and other factors that influence inshore waves.

Pyramid waves are higher than normal because they form at particular points where the crests of two wave trains, traveling in different directions, coincide. The pyramid waves, sometimes called short-crested waves, can appear suddenly and disappear just as quickly; the danger lies in the unexpected nature of their arrival.

In most cases when wave trains cross, the wave train being generated by the prevailing wind is usually superior to the secondary wave train. This reduces the chance of a combination of wave crests producing a very high peak, as could be the case if the waves were of equal height. There are situations, however, in which intersecting wave trains are of the same or similar height, and these can produce particularly vicious sea conditions. This might be the case when a low-pressure weather system is passing through and the rapid change in wind direction that occurs when the cold front passes leads to a wind swing of 90 degrees.

The situation can also develop when a wave train approaches a vertical harbor wall or cliff face that rises above relatively deep water. The approaching waves will hit

The sort of pyramid wave that occurs when two wave trains cross: these waves tend to be transient but can rear up without warning.

the vertical face and reflect back at an angle equal and opposite to that at which they strike it. This generates a mirror-image set of waves moving away from shore.

If the approaching wave train is parallel to the cliff, the reflected waves will also be parallel to the cliff, but moving in the opposite direction. If the approaching waves hit at an angle of 45 degrees to the cliff, the reflected waves will travel outward at the same angle, intersecting the arriving crests at 90 degrees. The intense collision between these two wave trains will produce what is called clapotic waves, or clapotic seas. These are pyramid-shaped waves that leap high in the air and then collapse in a welter of white water, resulting in seas that can be particularly dangerous for small craft.

Clapotic seas display a viciousness that is rarely found in other types of waves. They give a boat very little time to recover from negotiating one towering crest before it is hit by the next. Fortunately, areas of clapotic seas are usually local in nature and rarely extend more than a mile offshore.

Wave Refraction

Wave refraction is another inshore phenomenon that can throw up dangerous seas—and the risk here is that these conditions may appear just when you are expecting to find good shelter.

Wave refraction alters the direction in which waves are traveling, because of their contact with land or shallow water. The waves are refracted, or bent, because the part of the wave that is nearest to shore is slowed down when it arrives in shallower

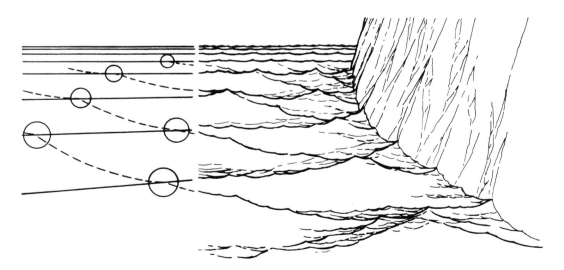

Expect to find higher than normal wave peaks where reflected waves cross incoming wave trains.

water. Gradually the entire line of the wave crest, under the drag of the slow end, pinwheels around to change the wave's direction of travel.

The effect of wave refraction can be seen on a beach when waves approach at an angle but tend to break parallel to the beach because the inshore end of each crest has been slowed down. The same effect can be seen when waves curve around a headland and change direction, even entering what might be expected to be a sheltered bay on the lee side—quite a surprise if you had expected a quiet anchorage.

For the powerboat driver, wave refraction can also create a problem in the way it cause waves to curl around isolated shoals and islands. A wave train approaching the shoal or island will divide to pass down either side, while the central part of each wave will break on the weather shore. The sections of the waves passing on either side will have their inner ends slowed by the shallow water so that the waves tend to change direction, heading in toward the shoal or island on the lee side.

Once they reach this lee side, these refracted waves will be traveling toward each other, possibly to cross at an angle of around 90 degrees. This could create clapotic seas in a place you might have expected to find sheltered water. This is likely to be a problem only in strong winds, however, when the initial waves are fairly large.

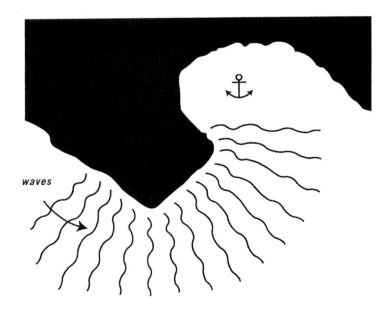

Waves refracting around a headland can make what should *be a secure anchorage uncomfortable.*

Sea Conditions and Fast Boats

A calm sea presents the perfect conditions for fast-boat operations, but once waves start to form, they will begin to affect performance. A regular wave pattern will usually allow the driver to find a speed that matches the conditions. Even in these apparently regular sea conditions, however, transient changes that produce higher-than-average waves must be expected.

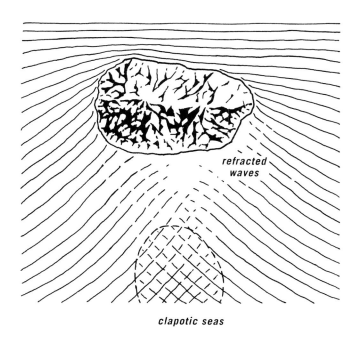

refracted
waves

clapotic seas

Seas can be chaotic in the lee of islands where waves reunite.

Equally, troughs that are deeper than the average must also be expected, and these deeper troughs, or holes, can be more dangerous than high crests because they will only become visible after the boat comes over a wave. A good driver will always keep something in reserve to cope with the unexpected, like an especially deep hole or high wave. Racing drivers will run at or close to the limit, but for routine driving, keeping a reserve in the performance of the boat could be a lifesaver (see the section "Performance Reserve" in chapter 7, "Driving a Fast Boat").

Statistics may not be particularly relevant when you are out on the waves, but bear in mind that one wave in 23 could be twice the average height, one wave in 1,175 could be three times the average and, most terrifying of all, one wave in 300,000 could be four times the average height. This is why a reserve is necessary.

Breaking Waves and Fast Boats

In regular sea conditions where the gradient of a wave is likely to be around 15 degrees, a fast boat will not have much difficulty adapting to the changing surface of the sea. Progress may be slowed as waves get larger, but the relatively shallow angle of the waves will help to smooth progress. When waves start to break, however, they demand a new approach.

A breaking wave tends to be steeper near its top, and in a head-sea approach this can look like a vertical wall. Because the wave top is relatively thin from front to back, the boat may be able to power its way through—but this invites the risk of solid water coming on board if the point of penetration is too low on the crest.

Waves tend to break in isolated patches, and it is rare to get a long breaking crest in the open sea. This opens up the possibility of driving the boat around the breaking area of a wave. This tactic requires skill and

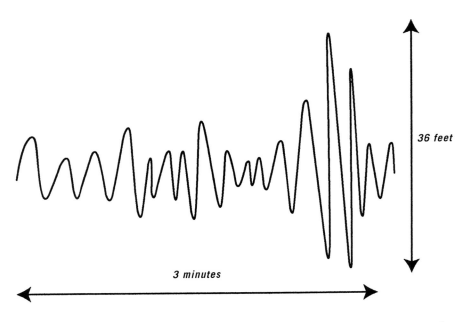

36 feet

3 minutes

The recording of an exceptional wave—a 36-footer—among waves averaging about 12 feet.

anticipation, and the driver will have to make some quick judgments about whether this is a better option than trying to power through the wave top.

In following seas, the area of a breaking wave crest can be used to give a smoother passage. When the wave breaks and runs forward, the height of the wave crest is lowered, which can permit a better ride if the driver chooses this point to cross the wave after it has broken. Waves rarely break in the same place consecutively, so this approach to transiting a following sea can work well.

If the wave in front of the boat breaks heavily, there is a risk that the hull will lose buoyancy because the water is fully aerated—a mixture of air and water rather than solid water. You want to avoid this, because then the boat will not lift readily to an oncoming wave. You will be aware of this problem if you feel the boat becoming temporarily sluggish.

Some breaking waves are generated solely by wind; others are formed by the combined influence of wind and other factors such as shallow water or currents. Breaking waves generated by the wind can be more difficult to drive around because they will be just about everywhere you look. However, this type of wave will tend to have a very thin breaking crest. Breaking waves

A wave crest poised to break. This would be one to steer around if possible.

in currents, shallow water, and tidal flows, on the other hand, will tend to be more local in extent—but can be more severe. It could be beneficial to try for a route around rather than through such waves.

Tactics in Fast Boats

Progress in a fast boat is hampered when seas are steep enough to prevent the boat from running in relatively level trim through the waves. Good driving techniques (see chapter 7, "Driving a Fast Boat") can help reduce some of the impact of wave height, while other tactics can be used to effectively increase the wavelength.

Instead of driving directly into a head sea, the boat can be driven at an angle to the waves. For given speeds of boat and waves, this will reduce the speed of encounter with the waves and, in effect, increase the wavelength, giving a better ride. If the destination is directly upwind, this tactic will mean traveling a greater distance, but it could become the best course when sea conditions significantly slow progress directly upwind. A course of 20 to 30 degrees off the wind can make a considerable difference in both comfort and progress. There are no hard and fast rules about the angle of deviation, and the only recommendation here is to

When running before a sea, adjust your speed to hold the boat on the back of a wave until it breaks, and then run forward.

experiment with different angles to find the one that best suits the conditions. Even quite a small deviation could make a helpful difference.

This tactic is less likely to be effective in following seas unless a significant deviation is used. However, it can be worth experimenting with if progress directly downwind becomes difficult—but you will need to be careful that you don't put the boat in a broaching position.

When traveling along a coastline, you can take advantage of the relatively sheltered water that may be found inside bays.

Rather than proceeding directly across a bay into the teeth of a headwind, a deviation of 30 degrees or so into the bay will open up the distance between wave crests (the wavelength) for faster progress. This route will take you inshore, where you can follow the edge of the bay until it eventually takes you under the lee of the next headland. This will be a longer route, of course, but it should be faster because you won't be heading directly into the wind and seas. Check your chart ahead of time to find places where such an alternative route might be helpful.

Weather

As a fast-boat driver, you can count on eventually finding yourself in any number of different weather situations. Weather forecasts and your own assessment of conditions will help you prepare for each trip. And knowing something about the general characteristics and behaviors of various forms of difficult weather will help you cope with them when they appear.

Weather Forecasts

Forecasts for sea conditions tend to be general rather than specific. These computer-generated forecasts are largely based on the relationship between wind strength and wave height. This relationship is established for open-sea conditions and may take a fetch factor into account.

Fetch is the distance over which a consistent wind has been blowing, and this has an important effect on wave height. Fully established waves consistent with the wind strength will only develop if there is a fetch of 100 miles or more. Closer to land, where the fetch will be shorter with an offshore wind, smaller waves can be expected. Waves will also grow in height with time if the wind is consistent.

Forecasts of swells are also available, derived from data that show what the wind has been doing over the past 24 hours

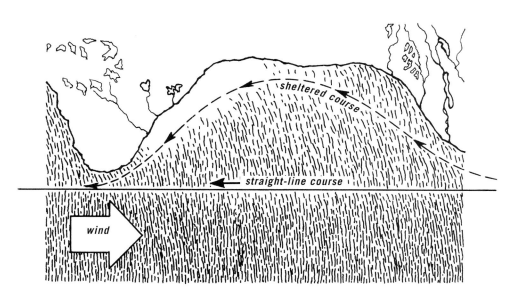

Take advantage of any shelter offered by headlands and bays. Even though the course alongshore might be longer, it may take less time and the ride will be more comfortable than driving into a headwind.

or so. When the wind stops blowing from one direction, the waves decay at a certain rate, and computer predictions turn this information into a forecast of the swell that will remain—or that will emanate to

Fetch

Wind Speed (Knots)	Fetch (Nautical Miles)					
	10	50	100	300	500	1,000
10	2	2	2	2	2	2
15	3	4	5	5	5	5
20	4	7	8	9	9	9
30	6	13	16	18	19	20
40	8	18	23	30	33	34
50	10	22	30	44	47	51

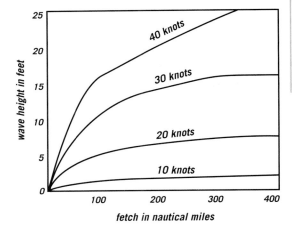

Duration

Wind Speed (Knots)	Duration (Hours)						
	5	10	15	20	30	40	50
10	2	2	2	2	2	2	2
15	4	4	5	5	5	5	5
20	5	7	8	8	9	9	9
30	8	13	16	17	18	19	19
40	14	21	25	28	31	33	33
50	19	29	36	40	45	48	50
60	24	37	47	54	62	67	69

other areas—after the wind ceases.

Wave forecasts tend to predict a range of expected wave heights; what you actually encounter as you travel should be somewhere between the two extremes. Be aware, however, that the predicted upper limit is not an absolute. Rather, it represents the *significant wave height*—that is, the average height of the highest third of the waves that are forecast to be present. This is a pretty good approximation of what to expect—but there is always a chance of higher waves.

Wave and swell forecasts do not take into account the local variations in sea conditions caused by currents, tides, shallow water, and topography. It's up to you to make an assessment of what conditions could be like on inshore waters; there may be a significant difference between what the

Top: *How the fetch, or distance to windward of the nearest land, will affect the wave height (in feet) at different wind speeds assuming that the wind blows long enough in each instance to achieve fully developed seas.*

Middle: *The approximate relationships among wave height, fetch, and wind speed assuming sufficient duration of wind. Given the wind speed and fetch, it is possible to get a good idea of the average anticipated wave height.*

Bottom: *The wave heights (in feet) that can be expected from different wind speeds over varying lengths of time and unlimited fetch.*

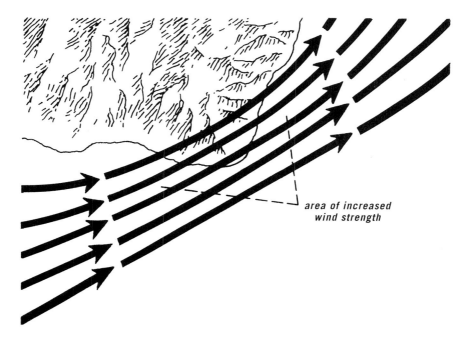

area of increased
wind strength

Wind sweeping past a headland tends to contour around the end of the headland even when the land is low lying. This tends to compress the wind, making it stronger.

forecast says and what you find. Forecast conditions provide a basis on which to build a personal assessment of what conditions to expect in a specific area, and local knowledge helps a great deal in making this assessment.

Weather Conditions

The effect of wind on sea conditions is the principal impact of weather on the performance of fast boats, but other factors—including rain, thunderstorms, and fog—are also important. The main influence of these conditions is to reduce visibility and put added pressure on driver and crew.

Rain

Rain can be anything from a light drizzle to a heavy downpour, of course. In most cases it will not restrict visibility enough to keep you from reading the waves ahead and operating your boat, but at higher speeds in an open boat, rain will get in your eyes or distort your view through goggles. Heavy rain or snow can reduce the ability of radar to detect weaker targets.

Thunderstorms and Squalls

Thunderstorms are areas of intense weather activity but should not present major hazards to a fast boat. Strong winds can exist within a thunderstorm, but in most cases they are too short-lived to generate any significant change in the sea. The heavy rain of a thunderstorm can in fact flatten the waves to a degree.

Thunderstorms are generally highly visible, and in a fast boat it's possible to drive around them. They may travel up to 30 knots, but most powerboats have the speed to avoid them. The direction of travel of a thunderstorm is indicated by the leading cloud that stretches ahead of the main storm. The radar will give another indication of the direction of travel. A thunderstorm will show up as a large, distinct target. Putting range and bearing coordinates onto this target will soon indicate whether the boat is on track to intercept the storm or will pass clear.

The electrical discharges in a thunderstorm are unlikely to have any significant effect on the boat or its equipment unless you're unlucky enough to receive a direct hit. The only real chance of this occurring would be in a harbor or narrow channel, where there may not be room to escape the storm.

Radar detection can be hampered by heavy rain in a thunderstorm, and this could also upset the link between your GPS receiver and satellites, leading to a temporary loss of position fixing. Visibility can be severely restricted in rain, which can be heavy enough to prevent a reading of the waves ahead, making visual navigation impossible. These disruptions of navigation will be temporary; if you get caught in a thunderstorm, the best solution might be just to hunker down and wait until it passes.

Squalls, particularly line squalls, can produce conditions similar to thunderstorms

successive positions and times of thunderstorms

bearing line

Thunderstorms and heavy showers show up well on radar, which can be used to plot avoiding action. Putting the bearing cursor on the target will show how it is moving relative to your boat. In this case, an alteration to port would be the best avoidance tactic.

except that they lack thunder and lightning. Squalls are usually associated with the passage of a cold front, so it is possible to anticipate them from a weather forecast map. Expect a change in wind direction as a cold front passes through; with a very active front, the change can be considerable, up to 90 degrees. The change in wind direction will normally be clockwise in the Northern Hemisphere.

A possible risk in line squalls is the presence of waterspouts, but these tornado-like phenomena are usually highly visible. I once saw a waterspout coming toward us in a narrow channel, and the sight of the highly disturbed water at the base and the towering, black, spinning cloud made me turn the boat around and run without hesitation. A fast boat should stay away from waterspouts; most of them travel relatively slowly, so there should be no difficulty in avoiding them. The base of a waterspout is rarely more than 200 yards in diameter. Waterspouts do not normally occur at night, but if they are present, they should show up on radar.

A roll cloud precedes a squall line, which in turn may precede a cold front by a hundred miles or more. (NOAA)

A mature cumulonimbus cloud spreading out into an anvil. This nasty-looking cloud can bring heavy rain, hail, and thunderstorms. (NOAA)

Fog

Fog can present a significant challenge to fast-boat operations, but much will depend on the visibility. If it falls to 100 yards or less, you could start to find it difficult to read the waves ahead. This is the time to slow down to reduce the danger of collision. Given the good maneuverability of a

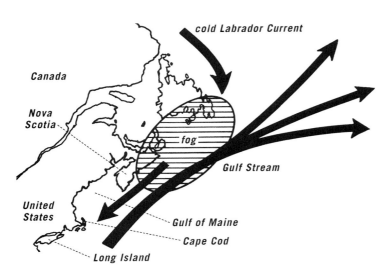

Advection fog is common off the eastern seaboard of the United States in the summer months. It forms when the warm, moist air of the Bermuda High—a persistent summertime atmospheric feature of the North Atlantic—is cooled by contact with the cold Labrador Current, causing its burden of water vapor to condense.

fast boat, you should be able to avoid collision with other boats provided you keep a vigilant lookout. Even if you are navigating with radar, a moderate speed is called for.

Radiation fog is the early morning fog created by temperature differences over the land. Sometimes termed a harbor fog, it is found close to land, so expect to encounter it in harbor entrances and channels; however, it can also drift out to sea. It appears only under calm conditions or when winds are light, and usually burns off during the morning.

Advection fog is formed by moist, warm air flowing over a colder sea, and it is only with this type of fog that there can be any significant wind. This is the fog you will find at sea, and it can persist throughout the day and into the night. Advection fog is only likely to disappear with a change in wind direction or sea temperature.

Fog conditions require intense concentration by the crew. Even if you have radar, one crew member should be dedicated to keeping a visual lookout. Watching the radar should be the sole task of another crew member.

7

Driving a Fast Boat

Driving a fast boat is all about balance. The forces of gravity, buoyancy, lift, resistance, thrust, and aerodynamics act on the boat, and the driver uses speed, steering, and trim controls to help direct and control these forces. The one variable you have no control over is the sea conditions in which you are operating. What you have to do is find a balance for the boat that allows it to cope with the prevailing seas.

Your objective is to drive your boat through and over the water in a level and true attitude, to produce a safe and comfortable ride for boat and crew, and at the same time to make the rapid progress that is essential to the fast-boat experience. On calm seas there aren't many obstacles, and an optimum balance is found simply by setting the controls to allow the boat to operate at maximum efficiency. Adjust the power trim so that the propeller is at its most efficient and the hull is running at its best trim relative to the water surface, and measure your success by the gain in speed. You should not need the trim tabs in calm conditions if the boat is well designed and not overloaded.

But calm seas are a rare luxury. When waves are present, they constantly interfere with the direct and level progress of a boat. Now the controls have to be used to try to find a new balance that maintains optimum trim for the conditions. As wave conditions get worse, this balance becomes harder to find.

Reducing speed is usually the last resort. This is not always the right solution, because if you slow down too much, the boat starts to contour the waves and you could find yourself operating at little more than displacement speeds—the low speeds at which the hull no longer generates the dynamic lift needed to climb out of its own wave-making hole for planing. It may require a bit of courage to go faster in rough seas, but the result could actually be a better ride.

In most sea conditions it is possible to use the controls to find a balance for the boat that will cope comfortably with the significant height of the waves. But every so often a larger wave or a deeper trough will come along to upset that balance. In most cases, however, you will not be driving the boat close to its limits; you should have performance reserves that will allow your boat to cope with these more difficult situations.

Driving a fast boat is a skill that can only be developed from experience. In this chapter, a variety of techniques will be presented to demonstrate how different sea conditions require different driving techniques and a different use of the controls. There are very few hard and fast rules in fast-boat driving, however. It's your responsibility as driver to adapt and use the various controls and techniques to find the optimum balance for the sea conditions you encounter.

Performance Reserve

The good driver will always keep a reserve of performance to cope with the unexpected. The driver's role is to optimize the boat's performance in the average prevailing conditions while holding something back for temporary changes in these conditions. In part this means that the demand for speed must be balanced against the stresses and strains it produces on boat and crew. To achieve this balance demands a concentrated focus on changing sea conditions and an instinctive reaction to the boat's controls to adapt to short-term changes.

This is one thing when the boat is simply trying to make comfortable progress through difficult sea conditions, but when you're attempting to push a fast boat closer to its limits, the balance can be harder to find. In offshore powerboat racing, the balance will be biased toward high-speed performance—toward driving the boat close to its maximum speed for the conditions, and accepting that the reserves for coping with larger-than-normal waves may be reduced. Because of these reduced reserves, there is a need for intense concentration and for reading every individual wave as it comes along. Even for the cruising boat, where comfortable progress is more important, concentration is essential—though the margin for error is greater.

When the object is to go as fast as possible in the prevailing conditions, this often means operating slightly below maximum speed potential. If you run right on the limits of a boat's performance, there is always the risk of encountering a larger wave than normal and having no reserve of engine performance to cope with it. Meeting the larger wave could make the boat come off the plane or be thrown off course, and such effects will dramatically slow progress. The fastest instantaneous speed in the average conditions will not always make the fastest progress overall.

What constitutes an adequate reserve is hard to define. With a fuel tank, you know just how much fuel is left and you can match this with how far you have to go to determine an adequate reserve. But there is no simple way to measure the reserves of boat and crew. Over a short distance you can drive a boat right to its limits and know that the boat and crew can handle the discomfort and pain for this brief period. For a longer distance, reserves are needed because the time scale is greater and the boat and crew have to pace themselves to have something left toward the end of the voyage.

The problem is that you do not know where the limits of performance are until you exceed them. Once you do, the boat will let you know. Fortunately, with modern boats it is the crew that will normally show the pain first, and they will give you an early-warning sign that you are pushing too hard. If the crew starts to suffer, don't carry on as an act of bravado.

Driving in Head Seas

Head seas present the most challenging conditions for fast-boat operations because, with the waves moving toward the boat, the speed of encounter with the

Driving a RIB hard in rough head seas on a rescue mission like this requires full concentration. (A. J. Young)

waves is at its highest. The situation is compounded because the boat is meeting the steepest side of the wave, its lee side. All in all, head seas are not the seas of choice for fast boats. Head seas give the driver little time to match the attitude of the boat to the approaching waves; reactions have to be faster and responses quicker.

Because head seas represent such a challenge, most of the controls available to a fast-boat driver are geared to coping with them. Trim tabs and power trim are used to keep the bow down in head seas; ballast tanks, in boats that have them, are also designed to cope with head seas.

Matching Your Speed to the Waves

Many times when driving a fast boat in head seas you can just select the speed you want to travel at and go. Calm conditions obviously qualify; apart from trimming the boat for performance, the choice of speed is wide open.

In slight seas, with waves just a foot or two high, even small fast boats should have no problem with the conditions. All you need to do is find a speed that suits the

The result of overenthusiastic driving coming over a wave in head seas. This gives the crew a rough ride and it also slows down progress because the propeller will cavitate and the boat will take time to pick up speed again. (A. J. Young)

conditions, set the throttle for that speed, and concentrate. Concentration is needed in all conditions because, while it might seem straightforward enough just to set the throttle, there can be surprises waiting. Lurking among those small waves could be the wake of a passing vessel; unless you're concentrating, you could be in for a nasty shock.

Once the waves start to get bigger, matching your speed to the waves is the key to high-speed, head-sea operations. For every set of wave patterns and every design of fast boat there will be an optimum speed of operation. There are no set rules or statistical tables that can show what this speed is, but it will become obvious as you work to match your boat speed to prevailing conditions.

Full speed can be comfortable in slight or even moderate seas, depending on the size of the boat. Small fast boats are obviously going to feel the impact of waves much sooner than larger boats, and the warning signs that you are going too fast will be felt when the boat starts to pitch and you start to feel serious wave impact.

For full-speed operations, the distance from one wave crest to the next—the wave-

Reading the waves ahead of the boat will allow boat speed to be adjusted before hitting larger waves.

length—needs to be short enough to allow the boat's hull to span the distance between the crests so that bow and stern are supported at the same time. The momentum of the boat will help it to travel between crests with little or no change in attitude, and progress can be rapid.

The larger the wave, the faster it travels; however, larger waves also have a greater wavelength. This means that while the larger wave may be traveling faster toward the boat in a head sea, there is also a greater distance between the waves so that the actual speed of encounter may not differ greatly. Where the difference becomes apparent is when the wavelength becomes

This RIB is struggling up the face of a wave and is going too slow for good control in these conditions.

longer than the length of the boat. Then the bow can drop into a trough while the stern is supported by a crest, and you will start to get the pitching motions familiar to fast-boat operators. When this happens, the attitude of the boat is poor for negotiating the next wave ahead.

In these conditions, the boat will start to contour the wave: it will want to follow the surface shape of the wave rather than leap from crest to crest. Once the boat starts to contour the waves, a driver's natural reaction is to slow down to give the boat more time to recover between each wave. But op-

erating at a slower speed is not always the best solution. At slower speeds the bow will tend to drop even farther between waves as it tries to contour them. Often, when slowing down like this, you'll get a comfortable ride only when the boat is fully contouring the waves, which will mean the boat is then moving very slowly.

A higher speed will keep the bow up so that, as the boat comes off the wave passing behind it, it will be in a better position to meet the next wave in front. The aim should be to meet the next wave with the bow slightly up so that the boat will ride over the wave rather than trying to plow through it. The boat should cut through the top of the wave so that it does not lift completely off. When you get it right, there should be a more or less level track for the boat through the waves.

Slowing the boat may seem the best way to cope with deteriorating conditions, because this slows the speed of encounter with the waves and gives you more time to think. If you want to make rapid progress, however, it's worth experimenting with opening the throttle to lift the bow. See if you can get the boat to ride over the waves in a level attitude, using the tabs, power trim, and any ballast to achieve the right balance for the conditions.

Head-Seas Throttle Control

Using the throttle properly is essential to successful operation in head seas. We've learned how to use the throttle to trim the boat, and this skill can be put to good use here (see the section "Throttle Control of Trim" in chapter 5, "Fast-Boat Controls"). Opening the throttle will lift the bow, and this is ideal when the boat is approaching a wave so that the attitude of the boat aligns with the slope of the approaching wave. This change in trim can be achieved with

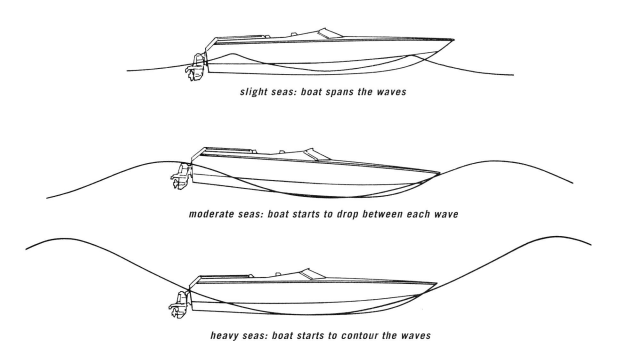

slight seas: boat spans the waves

moderate seas: boat starts to drop between each wave

heavy seas: boat starts to contour the waves

As waves grow in size, fast boats are less able to accommodate the wave shape.

Driving hard in lively seas, a boat should come close to leaving the water. Actually getting airborne, however, will slow the boat down. This boat is right on the edge.

little or no change in overall speed, as only a quick burst on the throttle is required.

If the power were kept on, the boat would accelerate up the face of the wave and likely fly off the top, but a quick burst of power is just enough to lift the bow. Then, by easing the throttle, the boat can be persuaded to cut through the crest rather than rise over it. Hopefully the boat is now in a level attitude that will allow it to drop into the trough in a comfortable way before the throttle is opened again for the next encounter.

The boat should pass through the crest with enough momentum that it remains level; closing the throttle too much as the bow comes through the crest will encourage the bow to drop into the trough. This is the last thing you want to happen, because then the boat will not have time to recover before the next wave hits.

Bearing in mind that wave encounters can occur every one or two seconds at high speed, this technique requires constant assessment and constant use of the throttle. This can only be achieved with a high level of concentration, which can be difficult to maintain for any length of time.

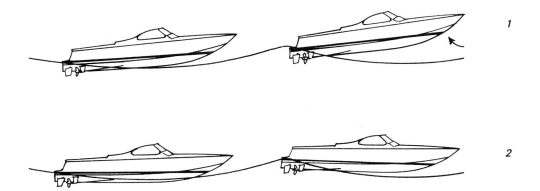

When running fast into a head sea, it is important to keep the bow down—in other words, to trim as flat as possible. If this is not done, the boat tends to fly off the tops of the waves (*1*). Driving through a wave (*2*), rather than bouncing off the top, will make for a better landing on the far side.

Rather than making constant use of the throttle in confronting average head seas, you may want to hold this technique in reserve for use when a larger-than-normal wave approaches. Meanwhile the tabs and the power trim can be used to find a comfortable balance for the boat to match the prevailing conditions. The tabs will then be your main weapon in counteracting the upward lift of the bow in head seas.

The design of the boat must also be taken into account. A boat with a fine, or narrow, bow section will

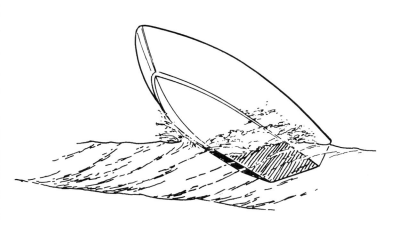

This duck's-eye view of a fast boat coming over a wave crest shows why a bow-up attitude at this point is uncomfortable and slow. The bow is going to slam into the trough before it meets the next crest.

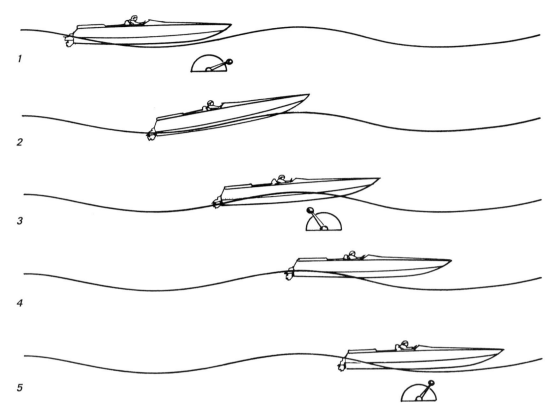

As you approach a wave, goose the throttle a few hundred rpm (1). This lifts the bow up so it won't plow in (2). On the crest, pull the throttle back to halfway between your current rpm and idle (3). This brings the bow back to a more level attitude and keeps the engines from over-revving if the prop breaks free of the water (4). As the boat drops into the trough, bring the rpm up to match your speed. This also keeps the bow slightly above level, so you are ready to set up for the next wave (5).

generate much less lift when it encounters a wave in head seas; therefore it should be able to achieve a more level ride, because the hull will be less sensitive to the passing waves. This is why high-performance boats are typically long and narrow.

A design with full bow sections, such as a sportfisherman or flybridge cruiser, will be much more sensitive to the passing waves and thus will need to be driven more carefully. You can't change the hull shape once you are on the ocean, but anticipating the reaction of a particular boat can help in finding the best operating solution.

If there is any doubt about what action to take in a head sea, open the throttle for a short burst of power to lift the bow. This is not an instinctive reaction—but you certainly do not want to close the throttle if a larger-than-normal wave is approaching. Closing the throttle will probably mean that the bow will go *through* the oncoming wave rather than lifting *over* it.

If you feel a need to slow down when approaching a wave, your boat is probably going too fast for the prevailing conditions. Even then the throttle should be opened with a quick burst to lift the bow for oncoming waves. The effect is more akin to trim control than speed control: these quick bursts of throttle lift the bow without creating any increase in forward speed and are key to driving a fast boat in head seas. This technique is most effective in a light and responsive boat, but even with a heavier boat it can be worth a try. You will certainly get some response; the question is, will it be quick enough to be effective?

Tactics to Improve the Ride

In most regular sea conditions you can find a speed at which reasonable progress can be made into head seas, and this progress can often be improved by optimizing the settings of tabs and power trim and fine-tuning the ride with throttle control. But there will be conditions, such as when the wind is running against a current, when the waves become very short and steep, and where the size of the waves prevents the boat from riding over them in a reasonably true and level attitude.

These conditions may be local in extent and it may be possible to navigate around them. If it is necessary to pass through them, a temporary change in course can often bring about a dramatic improvement in the ride. You may be able to make much better progress going upwind by tacking in the manner of a sailboat—repeatedly changing course from side to side in order to keep the waves approaching from 45 degrees on the bow rather than directly ahead.

This tacking, in effect, increases the wavelength because the speed of encounter of the waves is reduced, and boat and driver have more time to adapt to each wave as it comes along. This change in course will certainly produce a more comfortable ride and reduce the stresses on both boat and crew, and the overall rate of progress to windward may even be somewhat improved. With fast boats, the fastest route is not always the shortest route.

This is certainly a tactic worth trying when head seas become difficult; a course alteration of even 10 or 20 degrees can significantly improve forward progress. This tactic would normally be necessary only when you can't find the right balance and speed to head directly into the waves. However, it's also worth considering if you are

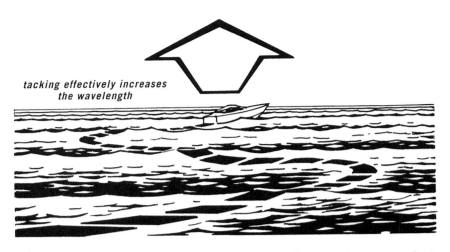

tacking effectively increases the wavelength

Tacking across waves in a head sea lessens the impact on boat and crew, producing a more comfortable ride.

just looking for a more comfortable ride on a long trip.

Avoiding Breaking Crests

When driving into head seas, try to avoid breaking wave crests. A breaking wave will have a near-vertical face, making it very difficult for the boat to lift over the crest. Because the water in a breaking crest is moving horizontally (and perhaps downward!) toward you rather than oscillating more or less in place, meeting it head-on could damage your boat and injure your crew.

Waves rarely break along the entire crest at once except in shallow water; rather, breaking wave crests tend to be in irregular, isolated patches. The best solution, then, is to drive around the breaking crests.

You should be able to anticipate a breaking wave approaching one or two wave-lengths away, giving you enough time to turn the wheel and avoid the worst of it. This alteration in course should be no more than 45 degrees, however, because you do not want your boat to end up broadside to the breaking crest—an invitation to capsize. A smaller angle of alteration should be adequate to avoid the crest so that it passes harmlessly down the side of the boat. If the crest cannot be avoided, it's better to open the throttle in a quick burst to lift the bow than to close the throttle and risk plowing into the wave wall.

In severe conditions when breaking waves are increasing, you may not be able to steer around them all. This may be the time to decide if continuing to windward is really your best option. Your tactics will depend on what you are trying to achieve by being out at sea in such conditions. When breaking waves start to endanger the boat and crew, your focus should be more on survival than on continuing a particular course. This is the time to head for shelter.

Driving in Beam Seas

With the wind and waves on the beam, the ride for a fast boat will be a lot easier than when trying to cope with head seas. In beam seas, with wind and waves coming at one side of the boat, there are none of the sudden changes in wave gradient that face the driver in head seas. The ride will be a lot smoother, but you still have to be aware of the sudden changes in wave conditions that can occur in any wave train. Breaking wave crests can be a danger in beam seas, and these can rear up suddenly alongside the boat. Also, with the wind on the beam, there is increased risk that the boat will land on the flat of one side of the hull rather than centrally on the V.

In slight and moderate sea conditions, there should be no problem in operating at full throttle in beam seas. The size of your boat will be less critical because ride comfort will not depend on the relationship of boat length to wavelength, as it does with head seas.

Here the boat is heading for a part of the wave that is lower than the high breaking wave on the right—this should help to smooth the passage through the wave.

breaking wave

Breaking waves on the bow can cause the boat to swing beam-on unless there is enough headway to maintain good steering.

In beam seas you will become more aware of the irregular nature of waves. Just when you think you're running comfortably along in a trough, you will find a wave crest coming right at you. This is partly because the waves are all moving down to leeward, and so each wave has to go past the boat on its way downwind. It can be disconcerting as you try to maintain a course at right angles to the waves to see the waves passing you on their way downwind even though they are beam-on to you. This will make it feel as though you are heading slightly upwind.

Matching Your Speed to the Waves

In beam seas there is less need to match your speed to the waves, but you still need to find a comfortable speed at which the boat can operate without risk of serious wave impact or dangerous changes of attitude in relation to the waves. The main risk is the possibility of a conflicting wave train coming in at a direction different from that of the wave pattern you are following. You are less likely to notice this in head seas, but in beam seas these secondary waves become more apparent.

Secondary wave trains can generate pyramid waves that rear up without warning. In moderate seas these pyramid waves may not be very big, but they can be a disconcerting change in what was an otherwise regular pattern of waves. There is also the possibility that the boat may have to cross over one dominant wave train and into the trough between the next two waves in order to maintain the approximate required course. In doing this you can experience conditions similar to those found when operating in head seas or nearly head seas.

Unless you are in a great hurry, it's best to operate in beam seas with some speed in reserve to give you the option of accelerating your way out of a problem. This problem could be the breaking crest of an oncoming wave or simply a pyramid wave that appears close by. In beam seas you will find yourself steering around difficult waves much more than you would in head seas.

Boat speed in beam seas should be in the middle of the planing range. If the boat has a top speed of 40 knots, a 35-knot speed might be appropriate. This allows the driver to drop down to around 25 knots if a difficult wave is approaching, or to accelerate to top speed in order to drive out of trouble around a wave—the latter being the preferred course of action when possible.

Throttle and Steering

Beam seas don't normally call for constant operation of the throttle to adjust the trim of the boat. In most beam seas the boat can be operated at a constant speed and will ride the waves comfortably. You should always keep one hand on the throttle, however, in order to accelerate or decelerate to avoid difficult waves. You can use steering in combination with the throttle to take action when a steeper-than-normal wave appears.

In the latter situation there are two options. The first is to steer upwind across a low section of the crest before the steep section arrives. The second, and probably better, option is to steer away from the problem wave by heading downwind. Steering away and opening the throttle at the same time will take the boat safely away. Once past the danger, you can bring the boat back on course and resume normal speed.

In rougher seas, good concentration is needed if you are to take timely action to avoid problems. Most of your attention will be focused on the waves coming from your weather side, but you also need to keep an eye on what is going on ahead. Beam seas may not demand the immediate response to

A slight alteration of course is usually all that is needed to avoid a breaking wave.

the controls that are required in head seas, but the ability to power away from trouble is still important.

The course and action you adopt in these conditions will depend to an extent on the course you are trying to make good. While constantly turning away downwind may be the easiest way to avoid problem waves, it could also take you a long way off course.

Looking along a wave crest, you'll see that the crest is never regular, but instead comprises a series of higher and lower sections. If you need to cross a wave crest in a beam sea, identify an area where the crest is low and aim to cross at that position. The gradient there will be less severe. But keep in mind that you may not be able to see what lies on the other side of the crest until you get there.

Chances are that a low crest will coincide with a gentle gradient on the other side, but the back of a wave can always have a steep gradient, particularly at a point where a wave crest has just broken. Select your crossing point with care, with the best position usually being at the beginning of a low section rather than toward the end, where the wave is starting to become steeper again.

Crossing the wave crest requires careful throttle control, easing the boat up onto the crest and only driving through and opening the throttle after conditions on the far side have been identified. A fast boat will always

tend to lean into the wind, and under the steering control of turning the boat into the wave crest, the boat may lean over farther. If the boat picks up a considerable heel as it goes through the wave crest, it could result in an uncomfortable landing on the other side. The transition through the wave crest should be done more by negotiation than by brute force.

Avoiding Breaking Crests

In a fast boat in beam seas, breaking wave crests can present a hazard. By looking ahead along the wave to windward, it should be possible to identify where waves have the potential to break. This is usually indicated by a steeper wave front and the presence of a rim of white breaking water at the crest.

The easiest way to avoid these waves is to turn downwind, open the throttle, and power the boat down and around the sections of approaching waves that appear to be breaking. Turning downwind offers a quicker response and lower risk than turning up into the wind and attempting to cross the wave in advance of the breaking crest.

There is an alternative solution, however, and the choice of which to use will depend partly on how far in advance a possible breaking wave can be identified. If you're on a long course into the wind, turning upwind and passing behind the breaking crest offers the benefit of maintaining a better course. Gaining ground upwind will always be preferred. But if you do not notice the breaking crest until it is almost on top of you, there is still hope—provided you have a responsive boat. Hit the power and turn away downwind from the wave, and there is every chance that you will outrun the breaking crest.

Driving in Following Seas

Operating in following seas appears to be an easy route for fast boats because the boat is running with the waves rather than fighting against them. In slight or even moderate sea conditions, this route is easier because you will have less wind effect and the rate of encounter with the waves will be slower than with head seas. In most conditions, you should be able to choose the speed at which you want to run. Only when the bow starts to drop between waves do you need to start taking control.

Once the waves start to build, however, following seas can provide a real challenge for fast boats. Following seas make it much more difficult to control the attitude of the boat. It's important to remember that the design of most boats is optimized for head-sea operations; the controls, such as tabs and power trim, do not help a lot in following seas. Your main weapon in following seas will be the throttle, and even this needs to be used with skill and care.

Running with the waves certainly reduces the chance of severe wave impact on the boat because, obviously, the speed of encounter with the waves is much slower. But it is just this slow encounter that tends to make life more difficult. Making slower progress over the waves means that the boat is more liable to contour the waves, which can result in considerable changes in the attitude of the boat and make it more difficult to control.

The fact that the boat tends to contour the waves rather than leap from wave top to wave top means it can end up pointing downward. This can be just at the point when the bow should be starting to rise to the next wave. No amount of throttle opening here is likely to produce the required change of trim to get the boat angling upward for the next wave. So the bow will bury itself into the wave in front. Although eventually it will lift, it will only do so after generating a huge amount of spray and possibly solid water over the bow. Easing back on the throttle may reduce this blow, but doing so will make the bow drop and go even deeper into the wave.

The way a fast boat behaves in following seas depends on several factors. The speed of the boat is one. At a speed that is more than twice that of the waves, the boat may be able to treat the waves in much the same way it would a head sea. With these higher speeds it's possible to maintain the attitude of the boat as it leaps from wave crest to wave crest, and rapid progress can be made. While 40 knots would probably be the minimum speed for this technique, it is only really effective at speeds of 50 or 60 knots and above. As always, much depends on the size of the boat and the size of the waves, and the relative speeds of waves and boat. The faster the boat relative to the waves, the greater the chance that this tactic will work, as long as the wavelength is relatively short.

The various types of following seas also have a significant influence on the way a boat behaves. Long, low waves are relatively easy to cope with. Following seas will not have a significant influence until they reach a certain height—around 3 to 4 feet for a 30-foot boat. Even at this height, the boat should be able to come cleanly through the waves at their crests and maintain full speed because the crests are relatively close together and the ends of the boat are not left unsupported. If they were, this would allow the bow to drop toward, and into, the wave trough.

Short, steep waves with a short wavelength make the worst following seas. This is particularly true when the waves are high enough to prevent full speed, and where the bow can start to drop into the trough before it has to lift to the next wave. These conditions can be very trying. Operating in them may require the techniques described in the following sections.

Matching Your Speed to the Waves

The speed at which a boat can travel in a following sea is not usually affected when the waves are just 3 or 4 feet high; full speed can be maintained in anything but a small boat. In these conditions, the ride is likely to be worse if speed is reduced, because the speed of encounter with the waves is reduced. This lower speed opens up the danger that the bow will drop as it comes over the crest of one wave and before it encounters the next. Once a boat starts this contouring between wave crests, the attitude of the boat is more difficult to control and the boat is likely to plow into the wave in front rather than ride over it.

As conditions deteriorate and the waves become higher, the boat operator is faced with two alternatives. One alternative is to maintain a speed considerably faster than that of the waves and attempt to lift the bow up over the waves with only a minimum of contouring. In this situation, keeping the tabs up and the power trim out will help to keep the bow up. Additionally, any ballast in the ballast tanks or any other movable ballast on board should be kept as far aft as possible. In this way it should be possible to maintain speed as conditions deteriorate, but eventually you will be forced to reduce speed as the bow starts to bury into the waves in front. Here, the second option becomes viable.

This second option is for the boat to travel at or just above the speed of the waves. In this way you can hold the boat on the back of a wave, matching the speed of the boat to that of the wave until you're able to open the throttle and drive over the wave when the wave crest becomes temporarily low. The boat will then cross over the lowered crest without fear of encountering a deep trough on the other side, because the lowered crest often means the wave has just broken, with water from the crest running forward to fill up the trough in front.

This type of driving requires considerable concentration because it is very easy to go too slowly and allow the wave behind to catch up. If this happens and the wave crest behind is breaking, the boat could get into a broaching situation. Wave crests have a nasty habit of appearing and disappearing without warning. Operating at these speeds requires the driver to look both astern and ahead. If there are any doubts about what is happening behind, the solution is always to open the throttle and drive out of trouble.

Throttle and Steering

A boat will accelerate naturally on the lee side of a wave in a following sea. The downward slope of the wave causes the boat to accelerate under the force of gravity, so opening the throttle in an attempt to lift the bow in this situation will have only a limited effect. A short burst of throttle might lift the bow a little, but there is a risk of driving the boat into the back of the wave in front, stuffing the boat into the wave, without enough lift to rise over it. (Some high-performance designs are fitted with anti-stuff planes at the bow to generate ex-

tra lift in this situation. These planes are a new concept and have yet to gain wide acceptance.) Short bursts from the throttle may also fail to produce the desired result as you come over the crest of a wave in a following sea, because at that point the propeller may not be operating in solid water.

In following seas your boat's performance will depend a lot on the shape of its bow. A boat with fine bow sections that have little lift could easily force itself straight into the wave. A boat with a full rounded bow or a RIB with a full-section bow tube will have much more buoyancy and so has a better prospect of lifting up over the waves. This is an issue on which the boat designer has to make compromises, because a fine bow is most effective in head seas and a full bow is most effective in following seas. No one style is going to be the ideal solution for all conditions.

Some cathedral hull designs can present difficulties in following seas. The bow shape may be very full, which might be optimal to lift it over the wave in front. However, the angle of the overhang in a cathedral bow often closely matches the angle of the wave it is encountering, which can produce a very hard impact on the relatively flat surface of the bow. The result can be a sudden slowing of the boat, because there is very little give when this type of bow encounters the back of a wave. A similar reaction can be found in RIBs with a squared-off tube at the bow.

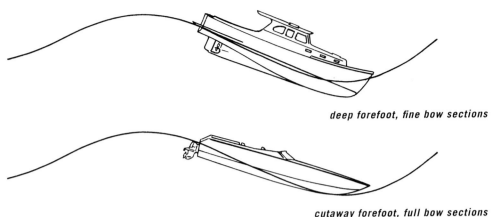

deep forefoot, fine bow sections

cutaway forefoot, full bow sections

A bow with a deep forefoot and fine sections (top) will bury itself in the backs of waves when running down-sea, gripping the water and in effect steering the boat by its bow. Such a boat can be hard to control and may even broach in a following sea. A boat with a cutaway forefoot and fuller bow sections (bottom) will be a lot more mannerly in a following sea but might pound you unmercifully in a head sea. In this, as in all aspects of boat design, you want the best compromise for all conditions.

Steering control can be used effectively in following seas, but it takes some care. Ideally the boat should never be more than 45 degrees from the line of the wave crests in case a wave behind starts to rear up and break. At a 45-degree angle to the wave line, there is ample time to correct the course and open the throttle to drive out of the potentially dangerous situation.

Steering can be used to drive around larger wave crests, but both throttles and steering need to be used for full control. Riding at an angle across the waves will stretch out the distance between wave crests, but because the waves affect first one side of the boat and then the other, the ride is likely to be uncomfortable. It may not always be easy to maintain effective control as the boat both pitches and rolls. The ride can be wild and exciting in these conditions—but it can be dangerous as well. There is always a risk of broaching or of meeting a larger-than-average wave when you do not have adequate reserves of performance to cope.

Broaching

Broaching can be a particular threat to displacement boats in following seas, but it must also be considered in fast-boat operations. Broaching can occur when a breaking wave overtakes the boat, lifting its stern. With the bow digging into the wave in front and acting as a fulcrum, the moving water in the breaking wave forces the stern to one side or the other and, unless corrective action is taken quickly, the boat will broach—will turn broadside to the wave. The boat then faces the risk of rolling over. It is a scenario that can develop very quickly, and once put into motion there is little the driver can do but concentrate on survival.

There is a lot a driver can do to avoid getting into such a situation in the first place, however. The best course of action is always to run at a speed at or above that of the waves. At these speeds there is no chance of a wave behind catching up with the boat and causing a broach.

Maintaining these speeds is not always simple, however, because even individual waves can move at different speeds. Just when it appears that the boat is safely on the back of a wave with the crest running just ahead of the bow, this wave can disappear and suddenly there is a breaking wave curling up astern. Even in this position, escape is still possible by opening the throttle and

driving the boat forward, away from the breaking crest. Of course, in order to do this you need to be aware of the breaking crest behind; it can be a wise precaution to have one crew member watching the seas astern.

A broaching situation only becomes really dangerous when the stern is lifted and the bow is down so far that opening the throttle will only drive the boat deeper into the wave in front, rather than away from the breaking crest. Fast boats operating at slower speeds are more prone to broaching because they have relatively little grip on the water to give them directional stability, and the weight of the engines concentrated at the stern will encourage the stern to swing into a broach if the bow becomes a pivot point.

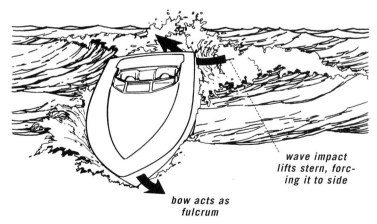

wave impact lifts stern, forcing it to side

bow acts as fulcrum

Broaching is a real threat in following seas, when waves can lift and swing the stern broadside as the bow drives low into the waves, acting as a fulcrum.

Avoiding Breaking Crests

The golden rule when operating in following seas where breaking wave crests are present is to travel faster than the waves, but difficulties can occur. The lee face of a wave is steeper than its weather side, so as the boat overtakes and crests a wave, the bow can become unsupported quite suddenly and start to plunge into the trough in front. The resulting downward angle of the boat will cause it to accelerate down the wave front. In slicing through the crest, the boat can also make the crest unstable, with the wash of the boat dragging the crest forward and encouraging it to break. Here is the boat, then, on the front of one wave, dragging the water forward, encouraging the wave to break—and with the boat at an angle that will bury its bow in the next wave in front—a broach in the making. Fortunately, a broach and subsequent capsize are only likely in very rough seas.

Another rule when operating in following seas is to turn the boat around occasionally to get a better idea of just what the wave conditions are really like. When running in following seas, waves appear much more moderate than they really are. By turning around to head into the waves, you will be exposed to the full reality of the conditions. This can help you decide whether it is in fact safe to continue in the prevailing following seas or whether it would be better to consider an alternative course.

In normal wave patterns it's possible to avoid breaking waves. The part of a wave crest that is likely to break will always be the highest part. Steer a course around these high parts, aiming for the lower parts and then overtaking the wave and passing through it to the next trough. Not only will this avoid any risk from a breaking wave, but it will give a smoother and more level ride that should enable you to make faster progress.

If it is not possible to drive around what looks like a potentially breaking crest, the solution is to ease the throttle, maintaining enough power to hold the boat on the back slope of the wave. Wait for the wave to break in front of you, then it will be relatively safe to drive over the crest and into the next trough.

Operating in rough following seas requires considerable skill and judgment, and the penalty for getting things wrong can be severe. You should be just as interested in what the waves are doing behind you as in front.

Running an Inlet

Traveling from seaward into a river entrance or a harbor can be one of the more exciting times when driving a fast boat. There should be no problem when the wind is off the land, because you will be coming into sheltered waters. But even then the flow of water coming out of the entrance can produce areas of breaking waves generated by the shoals in the entrance or by the narrow channel. The real challenge comes when the wind is off the sea, because then you have the wind blowing against the current, adding to the complication of the shoals or narrow channel.

Rather than rushing straight into the harbor, take time to think things through. You may not have any options if you are running short on fuel, but if you are concerned about the conditions, review the alternatives. Is it worth trying to raise someone on the radio in the harbor for more information? Are conditions likely to improve if you wait a while, perhaps for the tide flow to change or the wind to ease? Are you familiar with the harbor and its marks so that navigation will be straightforward?

For the actual run in, move forward without hesitation. The breaking waves over the shallow water of the entrance or the wind against the current present no good places to stop and reconsider if you aren't sure about things. Plan your navigation before you enter; make sure that the boat is well battened down and that fuel and electrical supplies to the engines are all

A breaking wave in an inlet. This is the time to apply full throttle and drive the boat away from the breaking crest.

in order. The last thing you want is a break-down as you run in.

After that it is largely a case of using the driving techniques given in this chapter for operating in following seas with breaking waves—riding in on the back of a wave and letting it break before you ride over it. This is one case where you really do need to watch out astern, because the waves will be unpredictable with the possibility of large standing waves. You need your wits about you and full concentration on the job at hand. It could be a wild ride.

Spinout

A spinout is one of the more serious consequences of bad fast-boat driving. In its moderate form, a spinout can be embarrassing as the boat turns end for end (but remains upright) and comes to a rapid halt. In serious cases that occur at very high speeds, a spinout can cause injury to the crew and damage to the boat.

One type of spinout can occur when the boat flies off the top of a wave and then reenters the water with the steering off-center. This is a driving problem and the solution—keeping the boat in a straight line—is largely in the hands of the driver (see the section "Dynamic Steering" in chapter 5, "Fast-Boat Controls").

A spinout can also occur when the boat trips on a wave crest, which usually only happens to high-performance boats being driven hard. It occurs when the stern of the boat lands on the crest of a wave after flying, with the bow still unsupported. The stern is held up by the crest but the bow will drop quickly and probably crash into the next wave, which will try to stop the boat. But with the weight of the engine and crew, the stern wants to keep going—resulting in a rapid swing of the stern to one side or the other. The spinout will almost certainly occur if the boat was starting to turn one way or the other when it leaped into the air—but if you're lucky, it could just stop suddenly and remain straight.

This type of spinout occurs most often when the boat meets a larger than normal wave or an irregular wave, putting the boat out of step with the wave. The spinout occurs so rapidly that there is no chance for corrective action. If crew members are not wearing harnesses, they are likely to be thrown around inside the boat or thrown out. A spinout can be a painful and dangerous experience.

Another type of spinout can happen when a boat is altering course. You see this happen quite regularly when race boats are turning a mark. It is usually a case of driving too hard in a situation that calls for moderation.

Picture the scene, with the driver turning the wheel to round the mark. Already, with the steering angled into the turn, you have one of the ingredients for a spinout. To round the mark, the driver will have re-

A spinout like this is usually the result of overenthusiastic driving. At best it will slow the boat dramatically and at worst it can cause damage and injury.

duced speed, so the bow has dropped a bit. Then there is the inertia of the boat making the turn, with most of the weight concentrated in the engines at the stern wanting to swing out as the boat is turning. It's easy to see that with a little too much enthusiasm going into the turn, the stern will break away, the bow will bury itself, and the boat will go into a spinout. In many ways this spinout is rather like a car skidding as it goes too fast into a turn. The back end breaks away under enthusiastic driving and wants to overtake the front end.

This type of spinout is rarely serious when racing unless it causes one boat to collide with another. The relatively low speed of the turn means the spinout is more embarrassing than dangerous. A spinout in a turn is more likely to happen with a boat that is fitted with dynamic steering, in which propeller thrust is used for steering. The boat will heel over as it goes into the turn and, with the steering angled, some of the propeller thrust will try to push the stern outward and upward. It is the upward component of the thrust that does the damage, lifting the stern and encouraging it to break away. You can see this

A spinout can occur when rounding a mark in a race. The driver may find himself going too fast, so he slows, the bow drops and may bury itself, and the weight of the engine tends to swing the boat wide, causing a spinout.

in pictures of a spinout, where it is invariably the stern that breaks away in the initial stages of the incident.

Concentration and Special Skills

Concentration is the key to driving a fast boat effectively. Situations change very quickly at high speed, and only if the driver is concentrating on what is happening can he respond effectively. The faster the ride,

the greater the need for concentration. In general, this concentration should be on the changing wave patterns ahead.

As speed increases, so does the degree to which the boat's safety lies in the hands of the driver. At slow speeds a boat will, to a large degree, take care of itself by adapting and conforming to the waves. At very high speeds, however, virtually all of the safety of the boat is under control of the driver, and the need for concentration becomes intense.

The driver should ideally concentrate on driving and not be involved with navigation or other tasks. In race boats, one crew member is dedicated to the throttle and one to steering, with the throttle man concentrating on the waves immediately in front of the boat and the helmsman taking a more distant view of the surroundings, such as looking for the next mark on their course.

In slight or even moderate sea conditions, when the boat can run effectively at full speed without constant throttle adjustment, concentration can be relaxed to a degree. However, the driver needs to be aware of unusual waves that can affect the boat. One big

Spinout with Deep-V and Stepped Hulls

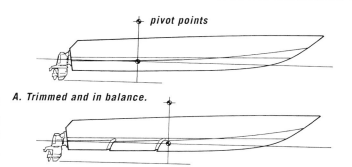

A. Trimmed and in balance.

pivot points

When you start to turn a deep-V or stepped hull at high speed you set in motion a series of events that could lead to a spin-out or, in a worst-case scenario, a barrel roll. To understand this let's look at the sequence of events that takes place.

Let's assume your boat is on a plane and running in a straight line when you decide to make a turn **(A)**. The boat will heel into the turn and swing around just as you want it to. In turning, the propeller thrust on the stern of the boat acts at an angle to the direction of travel and is pushing the boat around the turn. Provided the turn is not too tight and you are not traveling too fast, the boat will turn and you will eventually level out on the new heading.

Problems will start if you are traveling too fast going into the turn. Upon recognizing this, the natural instinct for a driver is to pull the throttles back to slow the boat. This will cause the bow to drop (by virtue of its design, the stepped hull will already be down—throttling back exacerbates this). Typically, when steering the boat around the turn, the pivot point of the hull

and the thrust from the propeller find a balance. When the bow drops suddenly, the pivot point of the hull moves forward, the propeller thrust has greater leverage, and the balance of the boat is upset **(B)**. This is the recipe for a spinout and is more likely to happen with a stepped hull, where the hull pivot point will be farther forward, than with a straight deep V.

Unless the boat is traveling very fast or the turn is very sharp the spinout will be more embarrassing than dangerous. But, in more extreme situations, the centrifugal force in the turn can cause a serious spinout or, even worse, it could cause the hull to roll over **(C)**. The remedy for avoiding this is simple: slow the boat down *before* you enter the turn—much like you should do when negotiating a car around a sharp bend.

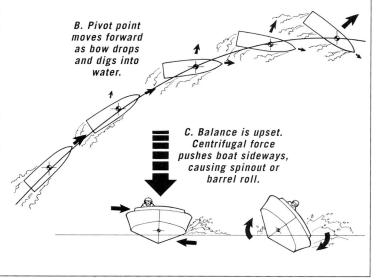

B. Pivot point moves forward as bow drops and digs into water.

C. Balance is upset. Centrifugal force pushes boat sideways, causing spinout or barrel roll.

danger can be the wake from passing ships and boats, and while you should be able to see these vessels and anticipate the wake, it can still come as a surprise. You should always keep one hand on the throttle for an instant response to changing conditions. The normal driving position is with one hand on the wheel and one on the throttle—even in apparently benign sea conditions.

You can be more relaxed in slower boats—those in the 25- to 35-knot range—and in larger fast boats. Here the impact of any change in wave pattern is not likely to be severe—and the poor throttle response often found on slower or larger boats is not likely to make much difference in the situation even if you do respond quickly. You cannot change the boat you are in, and you have to accept both its good and bad qualities. You will want to base your driving technique on the response you can expect from your boat.

Reading the Waves

A very important part of fast-boat operation is learning to read the waves: trying to anticipate which waves will rise higher than the prevailing pattern, which might have a tendency to break, and where the relatively low waves might occur. Much of the ability to read waves comes from experience. And simply watching waves at sea—how they form, how they develop, and how they dissipate—builds this experience. You'll discover that waves offer a constantly changing scenario, rarely with a pattern so regular you can predict them fully.

Heading into the sun will make it difficult to see and anticipate what the waves are doing; at night, reading waves becomes virtually impossible. In these conditions it's necessary to drive with caution and to hold a lot of performance in reserve to cope with the unexpected. You certainly won't be able to make the same rapid progress that is possible when waves can be seen and read easily.

Night Driving

There is rarely much need for driving a fast boat in the dark, and it's not something to encourage. I have done quite a bit of night driving when trying to break long-distance records, and it is a huge blessing when daylight appears once more and you can see what is going on. Night driving in a fast boat has to be done defensively. It usually consists of finding a speed at which the boat can operate comfortably without too many wave impacts or excessive motion.

A comfortable speed is quite easy to find in slight or moderate sea conditions, but the real difficulties occur in rougher seas where what *appears* to be a comfortable speed for the conditions could often be too slow for safe operation. In rough conditions at night, the only safe option might be to come right down to displacement speeds of 7 or 8 knots—but even then there is no guarantee that a planing boat can operate safely, because it is not designed to operate effectively at these low speeds. Rough following seas should be avoided at all costs at night because you really need to be able to see what is going on.

It is rarely completely dark at night, and at times, particularly in moonlight, it's still possible to read the waves to an extent. White breaking crests show up clearly at night and indicate the presence of larger waves, giving you a chance to take action to avoid them. Otherwise, there is a certain amount of guesswork involved in night driving. The ride will almost certainly be harsher and more uncomfortable than during the day, because you won't be able to anticipate many of the short-term changes in the sea.

Longer-Term Tactics

This chapter has been mainly geared toward the short-term operation of fast boats in varying sea conditions—essentially what is occurring within the time frame of a minute or so. But to operate a fast boat safely and enjoyably, you also need to think about the longer-term demands of the voyage. Planning for the longer term can help reduce stress on both the boat and the crew and have you ready to respond to any difficult sea conditions.

Before you set off, you should get a weather forecast. After relating this to the local currents and tides, you will be able to anticipate conditions that lie ahead. If you don't like the probable conditions, the possibility of tacking across the seas is an option—setting a course that tacks back and forth, perhaps 30 or 40 degrees off the straight-line course, for a more comfortable ride. This can be a particularly valuable tactic if it takes the boat into more sheltered waters inshore, where more rapid and comfortable progress can be achieved.

When proceeding along a coastline, where there may be a headwind running along the line of the coast, there is always the possibility of finding areas of sheltered water inshore. Projecting headlands can provide sheltered water; traveling within their protection may mean a longer distance traveled, but you will be able to maintain higher speeds. Part of your trip planning can involve identifying protected coastal areas on the chart.

In terms of longer-term tactics, it is always worth considering an alteration in course by 10 or 20 degrees off the direct route, just to see if the ride can be made more comfortable. This can apply to any conditions of rough seas, no matter what direction the wind is blowing.

As a part of looking ahead to the entire trip, have a strategy ready in case you need to seek shelter from a storm. When you're caught in a storm, the natural tendency is to try to get back home as fast as you can, or simply to head downwind to find shelter. These may not be the best options. Heading downwind toward land might give a more comfortable ride, but it will also take the boat toward an exposed coastline. Here the wind will be blowing directly onshore so that any harbor, particularly one with a bar or shallow inlet, could prove too dangerous to enter. Heading upwind toward land may give a rough ride to start with, but it should take the boat into steadily improving conditions as the shelter of the land starts to take effect.

When considering alternative routes for your planned voyage, bear in mind the fuel situation. Before you leave the harbor, calculate the potential distances and the extra fuel needed and be sure to have more than enough. While under way, keep a close eye on fuel levels and do your best not to let supplies get low. Running with little fuel in reserve can take away some of your travel options and force you into action you might really want to avoid.

I was on passage down the Florida coast, heading for a refueling stop, only to run into fog and a nasty sea while running the inlet to the harbor. Low on fuel, we had to go on in, even though the fog hid the buoys marking the channel and heavy breaking seas denied us the time to figure out precisely where we were. Once committed, we ran fast into the harbor. It was a bad situation that could easily have been avoided with adequate fuel on board. Better planning would have allowed us to wait for better conditions or to find an alternative harbor.

Driving a fast boat is serious business. Get it right, and it can be enormous fun and give a lot of pleasure. Using your skills to run fast in difficult conditions is a tremendous thrill. But get it wrong and a very painful experience can result. This chapter has provided a great deal of advice about driving a fast boat, but you can't drive with the book in one hand and the steering wheel in the other. Build up your driving skills by starting out in good conditions at moderate speeds. Hone your skills with experience. Along the way you will make mistakes, but these won't be a problem as long as you learn from them. There is no such thing as a perfect fast-boat driver, but the next best thing is a good driver who thinks things through. That is what you should be aiming for.

8

Driver and Crew

In a fast boat it is often the crew that can be the weak link. The boats and their equipment are generally tough and reliable and can keep going under severe conditions, while the crew can suffer from tiredness, lack of concentration, seasickness, and even injury. They can be the limiting factor in what can otherwise be a well-oiled machine designed to operate in a challenging environment.

In a way, that's a good thing. There's a good possibility that the discomfort and pain crew members may suffer under difficult conditions will prompt the speed of the boat to be eased or the trip strategy to be changed long before the boat itself gets into serious trouble. Crew complaints are the first warning sign that things are getting difficult and perhaps dangerous.

This may sound alarmist given that a boat is designed for pleasure, but when operating a fast boat, you need a warning sign that you are overdoing things. Call it a gut feeling, call it being frightened, but the crew will experience the first signs that the boat is going too fast for the conditions. Given a well-designed and well-built boat, you will probably not get any complaints from the boat until long after the crew starts to feel discomfort. So your body is the early warning system, and you really do not want to ignore the signs it gives you.

If you are just going to sea for an hour of fun, you will probably push the boat harder than you would if you were setting out on a hundred-mile passage to another port. When you are embarking on a passage you will want to take things more gently so that your reserves of fuel, stamina, and concentration last the voyage. It's easy to overtax your energy and resources in the early stages of a passage, only to find that fatigue sets in later. You need to pace yourself and your crew, to hold something back to cope with the unexpected.

The excitement of high speed can be great for the first half hour, but after that, pain and discomfort can take over. The driver will probably be the last to feel it because he will be preoccupied with operating the boat. It is the rest of the crew members who provide the warning signs that maybe you are overdoing things. A good driver thinks of his crew first and keeps an eye on their behavior and welfare.

Fast boating is a combination of skill and fun. The ride can be exhilarating, but it can also become dangerous if things go wrong. Your skill as a driver will be mainly aimed at making the boat go fast, but it should also be aimed at keeping things from going wrong. There may well be people on board with far less skill and experience at boating, and the line between excitement and fear can be narrow for the inexperienced. You need to be aware that

A racing catamaran.

what is exciting for you may be scary for others. Pace your driving needs accordingly.

The Driver s Role

In a leisure boat the chain of command is always rather vague, but custom dictates that the driver is in charge. Somebody has to make decisions about the driving of the boat—where it is going and how it is going to get there. This puts a lot of responsibility on the shoulders of the driver and leaves the rest of the crew with little to do but hold on tight.

If the boat is being pushed hard, this task will absorb most of the driver's concentration. The driver may not have time to think about the condition of the crew, the navigation, the fuel situation, or any of the other things that go toward making a fast boat safe. Most of the driver's mental and physical energy will be expended in reading the waves and working the controls. These are all short-term operations. This means that driving the boat and being in charge of it can constitute two conflicting roles, because the concentration and skills needed to drive do not leave a lot of time for longer-term tactical thinking.

In an ideal world, and depending on the size of the boat, there should be at least two people on board capable of driving. This provides a sensible backup in an emergency, and it also means that two competent people can share the work of making the boat go fast. Race boats provide a good example of the two- or three-person crew sharing the work as an efficient team. In the more casual world of leisure boating, this may not be possible; if the driver is alone in the boat, a more cautious driving style is called for.

We have emphasized the need for concentration when driving a fast boat, and it can be difficult to maintain the required level of concentration for more than an hour or so. Even after half an hour at the helm you can find yourself distracted from the job, and this particularly applies if you are trying to do all the jobs on board, including driving and navigating. With at least two people who can drive the boat, you can change drivers for a fresh hand at the wheel when you are traveling any distance.

The problem is that the environment aboard a leisure boat is much more casual than on a race boat, and even worse, the boat is invariably designed for one-person operation. Even if you want to share the workload, the design of the helm will not let you do so easily. It's understandable why the helm is designed like this: if you have paid for the boat, you want to enjoy its performance even if you're out on the water alone. I'm sure that car design, with its focus on the driver and passenger comfort, has a major influence in boat design.

The Navigator s Role

You may prefer to do everything yourself when you are driving the boat, but for those willing to share, let's have a look at how the roles could be divided if a second person is participating. This will often be the case in commercial and military fast craft, where every person has a role to play. Because one of the main jobs will be navigation, we will call this second person the navigator.

The navigator will work alongside the driver and will have the responsibility for longer-term planning: studying the weather and how it may affect sea conditions, considering travel tactics, and generally keeping an eye on what is going on. The driver will be able to concentrate on reading the waves and operating the controls.

The navigator can also monitor the radar and the chart plotter. A quick glance at these instruments may be all that is required in fine conditions, but it can be a full-time job when visibility is poor. Then there is the radio, which may have to be used as you approach harbor; and there is the fuel situation to monitor. The navigator could also help by handling the tab and power trim controls so the driver can keep his or her hands on the wheel and throttle.

This sharing of roles will help ensure that each job is done efficiently. Ideally the roles of driver and navigator should be interchangeable. With the navigator having so much to do, it's easy to see why, when a driver is out on the water alone, a lot of pretty important things just do not get done—or at best, get done casually.

Much of the role of the navigator depends on the layout of the helm. The navigator can't effectively use the electronic chart and radar if these are located immediately in front of the driver. The same applies to the tabs and power trim controls—particularly the latter, which on an outboard-powered boat are often incorporated into the throttle levers. The layout of the helm may prevent the driver and the navigator from sharing certain jobs. This will likely be the case in smaller fast boats, where the instrumentation tends to be concentrated in front of the wheel.

Having the instruments situated in front of the driver can be workable during daylight, if it is accepted that the level of concentration on the electronic screens will be cursory. But at night the screens of the electronic chart and radar can prove a considerable distraction to the driver, who is busy trying to read the oncoming waves and adjust controls accordingly. In these tougher conditions, the driver really cannot do both jobs satisfactorily. At night, splitting up the roles and driver roles is almost essential if the boat is to be operated effectively and safely.

In the short term, there is not much that can be done about the way a boat is laid out and the way its instruments and controls are installed. Crew members will have to split up duties and responsibilities according to what is practical aboard a particular boat. The navigator's role is going to depend on what instruments and controls can be seen and operated. This will usually involve picking up whatever tasks the driver cannot or does not want to do, particularly in the casual atmosphere that often exists on a fast leisure boat. Military and commercial boats have a much more disciplined approach to sharing the work. In either case, teamwork is called for.

The Rest of the Crew

There is nothing worse in a fast boat than having nothing to do. Just holding on tightly, trying to absorb the movement of the boat and its impacts with the waves, can sometimes give you little to concentrate on but the discomfort you may be enduring. In fine weather it should be fun, but once people have to start desperately holding on, the fun can quickly disappear. Without any positive task to occupy their minds, and perhaps with no good secure

A racing catamaran capable of 150 mph. The air flowing through the tunnel develops lift, which helps reduce the wetted surface and hence the drag.

seating, these riders will often be the first to show signs of fatigue and suffering in rough conditions. The constant pounding of the boat and the lack of secure seats and handholds can quickly make life uncomfortable, and they are likely to be the first to complain.

One way to make life on board a fast boat more enjoyable is for the whole crew to rotate roles at frequent intervals. In moderate conditions this can be a good way for relatively inexperienced people to gain an insight into fast-boat driving, and it's not a bad thing for a fast-boat owner to see someone else at the wheel. You can learn a lot about the boat and how it works by watching someone else drive. And if you have to sit in one of the guest seats or positions, you might be more sympathetic to what they are experiencing next time you are out. You might even think of ways to improve their experience with better handholds or better seating.

Fast performance boats are usually well outfitted with good seating for all the crew, though some seats may lack good handholds. Some of the worst boat designs, as far as crew facilities are concerned, are the flybridge cruisers and lower-speed sports cruisers. Here the provision of good facilities for use in harbor tends to take priority over good and secure seating at sea, and in some cases this can make life a misery for the crew. It should be a clear warning sign that the facilities on your boat are not ade-

quate if you find that your guests fail to come back for a second ride.

Communication on Board

One of the reasons guests can feel uncomfortable or even frightened when traveling at high speed in a fast boat is that they have no good way of communicating with others on board. The ambient noise levels can be high, which makes any attempt at talking hard work, and you soon lapse into silence rather than shouting. You feel left out of the loop, with little or no idea what is going on, particularly if you have no view forward.

An internal communications system on board, such as an intercom, can be a tremendous bonus and leads to everybody enjoying the trip much more. A headset with a microphone incorporated is the most effective means of internal communication and is a good investment. Being able to communicate makes travel more sociable, and it's also a good safety feature. Headsets can be a handicap if you want to move around in the boat. However, you are only likely to be moving around when the boat has slowed down, and then it will be possible to do without the headsets.

These systems will only be effective if they are reliable and if everyone on board is included. Being left out of the communications loop is not only very lonely for the person excluded, but can also be dangerous when that person is expected to react to a situation but doesn't know what is happening.

A good driver will always announce his intentions to the crew before he takes action. Before turning left or right, you can give a simple hand signal pointing the direction of the turn, so no one is taken by surprise. This can be particularly important in smaller boats: it's not unheard of for a passenger to be thrown from a boat when the driver executes a sharp turn without warning. There can also be a problem if the boat encounters a larger than normal wave, perhaps the wake of a passing ship. A good driver will shout a warning to the crew. Use of headsets can make these warnings much easier to communicate.

Personal Equipment

To provide the crew of a fast boat a comfortable ride and every chance to enjoy the experience, personal items such as clothing, life jackets, seating, and handholds need to be considered. Crew members are only going to be effective if they can switch off from the pain and discomfort produced by the motion of a fast boat and concentrate on the voyage itself or on the job they have to do. Small irritations can assume large proportions in the constant movement of a fast boat. While experience will dictate what works and what doesn't work, this section looks at some of the aspects to be considered.

Clothing

The type of clothing worn in a fast boat will be determined largely by the operating conditions. In warm or hot areas, light clothing is adequate and waterproof items won't generally be necessary. The freedom of light clothing makes it easier to move around the boat, but there are still some precautions to take.

Good coverage is important for preventing sunburn, which can be a serious problem in hot climates. The combination of wind and sun can be a killer, and the hot wind can be rather like standing in front of a furnace. The clothing will also reduce irritation from chafe between your body and fixed parts of the boat, such as the seats. Long-sleeved cotton shirts and long pants should be the normal wear in these conditions to give the right degree of protection. Shorts are OK in larger boats where you do not get the wind around your legs and chafe is not a serious problem.

In colder, wetter climates, a full waterproof layer can be essential to prevent exposure to severe weather. The wind generated by the speed of the boat can increase the risk of exposure considerably. If you use your boat for enjoyment, you're not likely to go to sea in conditions that risk exposure. Professional fast-boat operators can't be so choosy, however, and the crews need to think seriously about the protective clothing they use.

Victory 2, *one of the most successful racing catamarans built in the Middle East.*

With any clothing, the details are important. The constant movement of a fast boat make skin chafe a potential problem, especially clothing around the neck and wrists and especially if clothing becomes impregnated with salt.

Hands can also suffer from chafe, in this case caused by the constant need to hold on for safety. This can result in blisters, the pain of which can keep a crew member from holding on as tightly as usual, increasing the risk of being thrown overboard. The crew in RIBs can be particularly at risk, because the fabric of the tubes can chafe; the flexible handholds that are often used can be a real killer on the hands. Wearing gloves is the easy solution here and should be considered essential when going to sea for more than just a short trip, even in mild climates.

Often there are particular parts of the boat that can cause irritation or even bruising—perhaps the place where the driver rests an arm while running the boat. These problems should not be ignored, as the pain will pull your focus from the pleasure. In particular, a driver can do without this type of distraction while trying to concentrate. One solution is to apply firm padding to the area on the boat that is causing the trouble. Another option is to secure a piece of padding, with Velcro straps, around the arm or leg that is feeling the chafe. This can be particularly effective for a driver who is operating the throttle constantly and always faces the risk of chafe and irritation. Longer term, you may want to look for permanent changes that can eliminate the problem.

Unless you are firmly secured in a seat with a harness, there will always be a risk that you could be thrown about the boat if the driver takes some sudden action. To reduce the risk of injury, sharp and hard edges should be padded—or should not have been incorporated into the boat in the first place. This is initially the job of the boat designer and boatbuilder, but it's ultimately the skipper's responsibility to see that conditions are safe on board.

Headgear is another area of difficulty, and compromises have to be made. Even in small fast boats, more and more people are taking the sensible precaution of wearing a crash helmet. Helmets are mandatory on race boats, and what applies to race boats in the interests of safety should apply to very fast leisure boats. These can have the same level of performance as race boats, and although the driver may not push the boat quite so hard, he will probably also not be using the same level of concentration as a race boat crew. Simply stated, the risks can be just as high.

Helmets do have a downside, however. If you are thrown from a boat, the helmet's large surface area stresses the neck upon impact. If you go in headfirst, the sheer size of the helmet exerts pressure on the neck. If you enter feetfirst, the ridge around the base of the helmet acts as a brake. There have been instances in which a racer's neck was broken when a sudden blast of water under the helmet forced the person's head forward or backward.

A crash helmet can double as a way to wear a headset comfortably, with the earphones and mike being fitted as an integral part of the helmet—an excellent solution in boats that travel at very high speeds.

Eye protection is necessary in order to maintain visibility where there is no protective windscreen. You have the option of a helmet-mounted visor or goggles; in slower boats, sunglasses can be effective up to about 40 knots. You should wear a securing strap with sunglasses to keep from losing them overboard. To protect the rest of your face, which can be fully exposed to any blast of hot wind rushing past the boat, a good sunscreen is the best solution.

There is no perfect clothing that will meet the often conflicting requirements of water protection, sun protection, easy movement about the boat, and prevention of chafe and rubbing. Experience will show what works; in many cases local conditions and experience will guide you to the best choices for personal clothing.

Seats

Seating options were considered in a previous chapter, so the alternatives are considered here in terms of their effect on crew efficiency and comfort (see the section "Seating" in chapter 3, "Fast-Boat Features"). The two main choices are a saddle seat, or a bolster-type seat that offers the option of sitting or standing. Other types of seating are used in fast boats, most of them based on automobile seats, and they can be effective if they are designed for the marine environment. But they are second best in most respects, mainly because they do not provide for use of your legs for partial support.

Saddle seats and bolster seats are both designed to place the crew securely in the boat and reduce the need to hold on tightly, so you can have a more relaxed ride. With the saddle seat, most of the lateral security is provided by the knees gripping either side of the saddle; fore-and-aft security is provided by a backrest behind and a handhold in front. This works reasonably well, but there can be problems with chafing on the body where it is in contact with the seats. The seats tend to rely on softer foam padding in order to accommodate the shape of the body, but the insides of the knees are vulnerable to chafing. Velcro-attached pads can be a useful addition here.

There are almost as many styles of sad-

Sprung saddle seating and handlebar steering on an experimental RIB design. The handlebar steering can be too sensitive for fast-boat use.

This type of bolster seating gives excellent lateral support in a fast boat and is usually fitted with a tilting cushion that offers the option of a seated or standing position.

dle seating as there are designs of boats, with most boatbuilders producing their own proprietary designs. Styles vary from square boxes to shaped seats with sculpted foam padding combined with backrests shaped from stainless steel tubing. Many are more functional than comfortable—more in keeping with the macho image of rigid inflatable boats (RIBs) than with long-term comfort. The major drawback of saddle seats is that you cannot use seat belts effectively, and therefore you need to maintain a constant grip on the handhold for security.

In contrast, bolster seating can be much more effective for support and is more comfortable. Bolster seating provides good lateral support, particularly around the shoulders and hips—but unless a seat belt is part of the kit, you will still have to rely on a handhold for fore-and-aft security.

As with many things in a fast boat, seating involves compromises. While it may not be possible to alter the installed arrangement, problems with the seating can often be reduced by the use of portable padding or other minor modifications. Good seating is worth a lot of effort to achieve, because your seat is your primary interface with the boat. The right solution will greatly increase your enjoyment of fast boating.

Handholds

We have all seen it on a fast boat: crew members hanging on wherever they can—to the edge of tables, the undersides of seats, the steering wheel, anywhere they can get some sort of grip. These are not good solutions to the question of where to hold on during travel. Handholds are just as vital as good seating for secure positioning on a

fast boat. For handholds to be effective, their placement needs to be carefully thought out and fully integrated into a boat's design.

The main requirement of handholds is to provide good fore-and-aft security, but they are also called on to provide lateral security, especially with saddle seating. While the lower half of your body is well secured, the top half is not. Side-to-side movements can often be quite severe in a fast boat, particularly in RIBs. Good lateral security requires that the handholds be well spread across the boat. Narrow handholds, typi-

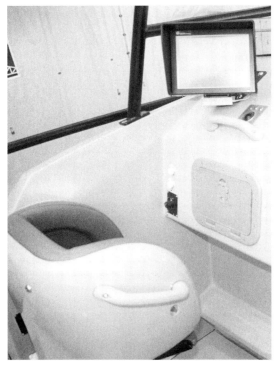

Seat back handholds (left) and a fast powerboat with several well-placed handholds on the seats as well as the dashboard (right).

cally mounted on the backs of seats, provide space for two hands—but placing two hands this close together will not provide worthwhile lateral support.

To get a wider spread for the hands, it's best to use the handhold on the adjacent seat as well as the one in front of you. Two passengers in an adjoining pair of seats could share handholds in this way to get better lateral support, although this may not always be comfortable for the two people. One cause of irritation on fast boats comes in the form of other crew members accidentally bumping or banging against you. The sharing of handholds could exacerbate this problem. In an ideal world, each seat would have its own handholds designed for the job.

As with seating, there is no simple solution to the provision of adequate handholds. These have to be arranged not only to give crew members security when they are seated, but also to provide something to hold onto when they move around the boat. Adjustable handholds that permit each person to find the most comfortable position are ideal, but this is rarely a practical proposition.

Handholds need to be rigid so that you can both push and pull on them. This rules out flexible handholds, which are compact but do little for the security of the crew—though you will often find them on RIBs. Handholds and handrails need to be carefully sized to ensure they permit a firm,

comfortable grip. Handholds and handrails that are either too small in diameter or too large can be very uncomfortable.

On some boats it can be practical to install vertical handrails between the deck and the deckhead; another solution is to fit handrails to the deckhead. These handrails protect movement about the boat but do not get in the way. The top frame of an open windscreen is often shaped to create a handrail.

To work their best, handholds and handrails need to be built into the boat as part of the original design. Only in this way are they likely to be given the priority they deserve and to make life aboard the boat safer and more comfortable.

Footrests

Like handholds, footrests are essential for good security, and they need to be integrated into a boat's design from the start.

Footrests come in two types: the loop type that is usually used in conjunction with a saddle seat, and the angled footrest that is usually used with a bolster or other type of helm seat. Both types are designed to give you additional security by using your feet to help stability and positioning.

The loop-type footrest enables you to either pull upward or push down with your foot firmly located. This enables some of the impacts and shocks to be absorbed by your legs.

The angled footrest creates a foot location that you can brace your legs against. If your legs are placed well apart, you also get lateral support. The shock-absorbing characteristics of the footrest can be improved by covering the deck with thick, hard foam rubber.

The use of footrests of either type demonstrates that in a fast boat, every part of the body needs to help in absorbing the shocks of wave impact. A boat moves in many directions: sideways, forward and back, up and down. A skilled driver can reduce the impacts from these motions but can't eliminate them. The final defense for the crew is to use their seats, handholds, and footrests in combination to help weather the jolts. You will get some idea of the impacts involved when you wake up the morning after a boat ride and feel the aches and pains. Fast boating is meant to be fun, but the fun only starts when driver and crew are comfortable.

Life Jackets

A ride aboard a fast boat can be rough. Common sense dictates that you wear a life jacket (also known as a personal flotation device, or PFD). Boaters have long been required to carry life jackets aboard a boat, but the choice of wearing them or not has been yours. Now it's likely that wearing life jackets in fast boats and most other boats may become mandatory under Coast Guard requirements.

In considering whether to wear a life jacket, bear in mind that the motion of a fast boat is often unpredictable; it only takes one momentary lack of concentration and you could find yourself heading overboard. In larger craft you may feel more comfortable because of the security of an enclosed cabin, but on some small fast boats, particularly RIBs, you are likely to be very exposed.

There is a choice of life jacket types, ranging from those that offer full inherent buoyancy to those that rely entirely on inflation to provide buoyancy. In between are types that offer a combination of inflation and inherent buoyancy, automatic or manual inflation, and a variety of attachment systems.

The type of life jacket that is buoyant without inflation is usually too bulky to be practical for wearing on a boat. Wearing this jacket, you may not fit into a seat or be able to move easily about the boat. However, the padding of the jacket can be quite comforting during a rough ride.

Even the semi-inflatable type of life jacket is bulky, although this is what the Coast Guard uses because even if you are unconscious when you go overboard, there is a degree of inherent buoyancy to keep you afloat.

A life jacket that must be inflated manually is not going to be much help if you are knocked unconscious when you go into the water. That's why some designs of inflatable life jacket inflate automatically when they hit the water—rather like the car airbags that automatically inflate upon impact. These are probably the best life jackets for fast-boat operations: they are compact, in most cases comfortable to wear, and most important, they will float you head up in the water even if you are unconscious.

Make sure your life jacket is adjusted to be tight fitting but comfortable. Picture

The sort of fully inflatable life jacket that works well on fast boats. Inflation can be automatic (on entering the water) or manual.

yourself in the water, depending on the support of the life jacket. If the jacket is loose, it could be free to ride up and even over your head. I once saw this happen to a first-time boater who was about to be strangled by her life jacket before she was rescued.

The crotch strap is a vital component of a life jacket, and you should not even consider using a jacket without one. The strap is particularly valuable in keeping the jacket from riding up on your body.

Fatigue

You can tire quickly on a fast boat, and this can lead to mistakes. The constant movement of the boat means that your body is working all the time, and you will discover muscles you never knew you had. Being fit is the best solution, but even a fit young crew will find the constant motion and the need to hold on or brace against the movement debilitating. After an hour in a fast boat with the constant pounding, your mind starts to go numb and you may find it difficult to cope with any sudden demands for action. This tiredness is both mental and physical, and you will notice that those people who have no duties to perform on board will be the first to show fatigue.

It helps to counter the physical fatigue by having the option to either sit down or stand up. The right seating, hand-holds, and footrests should permit either position comfortably. The ability to change position is a tremendous boost and brings into play new sets of muscles, helping to postpone exhaustion.

The operator of the boat can do a great deal to reduce the effects of fatigue by the way he drives. Considerate driving is the hallmark of a good driver. Severe bangs when the hull lands on the flat of the V or when the boat changes attitude rapidly increase fatigue levels. Just easing back on the throttle can make a big difference.

Signs of Fatigue

Fatigue builds up slowly, and its symptoms may not be readily apparent. Even the person who is fatigued may be reluctant to admit it, out of fear that others on board may see it as a sign of weakness. But rather than being judged a sign of weakness, fatigue should be considered a danger to the whole crew. A fatigued person may fail to hold on tightly and then get thrown around the boat. Fatigue can hamper the ability to make good decisions. But typically, nobody wants to be the first to own up to being tired.

The signs of fatigue can be subtle. A person whose head starts to roll from side to side rather than remaining upright may be exhibiting a sign of fatigue. If a crew member's grip on the handholds occasionally slips, it could be another indication of tiredness. A person who doesn't respond readily when his name is called could well be suffering from fatigue.

Mutual Support

Mutual support among crew members is essential in a fast boat. With the boat pounding along at sea, each person can contribute to the mutual support of all by keeping a watchful eye for anyone who looks fatigued or otherwise does not seem to be coping with the stress. The driver has a particular responsibility here, especially when there are people on board with little experience on fast boats. But the driver, busy at the helm, also needs help from other crew members in monitoring the condition of everyone on board.

Rather than putting a tired crew member in the position of having to admit to fatigue, the thinking driver could propose a change of positions in the boat. This can be readily accomplished without pinpointing any individual weakness. Moving to a new position in the boat will almost certainly bring relief, even though it may be temporary, to a person suffering from fatigue. This lets the person stand and move, use other muscles, and get a break from the old routine.

Seasickness

Seasickness is a fact of life for many people, and the ride of a fast boat can bring on the symptoms. Many of these symptoms will initially be the same as those of fatigue, but probably worse. It is only when vomiting starts that the difference is easily recognizable.

Seasickness is not too likely during normal fast-boat operations because the boat is moving so fast—above the lower-frequency motions that tend to cause seasickness. However, the ride of moderately fast cruisers can be a problem for sufferers.

The crew of a fast open boat usually has a good view forward, and being able to see and concentrate on the horizon forward can delay the onset of seasickness. At night, when the horizon is not visible, the risk of seasickness is higher. On cruisers there may be only one or two seats that face forward with a view through the windshield. People who have to sit in the saloon or some other place without an outside view will be more prone to seasickness.

Perhaps the highest risk of seasickness appears when the boat is stopped or is moving slowly. The slower rolling and pitching motions can bring on seasickness, so these periods should be reduced to a minimum unless seas are relatively calm.

Seasickness tablets can be effective if they are taken early enough. They may prevent seasickness but at the same time induce tiredness, which can increase the risk of fatigue. Fatigue is preferable to seasickness, however, because once started, seasickness will not go away until the boat is back in calm water. Any guests seriously at risk from seasickness need to be identified and watched carefully.

9

Navigation

Going fast is good, but going fast in the right direction is better. Navigation in fast boats always looks so easy when you just go out for a spin. You can see where you are in relation to the land, you probably know the local area well, and navigation is done almost by instinct because you know where you can go and where you can't. The local layout is in your head and you may not even need a chart.

Navigation only starts to get tough when conditions get difficult or you move out of familiar waters. Now you need to plan things more carefully and to think ahead. Combining unknown waters with the much-reduced time scale of fast-boat navigation leads you to focus your mind on the problems ahead.

The navigation challenge is primarily due to the speeds at which fast boats can travel. Response time and room for error are greatly reduced when you're traveling at 30 as opposed to 5 knots. However, the basic techniques for fast-boat navigation are not a whole lot different from those used at slow speeds, and in this chapter we assume that you have a basic grounding in navigation.

You need to find out where you are and look at where you're going, but as speeds increase, you have to make decisions quickly. The tools and information for navigation must be at your fingertips if you are going to be successful. As with most things in a fast boat, there is no time for a relaxed approach. At 30 knots you are covering a nautical mile (1.15 statute miles) in 2 minutes. At 50 knots you need to focus more carefully on what is going on, and when your speed rises to 60 knots, a nautical mile

Covering the Miles

			SPEED IN KNOTS		
	20	**30**	**40**	**50**	**60**
MINUTES					
1	0.3	0.5	0.6	0.8	1.0
2	0.7	1.0	1.4	1.7	2.0
3	1.0	1.5	2.0	2.5	3.0
4	1.3	2.0	2.6	3.3	4.0
5	1.7	2.5	3.4	4.2	5.0
6	2.0	3.0	4.0	5.0	6.0
7	2.3	3.5	4.6	5.8	7.0
8	2.7	4.0	5.4	6.7	8.0
9	3.0	4.5	6.0	7.5	9.0
10	3.3	5.0	6.6	8.3	10.0

Table shows the distance in nautical miles traveled at different speeds over different times.

every minute, you need total concentration to get the navigation right.

Two systems of navigation are used in fast boats: visual and electronic. Visual navigation is the use of visible clues such as buoys and land features to establish position. This is often called eyeball navigation, and in the days before electronics, this was just about all you had.

Electronic navigation is the use of instruments such as radar, the global positioning system (GPS), and electronic charts to provide information. With these aids you get a much higher level of accuracy and can navigate to close tolerances. Electronics can give you a great deal more confidence as you travel in a fast boat. The use of electronics has revolutionized navigation, transforming it from intelligent guesswork into a science.

You have to appreciate that the conditions in a fast boat are not conducive to accurate navigation. There is little chance of using traditional instruments such as a hand-bearing compass, parallel rules, or dividers. Even the steering compass can be hard to use due to the motion of the boat.

Electronic instruments aren't necessarily easy to use either. It can be difficult to get your fingers to press the right buttons on the instruments, and reading the small print on an electronic screen can be a challenge. At very high speeds, just getting your eyes to focus on the instruments can be a difficult task. The situation is compounded because you can't concentrate solely on working out the navigation while your mind and body are distracted by the duties and discomfort of traveling at high speed.

Electronics are fine for fast boats, and they do much that can't be accomplished by visual navigation, but the time has not yet arrived when you can rely wholly on electronics. It's still sensible to have a backup, so plan your routes on paper charts as well as on the electronic versions. It is much easier to get a good overall view of the route on a larger paper chart, and the paper chart can give you a lot of information that may not be obvious on the electronic screen.

Communications systems can be an important component of navigation and safety on a fast boat, and this chapter will also look at the use of radios and phones on board.

Fast boats are clearly a challenging environment for the navigator. With the advent of electronics, aspects of the challenge have become a lot easier; you don't need to focus quite so much on where you are but more on where you are going. High accuracy is not necessarily a feature of fast-boat navigation, but then high accuracy is not necessarily required except in certain situations. As long as you know that the boat is in clear water and not running into danger, your precise location is not that important. There are even benefits in traveling at high speeds because you can virtually ignore the effects of wind and tide on navigational accuracy—two factors that are critical to accurate navigation of slow boats.

In general, you will find yourself using visual clues from the land and from navigational marks, and combining these with information from electronic systems. There are a lot of these visual clues about if you know what to look for, and they can help to reassure you that the electronics are doing their job, giving you a high level of confidence in what you are doing. There is no doubt, however, that fast boats are a difficult place for navigation. The key is preparation.

Navigation Before You Leave

Your navigation preparation should be part of a general check that you perform before heading out to sea. Any work that can be done in the comfort of the harbor before you leave will be a great deal easier than trying to do the same job under way at high speeds. Away from the fast-boat environment there is time to plan and plot various alternatives. There is time to study a paper chart in detail and time to look at all the options, depending on the prevailing weather and where you want to go. If you are setting out on a passage, you can plan the proposed route both on electronic and paper charts. The whole purpose of preparation should be to reduce the workload at sea, where every operation becomes much more difficult.

Preparation is fairly straightforward if you have a precise route you want to follow, as when you are going from one harbor to another. On the way, you might think about a good place for lunch or where guests

Pre-Departure Checklist

might want to go to a beach for a swim. You can do a certain amount of preparation for these possibilities in your planning, but in relaxed situations like these you can also just stop the boat and work things out.

In offshore racing there is a set route that you plan to follow, but you might still want to look at alternatives in case these present a better option to make faster progress. I always said when I was racing that you need to do 100 percent preparation but you might only use 30 or 40 percent of what you prepared. The trouble is that you do not know which 30 or 40 percent you will need, so you have to prepare it all if you want to win.

Programming the Electronic Chart

When programming the electronic chart before you leave harbor for passage to another port, you can plan the entire route by entering consecutive waypoints as appropriate. From these waypoints you can identify the course needed to steer from one to the next, plus the distances between them.

With the proposed track thus established on the electronic chart, the only requirement when you get out at sea is to ensure that the actual route being followed is close to the planned track. The waypoints that you entered on the electronic chart will be linked by a line, showing the route you want to follow. There will be a second line, showing the track that the boat is actually following, so it is easy to compare them and apply heading corrections as required.

A waypoint is a position on the chart that you want the boat to pass through on your route. You can first establish this waypoint on the paper chart, marking the position, but you will probably want to transfer it to an electronic chart. To do this, find the latitude and longitude of the waypoint from the side scales of the paper chart and then enter these coordinates on the electronic chart. Alternatively you can do your plotting of the waypoints on the electronic chart directly, and this will show latitude and longitude so that you can transfer the position to the paper chart by the reverse procedure.

Selecting a waypoint is easy, but select them with care. On most electronic chart systems you simply set the cursor on the point you select and press the appropriate key. If you use a buoy or other navigational mark as a waypoint, keep in mind that they are usually in place to mark a danger. Set the waypoint a little off the mark, being sure to set it on the opposite side of the mark from the danger.

A waypoint can also be a random spot in the mid-ocean where you plan to alter course—simply a designated position of longitude and latitude—but it's always reassuring to have something marking the waypoint so you get a visual confirmation of where you are.

If you are working solely on a paper chart, you will need to join up the waypoints with lines that show the route to follow. You will then measure off the courses to follow along these lines and the distances between waypoints. Knowing the distances, you can calculate the time each leg will take at your proposed speed. With the electronic chart, however, most of the hard work is done for you. When the chart is interfaced with your GPS receiver, it will give you a readout of the speed you are making good, your course made good, and the time to go to the next waypoint.

In plotting routes on an electronic or paper chart through a series of waypoints, it's important to go over the route in detail to ensure that it's safe. It's so easy to plot the waypoints and assume that you will have clear water between them. However, the small-scale charts that are often used for planning purposes may not show up all the detail of isolated rocks and shoals. Therefore, once your route is plotted, the track line should be checked on a larger-scale display ("large scale" means "large" detail of a small area, and vice versa), looking along each side of the route to ensure that there are no navigational dangers close to your proposed line of travel.

When plotting the final track, you will want to build in safety margins. These should allow an adequate distance from any danger such as a rock or shoal so that you do not risk hitting it. Inevitably the boat will wander to one side or the other of its track, and you do not want these short-term deviations to take you into danger. Give a wider clearance to a sandbar or sandbank because the edge of the shoal may be poorly defined. On the other hand, you may choose to pass quite close to a headland, if there are no off-lying dangers, so you can see the land and get a good visual check on your location.

A buoy makes a good waypoint and can also be used to check the tide or current, which here is substantial.

Also consider the expected limits of visibility. In poor visibility a bigger margin might be in order to allow for unexpected course deviations. Judgment and experience play a big part here. While defining a waypoint is easy, getting it in the right position to give an adequate margin of safety takes more skill.

Unless you feel it's necessary to precisely follow a specific line, your route should be planned to pass fairly close to identifiable navigational marks or other features of navigational significance. Passing these features will give you a visual check on the accuracy of the information on the electronic chart and can be very reassuring.

This tactic also usually results in shortening the distance between waypoints, simply because there will be more of them. This can be an advantage in case there is any problem with the electronic chart and you need to proceed on visual navigation alone. The shorter the distance between

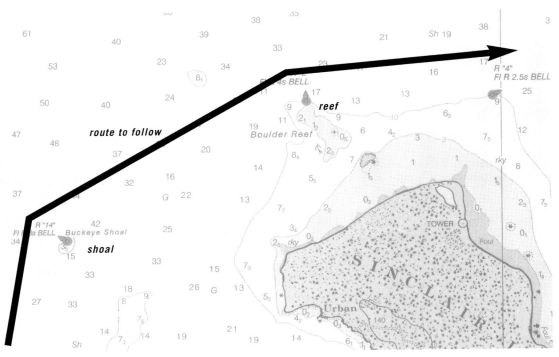

Plot your route well outside a buoy or beacon marking a hazard to provide a margin for error.

waypoints, the more accurate will be your course made good between them, because any steering errors will have less effect over the shorter distance—meaning less risk of missing a mark.

Preparing the Radar

Getting your radar unit up and running before you go is much easier than trying to do it at sea. Setting up the radar means that you optimize the display for the conditions you'll be in. The main controls to adjust are the tuning, the gain, and the sea clutter. This can be a fiddly job, and the control knobs can be difficult to adjust precisely

when the boat is bouncing about. Once you have optimized the tuning and gain in the harbor, these can normally be left on the same setting, but changing conditions at sea, such as increasing wind, may demand that the sea clutter be adjusted while you are under way.

Some modern radars have automatic settings for these parameters—a highly desirable feature because the less you have to mess with while under way, the better. These automatic settings ensure a pretty good picture at all times so that the only thing you may have to adjust as you go along will be the range. Modern radars are

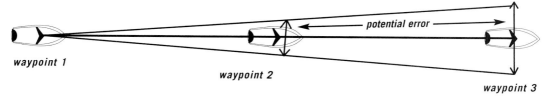

waypoint 1

waypoint 2

potential error

waypoint 3

The potential error when steering a course increases with distance. Here the potential error distance doubles between waypoints 2 and 3.

Having the paper chart alongside the helm and the electronic systems can provide a good check of progress.

usually linked to the electronic chart display so that waypoints you have plotted show up on the radar display as well, allowing the radar to be used as a check on navigation.

Preparing the Paper Chart

With the advent of electronic charts, paper charts have taken a back seat in fast-boat navigation. I still like to have them available because they can show a broader picture. The small size of electronic screens imposes a limit on what they can show, so for me the paper chart is a vital extra display to have on board. A paper chart can also play a valuable role as a backup to the electronic version in case of malfunction.

Out at sea, when a fast boat is bouncing around in waves, it can be extremely difficult to read the fine detail in either an electronic or a paper chart. It's not possible to make electronic charts easier to read except by changing the scale. On the paper chart, significant navigational features can be highlighted, and you can write in comments and additional details as you wish. This should all be part of your preparation work. In this way, the chart can be tailored to your requirements.

There are many ways to highlight a paper chart to make it easier to read and more useful. You can put pencil rings around important navigational marks such as buoys and beacons, with a letter to indicate their color so that they stand out on the chart. If you will be running at night, you can highlight navigational lights and mark their flashing characteristics in large letters or

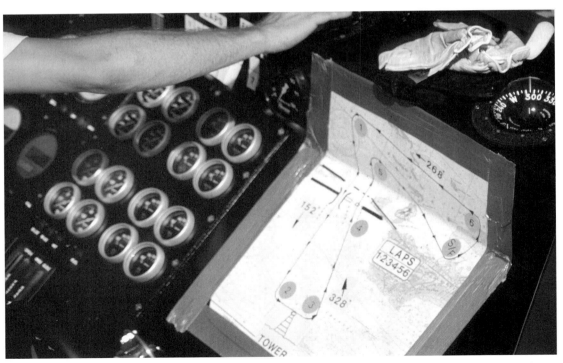

The paper chart in this race boat has been modified to highlight buoys and other marks so that it can be read easily at high speed.

figures. Obviously, all waypoints should be plotted, with courses and distances between them written in large figures. Any danger areas such as shoals and rocks can be highlighted with ringing or shading.

Marking the paper chart in this way presents significant information in a manner that can be easily identified even when operating at high speed. Conditions probably will not allow the chart to be opened to its full expanse, but it can be folded so that your current area of interest is visible. Carefully highlighting the paper chart makes it a valuable part of the navigator's equipment, and it should be stowed away only when the boat is operating in familiar waters. Even then, when you are perhaps just out having fun or trying out a boat, it's quite easy to become disoriented and lose touch with your current position; the paper chart can still perform a useful role in reestablishing where you are. I'm a great fan of having a paper chart in a fast boat, and I consider it an essential part of the equipment for navigation.

Navigation on the Water

Having done as much preparation work as is practical, you now need a routine for navigation when you are under way. This does not have to be formal, but on the other hand you can't afford to be too casual about navigation because things can change rapidly. Running aground in a fast boat can be painful, and your insurance company will not thank you for it.

While under way, you may navigate a variety of routes. One might have you heading toward a waypoint on the electronic chart, the next running inshore along a familiar coastline, and another proceeding port to port or to a favorite fishing spot. The main thing to remember in fast-boat navigation is to keep things simple, bearing in mind that the work that can be done under way is limited. You don't want to get involved in complex calculations and fine navigational techniques in a fast boat. The simple solution is usually best, even though it may not always result in the most direct line of travel.

Heading to a Waypoint

Waypoint navigation is ideally suited to fast-boat operations, making navigation relatively simple even in the sometimes hostile environment of such a boat. The waypoint can be programmed into the electronic chart before departure, and the displays will indicate the courses to the waypoint and the distance to go. These give you a check on progress. As your position moves across the chart display, it's easy to see when you might be able to pick up the waypoint visually if there is a buoy or other mark there. Of course you can always change a waypoint or select new ones while under way, if you wish.

The electronic chart also shows your cross-track error, which is a measure of how far your boat is off its planned route. The straight-line route between each waypoint is shown, with the actual track you're following displayed alongside. The difference between the two is your cross-track error. With this information in hand, it's a simple matter to correct the course being steered so that eventually you end up at or close to the selected waypoint. Not only will the clever electronics show the cross-track error graphically, but they will also give you a precise measurement of the distance you are off course.

To begin your trip, simply follow the course to the first waypoint along the route to your destination. When the boat reaches the first waypoint, you then set course along the track to the second waypoint, and so on.

To prepare for a possible failure of the electronic chart system, the courses and distances between the waypoints should also be noted on a piece of paper or paper chart. This will give you enough information on board to follow the projected route. When you revert to visual navigation in this way your navigation will be far less accurate,

but if you have planned things well you should still be able to get where you are trying to go.

When navigating by "eyeball" you will be relying on your accuracy in steering the compass course to the next waypoint—a skill that we will explore later in this chap-

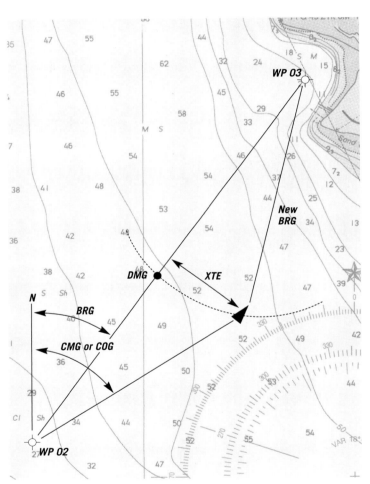

GPS units supply a great deal of information about your current position and your distance and bearings to waypoints. Displays on GPS units vary greatly, but the terminology and abbreviations are universal.

If a radar target is thought of as a waypoint, it can be used in an alternative form of waypoint navigation. One important point with using radar in this way: targets on the radar display are not named and identified as they are on an electronic chart display, so you need to make a very positive target identification before heading toward it.

On fast boats, radar is generally used with a head-up display—that is, with the heading marker always pointing to the top of the screen to indicate the direction in which your bow is pointing. All targets are pictured in their positions relative to your heading.

An alternative is a north-up display, with north always at the top of the screen.

This requires a compass input into the radar; the heading marker will then point to the relative direction in which the boat is moving. Because this type of radar display is compass-stabilized, if the compass swings about, the radar picture also swings.

With both of these displays, your boat remains at the center. All the targets on the screen are shown in relative motion: the target returned by a ship moves across your screen in a vector combination of this motion with yours. With your boat remaining in the center of the display, it appears that instead of the boat moving past land, the land moves past your boat.

The computer on a type of radar display known as true motion uses the speed and heading of your boat in order to draw your track, with the land remaining stationary. Other vessels move past as you would see them in real time. This is perhaps the ideal radar display, but accurate speed and heading inputs are not easily obtained on a fast boat, and these units are expensive. They are usually found only on larger fast boats.

There is a lot to be said for a north-up display, because the electronic chart also has north up, permitting a direct comparison of the two displays. On modern

Dual-screen color radar allows two radar pictures of different scales to be displayed side by side, an ideal arrangement on fast boats.

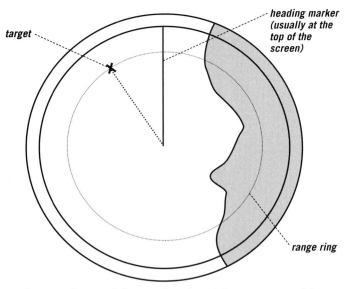

target

heading marker
(usually at the
top of the
screen)

range ring

Radar can be used for navigation. The range to objects on the screen (such as headlands and buoys) can be measured directly. In order to determine the course to steer to Target X, the compass heading of the boat is added to the bearing measured on the radar when you are using a head-up display. If your compass heading is 350 degrees magnetic and the relative bearing to Target X is 330 degrees magnetic, the course to steer is 350 plus 330 = 680 minus 360, which is 320 degrees.

units the range of the two displays can be made the same. This comparison of displays is useful when you need to identify a fixed target. On some units it's possible to lay the radar display over the electronic chart for direct comparison. This sounds like the perfect arrangement, but in crowded waters the screen can get quite cluttered, making it difficult to see what is going on. Combined units are available that have the radar and electronic chart displays side by side on the same screen, and this can

be one of the best layouts for fast-boat use.

Another type of radar uses a split-screen display to show two radar pictures, covering different ranges. You can select the ranges you want to use. For fast boats, a 6-mile range could be used for early detection of targets; a 1-mile or 3-mile range on the adjoining display could be used for closer maneuvering. These would be ideal settings for use in fog.

Radar is the one piece of electronic navigational equipment that provides information that is not positively identified. Electronic charts give you well-defined information and positive speed and course readouts. With radar you have to interpret the information shown on the display. Targets are not labeled, and you have to work out what they are. You cannot be sure that you are picking up every target that is within range, because weak targets might not be detected or might be lost in the sea clutter.

You need skill and experience to operate radar successfully. It's easy to take what you see on the radar for granted, to make what you see on the display fit with what you expect to see. This can lead to disastrous mistakes in difficult conditions such as poor visibility.

Radar for Collision Avoidance

Radar comes into its own in poor visibility because it is the only electronic instrument that shows the locations of other vessels. Using radar for collision avoidance requires considerable skill. You will always need to proceed at a safe speed, a requirement of the International Regulations for Preventing Collisions at Sea (often referred to as COLREGs, for Collision Regulations). The determination of that safe speed is left to your own judgment, but it must be based on prevailing visibility and the stopping distance of your boat.

Fast boats are generally very maneuverable, enabling you to steer around any vessel that looks like it's coming close. But first you have to be able to see it. This sounds easy, but if you are looking through the windscreen, visibility is likely to be reduced by reflections; you can also be distracted by the electronic screens in front of you. Even at an open steering position, staring out into the fog is not an enriching experience; it's difficult to maintain concentration because there is nothing to focus on.

Locating other vessels on radar is not too difficult. They can usually be identified for what they are because of their locations relative to the land or by the way they move on the screen. The problem is that while you can be reasonably confident of locating larger vessels by radar, there is no guarantee you will see all the smaller boats that may be around. They may be just too small to show on the radar except at close quarters, and at close quarters they can be easily lost in sea clutter. If your boat is on autopilot, you should get a much steadier radar picture. The autopilot also leaves you free to keep a better visual lookout or to concentrate more on the radar.

Given the limitations of radar detection, the driver of a fast boat has no right to go steaming along at high speed on the assumption that he can detect and avoid anything in his path. Caution must be the watchword in poor visibility. Other vessels might not see you on their radars. They may not be using radar at all, instead relying on a sound signal from your boat to indicate your presence.

When you do see a ship or boat target on the radar, you then have to assess whether it is a collision risk. There are well-defined ways of plotting target tracks, but these are not practical in a fast boat, and you probably will not have the luxury of a true-motion radar that does the job for you electronically. You only need to determine whether the target is coming toward you or whether it will pass clear, and you can do this by watching the movement of the target in relation to you. If the target is moving in toward the center of the display along a more-or-less steady bearing, it probably presents a danger; if it is moving parallel to your course line, it should pass clear but possibly quite close; if it is moving away from the center of the display, you're all set.

Another way of checking is to put the bearing cursor on the target. If the target stays on the cursor, collision is a distinct possibility; if the bearing is changing considerably, the target should pass clear, either ahead or astern. Remember that what you see on the radar is the relative motion of the target, as it moves on the display with a combination of your course and speed as well as its own course and speed, because your position remains in the center of the screen.

You might want to just keep out of main shipping channels when it's foggy. In crowded waters you can reach a point of target overload, with so many targets on the display that you lose track of the ones that are important, and that could pose a collision threat. By keeping out of the main channels, you will have fewer targets to deal with, since many of them will have to stay in the deep-water channel. Even if there are no obvious main channels, simply restricting your travel to shallower waters will ensure that the bigger vessels are not in the way.

You can use a similar technique when entering a harbor in poor visibility. The buoyed channels at many harbor entrances show the limits of deeper water. On either side of this main channel there will probably be water that is deep and wide enough for your boat; navigating there will keep you out of the way of much of the harbor traffic. You need to study the paper chart carefully before adopting this tactic, because there may

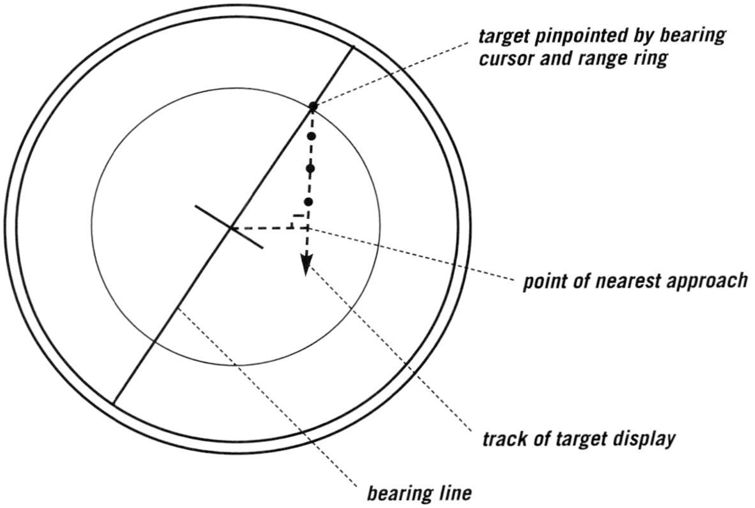

Labels on figure:
- target pinpointed by bearing cursor and range ring
- point of nearest approach
- track of target display
- bearing line

Tracking an approaching target on the radar to avoid a collision: Fix the initial position by pinpointing it with the range ring and bearing line. The closest approach of the target is shown by the imaginary line at right angles to the line joining successive target positions fixed in this way. If the bearing of the target does not change a great deal as its range decreases, then you are on or close to a collision course.

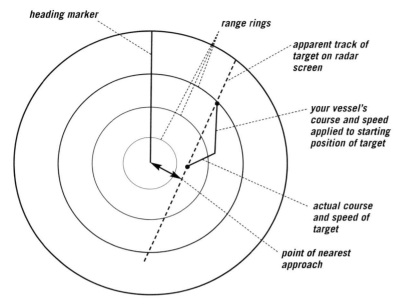

Labels on diagram:
- heading marker
- range rings
- apparent track of target on radar screen
- your vessel's course and speed applied to starting position of target
- actual course and speed of target
- point of nearest approach

Using a relative-motion radar, it is possible to work out the actual course and speed of an approaching vessel.

Steering a Course

Steering a fast boat can be quite a challenge. You steer not only to keep the boat on the required course, but also to help smooth the ride. The most comfortable ride will come with minimal adjustments to the wheel. However, the compass on a fast boat is never very steady because of the pounding of the boat, so you can see why following a desired course is not easy.

A driver who tries to follow each gyration of the compass can cause the boat to change direction repeatedly as it chases the compass needle. Instead, the driver should average out the swings of the compass, maintaining a steady heading with the minimum of corrections. It takes considerable skill to find the right balance between letting the boat find its own headings and applying corrections as required by the compass.

Many people steering a fast boat will show a bias to one side or the other. If the wind is on the beam, a helmsman may show a course bias toward the downwind side, perhaps just coming onto the required compass heading at one end of the heading swing. When steering a compass course,

be points where the buoys come close to dangerously shallow water. You should also check the tides. A bit of thought before you take on a challenging navigation situation in poor visibility can help you find a safer route to your destination.

Because nothing you see on the radar is 100 percent certain, you should use the information it presents with caution. Radar can be great for detecting other vessels, but if they look like they are getting anywhere close to your position, slow down, sight them visually, and then take avoiding action if necessary. And keep in mind that there may be small boats in your area that you don't pick up on radar at all.

this bias can have a 5-degree or more cumulative effect on the actual course made good. If you are trying to maintain a good compass course to the next mark, this bias needs to be identified and allowed for. On an electronic chart plot, such a bias will show up clearly as cross-track error and can be corrected. But without electronic navigation, the biased course could proceed right on past the buoy or other intended destination.

Steering by GPS

It is the magnetic compass that creates many of the steering problems on a fast boat. Now there are ways to make the job a lot easier using information from GPS satellites. The heading marker, a feature of many electronic chart displays, can be used as a steering indicator in preference to the compass. The heading information is based on incoming GPS data. The main benefit of steering using the heading marker on the electronic chart display is that it allows a course to be steered toward a point shown on the chart, but without the constant swings that make a magnetic compass difficult to follow.

One type of heading marker gets its information by interpolating between two positions previously established by the GPS. This type of heading marker has a very slight delay compared with compass steering, which can make course-keeping difficult.

Another type of GPS heading marker processes information in real time and is more accurate and expensive. Here the signals from two or more GPS satellites are analyzed and, from the change in frequency of the signals—the Doppler effect—the heading can be determined. The calculations are complex, as you can imagine, but the result is that the heading marker shown on the display is the actual heading of your boat and can be used like a compass with confi-

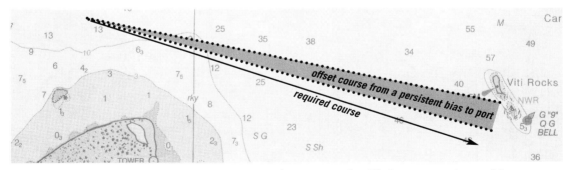

Many drivers find it hard to steer a required course and will show a persistent bias to one side or the other.

dence. The only snag with both of these "satellite compasses" is that they will not work when the boat is stopped.

Another type of satellite compass uses two GPS antennas that are mounted a known distance apart in the fore-and-aft line of the boat. These give two positions, and the relative angle between these positions is the course. This approach will work even when the boat is stopped. Any GPS compass can show the course in degrees true, so no corrections for variation and deviation are needed, as is the case with a magnetic compass.

Autopilot

We have talked about steering as done by the driver, but autopilot steering is also something to be considered. I have used autopilots at speeds up to 70 knots on large fast boats, and have conducted trials in a 16-foot RIB in which the autopilot worked fine at speeds up to 40 knots in lively seas. You do need to watch the autopilot carefully at these speeds, and I would hesitate to use one when there's any risk of big waves because of the possible need to make quick course alterations. You should have the autopilot disconnect button ready. On one fast boat we had a large red button for just this purpose.

Even at high speeds a properly adjusted autopilot will maintain a course accuracy of 2 or 3 degrees, much better than any human driver can hope to achieve. This steering accuracy is achieved with a minimum of rudder corrections, so the boat should have a better ride. It takes a degree of confidence to use an autopilot at high speed because it would be very easy to suffer a spinout if the autopilot failed. However, testing has shown that autopilots can work satisfactorily even in small boats such as RIBs.

Apart from the obvious advantage of maintaining a straight course, an autopilot offers other benefits. The driver does not have to concentrate on the movements of the compass and has more freedom to operate other controls or to study approaching waves. Under steady autopilot steering, the radar display will be more stable and should be easier to view and interpret at high speed.

At night the steady course maintained by an autopilot means that any lights, vessels, or navigational marks will maintain a steady bearing relative to the heading of the boat. This will make them much easier to identify, as they will not be swinging around the horizon. This can be particularly important in the case of flashing lights, whose heading could change considerably between flashes, making it hard to identify them. In fog, using an autopilot will permit more time for maintaining a good lookout.

The limit for autopilot use in a fast boat is probably reached when the boat can no longer be operated comfortably under a steady throttle opening. Once the throttle has to be used to adapt the trim of the boat to approaching waves, it's time for a human driver to take over. Manual control is also needed for steering around large waves.

Visual Navigation

Visual (eyeball) navigation, the system used before electronic charts became viable for fast-boat use, largely involves plotting courses between known navigational marks, then steering those courses until the marks are located visually. Success lies in selecting suitable marks as your visual waypoints.

Not only do you want to be able to identify marks such as buoys and beacons along the route, but you also need to identify land features such as distinctive buildings, TV masts, and prominent headlands to help keep you on track to your waypoints. It is a bit like detective work, and there are plenty of clues out there if you know what to look for.

Knowing the approximate route you want to follow, start your preparations for visual navigation before you leave on a trip. Draw lines on the chart to link what you believe will be the best waypoints. Now look along these lines between waypoints to see if there are other marks or features that can be readily identified and that you might want to use as secondary waypoints.

These alternatives could involve a small

Transit marks like these two lighthouses can give a useful visual check on progress.

deviation from the direct line, but anything you can do to shorten the distance between consecutive waypoints will help you maintain an accurate course. If you steer a 5-degree error, you will probably still be within visual range of your waypoint after 5 miles. But if you double that distance to 10 miles with the same course inaccuracy, you could well pass the mark without seeing it.

Clues on the shore can help you steer a better course. Extend your course line between waypoints toward the shoreline, if it's close enough to be visible, and there could well be a distinctive building or some other feature close to the extended line that you can steer toward—an easier proposition than following a compass course. It could be a distant headland that is the heading mark, and it does not have to be in a direct line with the course extension: anything within about 5 degrees of your course will give a steering mark that is good enough.

Remember that the buoy you are aiming to use as a waypoint may only be visible when you are a mile or so away. But a good shoreline feature that is in line with your route might be visible for 10 miles, keeping you on course toward the buoy.

Be careful in choosing your identifying objects, because your chart will not always be up to date with respect to shore features, and one tall building can look very much like another. But it is so much easier to steer toward a mark than to steer a compass course. I have seen drivers even pick out a cloud (or

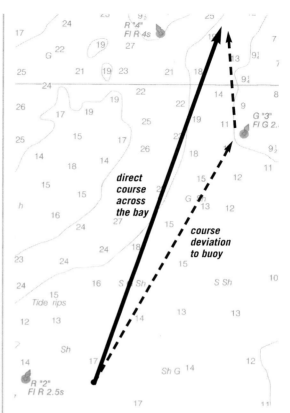

Deviating from a straight course in order to sight an intermediate buoy shortens the distance between sightings and reduces the chance of steering errors.

a star!) as a temporary steering mark.

Even if shoreline features don't offer precise positioning and can't provide help on the correct course to steer, they can be used as clues to your progress along the chosen route. Clues such as waves breaking along the edge of a shoal can give you an idea where the boat is, if the line of the shoal marked by breakers can be related to the line of a shoal on the chart. None of

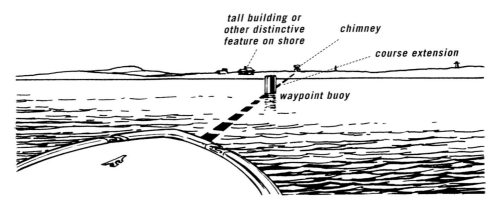

Finding a buoy is much easier if there is a distinctive feature on the land behind. By extending the course over the land it is easy to find a point to steer toward.

these clues may give a positive fix, but when you add them together, an accurate picture can emerge.

Night and Fog Navigation

Navigating in fog without the benefit of electronic systems presents a real challenge. Again, the key to success is to reduce, as much as possible, the distance between consecutive waypoints, even if this means taking a longer route.

When you are heading toward a harbor entrance, for example, it can be beneficial to steer a bit to one side or the other of the intended waypoint, so that when the elapsed time has been run there is only one way to turn to find the waypoint if it is not in sight. Much will depend on the mark being used, and this offset technique will not offer much benefit in trying to locate a buoy or isolated mark.

If a buoy or isolated mark is the waypoint, it's best to head directly for it. If you don't find it after the distance has been run, turn and reverse course. There is no benefit in making random alterations in course, hoping you will find the mark; unless you're lucky, you will just end up lost. Only a planned search pattern will locate the mark. The best pattern is a square search, starting at the point where you expected to find the mark. The buoy should not be far away.

When seeking a mark in fog, the tendency is to look ahead and not to the side. However, the maximum detection range will always be on either side of the boat, not ahead. Crew members should be detailed to keep watch abeam when approaching a mark so you have the best chance of finding it.

Navigating a fast boat in fog may demand a speed reduction to conform to the

International Regulations for Preventing Collisions at Sea (COLREGs). A reduction in speed could also be required when approaching a mark such as a buoy, so that a positive confirmation of the position can be made.

On a boat with electronic navigational systems, an electronic chart is used at night or in fog in exactly the same way as in clear visibility to give precise position and route information. Radar is a particular benefit, because your own ability to see how the boat is doing is so hampered. It can also be beneficial to use autopilot in order to free the driver to help with the radar.

Making Landfall

Without electronic navigation, making landfall—sighting and identifying a coast—can be difficult in poor visibility. You may never travel out of sight of land, in which case you should always have some visual clue to where you are. But even in local waters the visibility may deteriorate and cause you to lose sight of land.

You need to get close enough to make a visual identification on land—but at the same time, getting too close could take the boat into dangerous waters. Traditionally, making landfall has always been the moment of truth for navigators, but there are techniques to make the job easier and safer.

The solution lies in carefully choosing the point at which you close with the coast. This is where paper charts are most useful. A careful study of your chart should enable you to identify a stretch of coastline devoid of off-lying dangers such as rocks or shoals. A bold coastline where the seas move gently toward shore should enable a safe landfall even if your position accuracy is not good.

When your calculations show that you are approaching land, turn the depth sounder on and slow down so that it can work properly. A speed of 20 to 30 knots should be fine. Watch the depth sounder like a hawk,

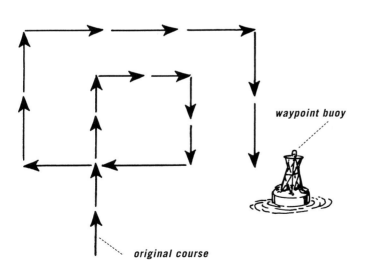

waypoint buoy

original course

Use a box search to locate a buoy in the fog.

because it becomes your main guide to safety.

Set yourself a lower limit on the water depth that you consider safe. If you get to this limit without sighting land or markers, it's probably time either to run parallel with the coast—you know the direction of the coastline from the chart—or head out to sea again and try a landfall at another place.

A technique to use when you are trying to make landfall at a headland is to set a course to a point a mile or two inside the headland. You need to see and identify the headland, and if you set the normal course to pass clear outside it, any error in steering could mean that you pass so far out that you see nothing. Steering to a point inside the headland should provide enough latitude for error. Of course you need to check that the coastline inside the headland is clear of off-lying dangers.

When making landfall on a coastline in poor visibility, try to approach the coastline at an angle rather than head-on. Then if a difficulty is sighted ahead, there will be only

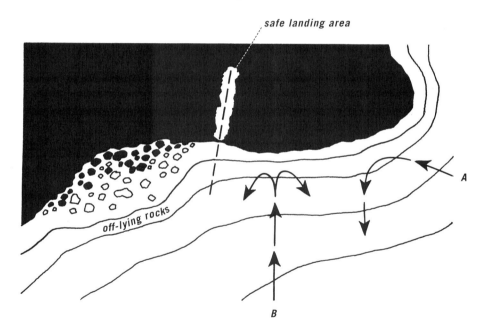

Instead of heading directly for a headland or landfall in poor visibility, it is better to approach at the angle shown in A. Approaching directly, as in B, means having to turn through a greater angle if sudden shoaling is detected and you will be unsure which is the safest way to turn.

one way to turn to head to seaward. If you approach directly into the coastline, you are faced with the option of turning either way to get clear, and the best way to turn may not be immediately obvious. In addition, the turn will then have to be made through a full 180 degrees to reverse course.

Techniques like this can be used to reduce the risks inherent in making a landfall in poor visibility. Much will depend on the circumstances, and only a careful study of the paper chart will show what the possibilities might be in a particular location.

Using electronics will allow you to make landfall with greater confidence, but even then you need to use caution. Check the paper chart to ensure there are no off-lying rocks or shoals; these may not show on the electronic chart at some scales. Use both radar and the chart to confirm the approach, and keep the depth sounder on as an added check.

Tactics under Difficult Conditions

Without radar and electronic charts, you need to give careful thought to the best tactics for determining your current position or to find the way to a reference point that can help determine that position. It's hard to plan future action if you don't have a point of reference.

Hopefully you will never get into a situation where you don't know your position. But when you're having fun, it's easy to get carried away and not think ahead. You could be out there setting up the boat or just making high-speed runs when the mist comes down and you lose touch with navigational marks. You could be out of sight of land, with no position reference.

A possible solution is to head in the general direction of land until it is sighted, using the depth sounder as a check, and then to run parallel to the coast until you can make positive identification of land features. From this point you should be able to establish a course to your desired destination.

There can be a variety of clues to your position, including a change in sea conditions that could indicate shallow water, or a change in the color of the water that in some areas can be significant. You might stop a passing fishing boat to ask information. Or look for a ferry that is known to operate on a specific route: the ferry can be a clue to your position and its heading can point you to a particular port.

None of these indications may give the positive position you would like to have, but they offer clues. If things work out, your confidence should improve as you close with the land.

Returning Home

When it's time to head back to the harbor, the boat with electronic navigation has it easy. The entrance to the harbor can be established as a waypoint to steer toward. Simply call up the waypoint, and you have the course and distance to go. In poor visibility, previous knowledge of what the entrance looks like on radar can be a help in identifying it.

It's another matter for a boat without radar or an electronic chart. Rather than trying to head directly to the harbor entrance, it's often better first to find the coastline, then follow it until you reach the harbor. If you try to head directly to the harbor entrance and you see the coast but no harbor, you will not know which way to turn to find it. But if you've set a course to the coastline that is deliberately offset to one side or the other, you will know which way to turn after you spot land.

Because your home harbor is a regular destination for your boat, the techniques of a return without electronic navigation assistance should be well practiced. You also need to become familiar with local landmarks so you can readily identify them as you motor home.

Communications

Radio communications are important to a fast boat for keeping in touch with what is going on around you—for instance, hearing navigation warnings or even distress messages, or sending them. You expect other boats to keep a listening watch on the radio so they can help if you get into trouble, so do the same yourself when you are at sea. Radio links are also useful as

you enter a harbor for contacting the marina to announce your arrival or secure a berth.

Cell phones have revolutionized communications at sea, and the ability to simply dial up a number and get a response has opened up many possibilities. However, a cell phone is not the best communication tool on a fast boat. It should not be your first recourse for sending distress messages (the Coast Guard does not monitor cell phone frequencies as they do emergency VHF channels) or even for routine marine calls.

A cell phone allows private conversations, but this can be a disadvantage when it's a conversation about marine hazards or other subjects that other people or boats at sea should be aware of. The big advantage of cell phone communication is that it links directly into the phone network. But you cannot talk to another vessel unless you happen to know its cell phone number. A cell phone may only work up to about 10 miles offshore, and there can be blind spots without coverage. It's a good idea to determine the areas of coverage in advance in case you need the phone in an emergency. So by all means use a cell phone to call your friends and to make private arrangements, but don't use it as a substitute for a good marine radio.

For marine work, VHF radio provides a reliable link. But bear in mind that VHF links only operate in a direct unobstructed

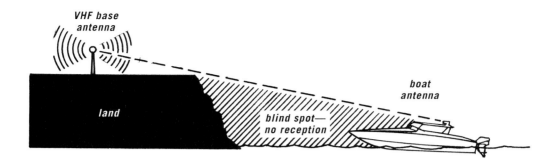

Communication with shore can be lost if high land gets between the VHF base antenna and the boat's receiver.

line between two antennas—the one on your boat and the one on the other boat or on shore. It is the high antenna on shore that helps to increase the range of VHF radios, but if high land intrudes between this antenna and the boat at sea, communication can be lost. You are likely to find a blind spot under high cliffs where there could be no link for a mile or two out to sea.

VHF communication between boats and a good shore station should reach 20 miles or more. The range will depend a lot on the antenna that is fitted to your boat. Fast boats usually have a low profile, so you want the antenna as high as possible to improve both reception quality and range. Most marinas do not have very high antennas, so don't expect radio contact with the marina over more than 10 miles, and more likely only 5 miles. Boat-to-boat commu-

nication is usually limited to a range of 5 miles or less.

Communications at High Speed

The constant pounding of a fast boat moving through the waves can knock the breath out of you and make it difficult to talk clearly and coherently. Add to this the noise of engines and wind, and you can see why voice communications over radio or phone should be limited to short, concise messages, unless you slow down to make things easier. The high noise levels can make it difficult to hear what is coming over the radio, so keeping a listening watch for other people trying to communicate with you and your boat is not easy.

You can always slow down in order to improve radio or phone reception, but you should always start with a good communications installation. An external antenna will improve the quality of the cell phone link, just as a tall antenna will help with the radio. Most VHF radios use either a telephone-type handset or a fist mike that you talk into, with a loudspeaker for the listening watch. Headphones are better for keeping a listening watch, but they can make it difficult to hear what others on board are saying. Be sure the microphone can be operated with only one hand so that the other remains free for holding onto the boat.

With all the products available, radio and cell phone installations can be tailored to suit you and your boat. In an open boat, the options may be limited by the requirement for waterproof equipment, and this rules out most cell phone fittings designed for car use. It's worth taking the time to set up good radio and phone installations, because they are important for more than just social chat and confirming a berth at the marina. A reliable radio or phone could mean the difference between rescue and disaster if you get into trouble.

10

Emergencies

In any fast boat there is always the risk of an emergency situation. Colliding with floating debris, grounding, fire, and even capsizing are risks at sea. In a fast boat you may be pushing the limits, and the trouble is that often you will not know where the limits are until you reach them. Caution should make you err on the side of safety, but you must accept that there are always risks.

Most of the obvious risks are well understood. Experience has led the way to vastly improved boats to the point where construction failure is minimized, risk of fire is reduced, hulls are sound, and even engine failures are unusual. There are still unpredictable elements in fast boating, and colliding with floating debris is high on the list. You can't do much about this except keep a good lookout.

The first priority in any emergency sit-uation is to let somebody know about the problem, perhaps through a priority call to the Coast Guard. In any such call it's important to explain whether you can cope with the problem using the resources of the boat and its crew or whether help may be required. In dire situations a full emergency distress call may be necessary.

In all messages of this type, the people you call will need to be told your position, so they can find you; the number of people on board, so they can account for everyone during any rescue; and the type of boat, so they know what they are looking for.

Fire, capsizing, or serious collisions with debris create immediate emergencies. Less urgent problems such as engine and steering failures may dent your pride but are unlikely to lead to full-scale emergencies. Even an electrical failure can put a boat out of action, and the only way to prevent this type of problem is by a sound installation in the first place and good maintenance after that.

The real challenge for fast-boat owners is to keep minor problems from escalating into major ones. If the engine fails, you probably have a second one to get you home slowly; if the steering fails, you can use the engines for steering sufficiently to get home. Fuel and electrical failures can affect both engines and may be harder to deal with, but with the right knowledge and tools, you can fix the problem.

These relatively small problems can escalate, however. I once came across a boat on fire—and it all started with steering failure. The steering was the old wire-and-pulley type, and the flexible steering cable had frayed and then broken. Not too difficult a problem to fix—but the loose ends of the wire had, unknown to the driver, fallen across the battery terminals. The result was sparking, and a fire that destroyed the boat.

In another incident, the batteries came loose, the boat caught fire, and then the situation escalated even further as the fuel started burning. An engine failure that might not be a major problem in calm conditions could put you in serious danger if the weather happens to be severe or you are running an inlet. Beware when you have what looks like a simple problem, because it could quickly become serious.

We have talked about the importance of maintaining reserves: reserves of distance from dangers when you are navigating; reserves of speed when operating a boat in waves. You also need reserves for coping with emergencies. Try not to push yourself or your crew to the limit; if something unexpected happens, you need the physical and mental reserves to deal with it. When things do go wrong, take time to think through the problem in a logical way to find a solution. And be sure let someone know of your predicament, even if it is not urgent or desperate.

Major Emergencies

Virtually all emergencies at sea are preventable, but that does not stop them from happening. Careful maintenance of a boat's operating systems should give you the required reliability. After that you need to drive your boat with respect for the conditions and navigate with a bit of forethought and planning. But you can't take all the risk out of fast boating.

Collisions or groundings are possibilities if you get your navigation wrong; fire can be a distinct risk in a fast-boat; capsizing is a danger, though it's only likely to be a problem in *small* fast boats. Being aware of these possible major emergencies and ways to counteract them will put you in a better position to come through such an incident without serious harm.

Colliding with Debris or Grounding

Fast boats have strong hulls that are designed to take the battering of high-speed wave impacts. In either a grounding or a collision with debris, this strong hull will probably survive the initial impact. Floating debris tends to ride low in the water, and if you hit it there is every chance the hull will ride up over it rather than collide directly with it. You could find the same happening if you ground on a sandbank. You may come to a fairly rapid halt, and this opens up the possibility of people on board being injured or even thrown overboard, but the hull is likely to survive and stay intact.

The risk when you hit debris or go aground on a soft bottom is that you will almost certainly damage the propeller or possibly the entire drive unit. The propeller is the lowest part of the boat, so this will be the first to go. There is a good chance that the drive unit will also suffer, particularly on stern drives and outboards. Even when it is only the shaft or drive unit that is affected, there is a risk that the hull will be damaged around the transom area. With luck the bilge pumps will be able to cope with this, at least until help arrives.

If only one unit on a twin-engine boat is put out of action, the boat can return home at slow speed. If both units are knocked out, there is little to do but radio for help and await a tow. If the depth of water allows, put out an anchor to keep the boat from drifting into further danger.

Colliding with rocks can be a different story. The constructed hull is rarely subdivided enough for the boat to stay afloat in the event of serious damage. There is usually a watertight bulkhead at the bow but, in my experience, grounding damage is usually on the bottom of a boat rather than at its bow. In such a situation you will be glad you are carrying a liferaft and other safety equipment.

Fire

There are two likely types of fire on a fast boat. One is a fire in the engine or engine compartment, and the other is an electrical fire; of course the two could be combined.

Inboard engines should have a built-in fire extinguishing system that can be activated to kill the fire with an inert gas. For this system to be effective, it's necessary to seal off any air intakes to the engine compartment so that the fire is starved of oxygen and the smothering gas cannot dissipate. Sealing the compartment is not easy, and provision for doing this is rarely included in the design of a boat. Such a built-in extinguishing system can only be operated one time in any emergency, so it is important to close off the air inlets as much as possible. The system is activated by a dashboard control; be sure to switch off the engine first.

Turn off the fuel supply if you can get to the valve, but don't open the engine hatch to do this. After you have set off the built-in fire extinguishing system, don't be in a hurry to open up the compartment again, because this could introduce oxygen and get the fire going anew. When you do open it, have a portable extinguisher ready in case of a flare-up. With outboard motors you will use a portable fire extinguisher. Cutting off the fuel supply to the unit should quickly extinguish the fire, because there is very little inside an outboard motor, apart from fuel, that is capable of burning.

An electrical fire could occur anywhere there are electrical circuits. Chafing on the wiring, loose terminals, or a short circuit are the most likely causes. With the wiring hidden away it can be difficult to get to the root of the fire. A good starting point is to turn off the electrical circuits in order to disconnect the initial cause of the fire; then tackle the fire with portable extinguishers.

I once faced an electrical fire in the foam insulation behind some paneling. Every time we opened up the paneling to get to the source, it would blaze up, and it took us some time to put it out. This fire was difficult to cope with because the circuit that caused the trouble bypassed the main electrical switch, so we could not turn the circuit off.

Once again, call for help as soon as a problem is discovered and while you still have battery power. Try to keep the people on shore fully informed about what is happening so that help can be dispatched if necessary.

Capsizing

There are two likely scenarios in which a fast boat could capsize: being caught in surf, or traveling in rough seas. It is usually only small boats that get into a situation where they might capsize; there should be little or no risk with a larger fast boat. You might be tempted to run into a beach, where a surf is running, and drive in too cautiously—allowing the breaking waves to overtake you and causing the boat to broach, turning sideways to the waves. It could be the same in rough seas, if you are going too slowly in breaking waves. In either of these situations, careful but forceful driving is the best prevention.

If you do get caught in one of these situations and the boat capsizes, it will happen suddenly, with little warning. There will be no time to make an emergency radio call, and once the boat has gone over, the radio will probably not work. The suddenness of the incident will leave you and your crew in a state of shock; even in warm water it can take some time to appreciate just what has happened. One minute you are looking forward to a barbecue on the beach and the next you are in the water.

The first thing to check after a boat capsizes is that no one in the crew is trapped under the boat; a head count is essential to establish that everyone has escaped. Stay with the boat; it's often possible to climb onto the overturned hull, using the outboards, stern drives, or stern gear as ladders. Getting onto the hull will not be easy because there is not much to hold on to, but it's better than staying in the water.

If you capsize in surf, there is every chance that the boat will be washed into the beach and that you can walk ashore. If you capsize in the open sea in rough conditions, there is little choice but to wait until someone reports you missing and a search is initiated, or until you are spotted by a passing boat or from the shore. If the boat carries an EPIRB (emergency position-indicating radio beacon), activate it; the beacon should generate an immediate response to the situation. A portable, waterproof VHF radio will be even better, because then you can explain the problem to someone.

The trouble is that the EPIRB and the radio are likely to be inside the capsized boat. Consider the situation carefully before diving under the boat to retrieve them. The rough conditions in which the boat capsized could make this a risky operation. And keep in mind that you can't dive with a life jacket on.

Towing

An emergency situation at sea may result in the need for your boat to be towed, or for your boat to tow another. In calm or moderate conditions, towing should be a straightforward operation. The only problem might lie in finding a suitable line for towing and securing it to something strong enough to handle the stress. It can pay to have one good length of line on board for towing; if nothing else is available, the anchor line may be the best option.

If your boat is doing the towing, you can spread the load between two mooring cleats at the stern by making up a bridle to string between them. The same applies if your boat is the one being towed: try to spread the load between a couple of cleats (although the anchor windlass on larger boats could be a good option). Watch out for chafe on the line where it passes over the edge of the boat; put some padding at this point if the tow is likely to last more than an hour or so.

Use moderate speed when towing; probably little more than idle is required. This can mean a long journey home, but at least you will get there without too much stress and strain. The aim should be to keep a steady pull on the towline rather than have it repeatedly jerking and releasing. The optimum speed will depend on the prevailing sea conditions and the boats involved.

11

The Future

Rapid development has been the story in fast powerboats over the past two or three decades. It's a chronicle of innovation that shows no signs of coming to an end.

Most new boat designs have managed to gain in particular areas of performance by emphasizing certain features, but the gains are often countered by a downside. This balancing act in design is now bringing slow and steady progress in the refinement of hulls. We are seeing a number of hybrid designs that promise better seakeeping and/or better efficiency.

The development of new fast craft is coming not just from the leisure sector, but also from designers of fast ferries. Ferry designers have produced concepts like the wave-piercer catamaran and the long, thin monohull (the very slender vessel, or VSV), and it is from such designers that we can

look for some of the future developments in fast boats.

Monohulls

The fast-boat market is focused on the deep-V monohull, a well-tried and well-tested solution to high performance. The vast majority of fast boats on the water are deep-V designs. Looking into the future, it's difficult to see much in the way of changes in the monohull concept. Most of the options have been exhaustively tested, and designers know enough to design a hull for the speed and the job it has to do.

The VSV is one new development, and military versions of this design have been successfully evaluated. Being long and thin, these boats tend to go through the waves rather than over them, which certainly makes for an exciting ride.

When you first try a VSV in rough water, it can be scary to experience the boat heading directly into a wall of water. But the bow simply knifes through the wave, and the boat comes out the other side, smiling. Torrents of water may pour over the deck, but the ride is almost level, with virtually no pounding. And you can make much faster progress in rough seas than you ever could with a deep V.

The downside of this concept is the very limited amount of space inside the boat and the fact that the boat has to be built super-strong to stand up to the punishment. There is also a problem in seeing where you are going, with water rushing over the vessel as it attacks the waves.

For the military, the VSV offers the possibility of going faster and in rougher conditions than conventional designs. For leisure use, the internal space limitations are probably too severe. For ferry use as an all-weather fast commuter, the designs go up the size scale; this permits more usable internal space and makes them a viable proposition.

Catamarans

For ultrahigh performance, the asymmetric planing catamaran is the most favored boat, as seen on the racing circuit. But outside of racing, the catamaran has had only limited popularity despite its several advantages.

The use of planing catamaran hulls is likely to be restricted to racing boats because these hulls are difficult to design with enough space inside for sensible accommodations. On the other hand, there is increased use of the displacement catamaran that offers modest speed and a long range for cruising. With this concept you can cruise at 30 knots and not have to stop and refuel every 200 miles or so.

The catamaran still has a lot of potential, and several new ideas are being tested. The long, thin displacement hull, whether used in monohull or catamaran form, is very fuel efficient. Cruising catamarans, while they can cut through the water like a VSV, have comfortable accommodations, mainly above the hulls, and they are not designed to be pushed hard. Sixty-foot catamarans of this type are being built with a 30-knot speed and a 2,000-mile range, enough to cross the Atlantic with one stop in Bermuda or the Azores. If fuel shortages become a problem in the future, this could be the best route to economical boating.

An extension of this type of catamaran is the wave-piercer design. The wave piercer rides on two displacement hulls that are designed to pierce the waves, a concept widely used on fast ferries. The design has not translated well into smaller sizes, but this may change. Designs down to 60 feet in length, with impressive seakeeping qualities, have been developed for sportfishing.

A wave-piercer design that has very long, thin hulls to reduce resistance. These hulls tend to go through waves rather than over them, making life more comfortable on board.

Another modification of the basic catamaran design is to add foils. Hydrofoils, as such, have gone out of fashion; they have been superseded by less complex, hybrid designs that offer similar or better performance. The foil-assisted catamaran is being used in many applications to improve performance of the basic catamaran hull. Foils are shaped in cross section like an aircraft wing, and they do a similar job by translating the forward motion of the craft into lift. This lift supports a portion of the boat's weight, reducing the surface area of the hull in contact with the water and thus its resistance.

Adding foils between the hulls of the catamaran provides additional lift without going outside the envelope of the hull shape. The hull itself provides the support for the foils, so the whole layout can be designed for maximum efficiency. Of course the foils themselves add resistance, but on balance the foil-assisted catamaran is more efficient and has better seaworthiness.

A combination of foils is normally used for this application. The usual configuration includes a full-width fixed foil between the hulls at the aft end, where most of the weight is concentrated. This is balanced by a pair of canard foils that extend from each hull into the tunnel forward. These forward foils can be either fixed or hydraulically adjustable. Adjustable foils provide a way to adjust the boat's trim for ride control and they also act as dampers to reduce pitching.

The foil-assisted catamaran design has been used for craft as small as rigid inflatable boats (RIBs), although in these smaller sizes only the single full-width foil is normally provided. Foils are becoming more common on catamarans of 60 feet and above, where the cost and complication of the system can be justified.

Trimarans

Trimarans are attracting new interest. There are a few smaller leisure craft in this configuration, but the main application is for fast ferries. The main attraction of trimarans is their ability to operate well in rough seas. The center hull is long and thin, like a VSV; the two side hulls improve stability, particularly at rest or at slow speed. The side hulls can be attached amidships or, more commonly, at the stern, where there is less chance of waves striking the underdeck between the hulls.

There are several approaches to modern trimaran design, with both planing and displacement types being developed. The planing type uses a long, narrow center hull that has a V bottom to cushion the ride; the side hulls or sponsons provide stability and allow for deck accommodations to be spread over a larger area. This approach is favored for smaller trimarans.

Larger trimaran designs are adopting a wave-piercing displacement center hull. These displacement trimarans are showing considerable potential as fuel-efficient designs with good seakeeping ability. The long, thin center hull is designed to go through waves in wave-piercing fashion for a level and comfortable ride. The side hulls are designed to just skim the surface at high speed to offer minimum resistance; in one version the side hulls ride completely clear of the water at upper speeds, with foils extending below them to offer stability.

A more highly developed trimaran concept has foils also under the center hull, resulting in a considerable decrease in the wetted surface area of the hull. The efficiency of this concept is not in doubt, but installing the equipment within the narrow beam of the center hull can be a challenge in smaller sizes and when high speeds are required.

Hovercraft

Hovercraft have been around a long time. They can be a great way of traveling on the water, because they ride on the surface with virtually nothing below water. Because of their almost nonexistent draft, you can land on a beach without a care in the world. In the pure hovercraft, the air cushion on which the craft rides is contained by a flexible skirt. On a sidewall hovercraft—or surface-effect ship, as it is more commonly known—the cushion is contained by the sidewalls of a catamaran hull, with flexible skirts at the front and rear.

Hovercraft are severely limited as to sea conditions under which they can operate safely, and it seems likely they will remain only a small niche sector of the fast-boat market. However, new types of craft based on the hovercraft principle hold promise for wider use.

One new design does away completely with flexible skirts, where most of the wear and tear on a hovercraft takes place. Instead, the air cushion is contained within a hollow chamber molded into the underside of the hull. This cavity hull is shaped above water more like a monohull, a shape that promises better seaworthiness. The underwater shape is reversed in form.

The air cushion in the cavity hull, pressurized to around 2 psi, supports about half the weight of the craft. This serves to lift the boat in the water and dramatically reduces the hull's contact with the water. But it lifts the craft only to a certain height, in order to keep the propulsion system in the water. The pressurized air acts as a partial cushion against slamming in waves. And with the hull shaped like a conventional monohull above the waterline, these craft have a similar level of seaworthiness.

A more recent development of this cavity hull concept has the forward part of the underbody shaped like a deep-V hull to give a clean entry to waves and places the air chamber along the rear two-thirds of the hull. This configuration in effect introduces a step in the hull amidships, with the cavity behind it. This creates another type of hybrid design—a cross between a deep-V and a surface-effect ship. The future of fast-boat hull design could well lie in the development of similar hybrids.

Flying Machines

With an unpredictable, ever-changing surface, oceans and seas provide perhaps the worst medium in the world for high-speed travel. One new concept meets the challenge of high speed on water with a craft that skims a few feet above the surface. This is the creation known as a ground-effect craft or a wing-in-ground (WIG) vehicle: it's a boat that flies—or a flying machine that travels on water.

The WIG has wings that generate lift for flight only when they are close to the surface. The lift is created by the air squeezed between the wing moving forward and the surface below. This is high-efficiency lift, but as the craft rises, the lift starts to dissipate. The lift is only sustained close to the water or ground and is only effective over relatively smooth surfaces. The craft can only take off and land on water.

WIG designs tend to look like aircraft but do not have the control surfaces of an airplane. They are designed to be inherently stable, taking off from the surface when the speed is high enough to generate the required lift and landing when the speed slows and the lift reduces. They are stable in level flight, with the only controls being the throttle and the rudder, the latter usually being an air rudder mounted behind the air propeller.

These craft can cope with moderate waves. You can feel the resistance of the waves until around 40 miles an

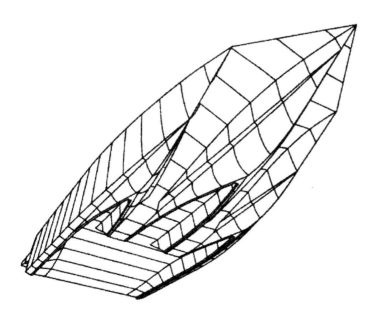

New cavity hull designs combine a forward deep-V hull shape with a recessed rear section into which air under pressure is injected to generate extra lift.

A cavity hull catamaran that has air cushions under the side hulls to reduce resistance and increase efficiency. A separate blower maintains the air pressure under the hull.

hour, when the hull lifts free of the water and accelerates rapidly. Once airborne, the ride is level and smooth. Top speed depends on the power, but 80 to 100 miles an hour is quite common. Such speeds are achieved with relatively small engines, demonstrating the efficiency of these craft. WIG designs come in a variety of sizes, from single seaters up to huge passenger and cargo versions that were developed in Russia.

WIG craft are quite rare, but if the concept becomes more accepted, an interesting question arises: are they boats or planes? If many of them begin to appear above the waters of the world, there will probably be a need for stricter control of their operations. In most countries they are classified as marine craft, and the level of regulation is relatively low.

Ride Control

Any number of components and features are available to help generate lift or govern trim on a fast boat, such as foils, planing surfaces, trim tabs, and interceptors. The designer can select those that do a particular job or add a particular characteristic to a hull—tailoring the hull to the work it will perform or the conditions under which it will operate. An alternative approach to designing a hull that can cope with constantly changing sea conditions is to use variable geometry. This approach is employed in RIBs, which automatically adapt to the changing shapes of waves through the medium of their inflatable tubes.

Some designers are now working on hull forms that can change shape in significant ways to face different sea conditions. These changes in shape mainly relate to a change in the angle of the stern section of the hull, akin to an aircraft wing that is extended in area for takeoff and then retracted for fast flight. This type of variable geometry is like an overgrown trim tab—and when you start to think along these lines, other possibilities open up.

Think about a hull with tabs or interceptors not only at the stern, but also at a point halfway along the hull. If these forward tabs are lowered, the bow will lift. With two sets of tabs installed, you have the possibility of lifting or lowering the bow or stern, either together or in opposition. Now you start to get better control of fore-and-

A Russian WIG craft that uses the lift from the short wings to skim the surface, allowing very high speeds with low power.

aft trim, opening the door to a form of ride-control system.

Ride-control systems are widely used on the new generation of high-speed passenger ferries. Rather than having tabs on the hull, these systems use a T-foil—a strut extending below the hull, with a cross foil at its bottom. This cross foil generates lift; it also has trim surfaces that can be adjusted under computer control to trim the hull at high speed to maintain a level ride.

The technology is there, but how much of this will be applicable to smaller, high-speed craft is the question. Many people like to have the control of a fast boat in their own hands and would not like to turn the job over to a computer. And such systems are expensive. They can be justified on a large ferry because they are a small part of the overall cost, but is the cost and complication worth it on a smaller boat?

Ride-control systems will have a place on high-speed boats, and we already have them to a certain extent in the form of tabs and interceptors. On some craft, these are already being put under computer control,

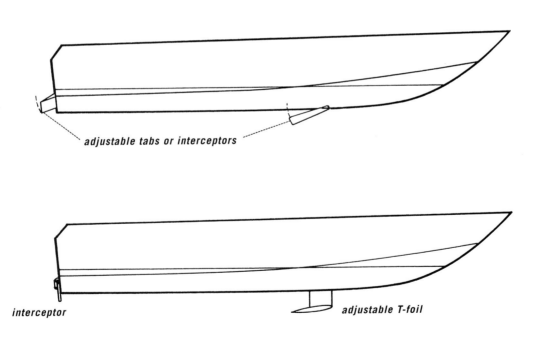

adjustable tabs or interceptors

interceptor   *adjustable T-foil*

Alternative ride-control systems include adjustable computer-controlled T-foils and/or tabs under the hull to help control lift and produce a level ride at speed.

leaving the driver free to concentrate on throttle and steering.

We will certainly see more fast-boat systems operated by computer now that quick-acting interceptors are being introduced, but it's difficult to forecast just how far this trend will go. You may get a more comfortable ride, but you give up the thrill of being in total control. And it can be a bit unnerving to ride on a fast boat under computer control: you have to pray that the person who developed the software got his sums right.

Fast-Boat Engines

There have been tremendous strides in engine development in recent years. In the early days of fast boats, the gas engine was king because it offered a considerable weight advantage compared with similar power from a diesel. Now the diesel engine is catching up and can compete with the gas engine on almost equal terms. This is because road transport has demanded more efficient diesels; this has led to a development spin-off for marine diesels, which are now highly efficient and reliable.

The gas turbine has long threatened to challenge diesel and gas engines, but its high cost has always been a deterrent. There is no doubt that the light weight of the turbine can be an important advantage for high-speed boats, but that is not the end of the story. The fuel consumption of a turbine is higher than that of a diesel, so more fuel has to be carried. When you add in the weight of the extra fuel and all the ancillary components required for a turbine, the weight savings may not be all that much. You also have to consider the response of the turbine, which can be quite slow. It looks as though the application of turbine power will be restricted to larger fast craft, and this is a relatively small market.

A new hybrid marine engine is being developed: a diesel version of the rotary, or Wankel, engine. This has the simplicity and smoothness of the turbine, with a single rotating component, and most of the early problems with seals seem to have been resolved. These engines are going into production, and if they prove successful they could be the next step beyond the reciprocating diesel engine. The rotary diesel has a considerable weight advantage over its reciprocating counterpart. If this engine turns out to be reliable, it could open up a new market in fast boats.

Fast-Boat Propulsion

There is no one propulsion system that meets all the requirements for high-speed craft. We have looked at some of the drawbacks of each system earlier in this book, and there is plenty of scope for new development.

Surface propulsion seems to be the way to go, at least in the short term, and a new drive system under development could advance surface drives from where they are now. Instead of having a universal joint in the drive shaft to adjust propeller height in relation to the water surface, this new system controls the water height in relation to a fixed propeller shaft. This replaces the universal joint of the drive shaft, the weak point and most expensive feature of some surface drives, with a simple water-controlling tab.

A surface-piercing water jet is also under development. Because most of the work of a water jet impeller is done by the lower half of the rotor, it was reasoned that if the water were ducted only to this lower half, greater efficiency would result. This system is in the development stage and could lead to more efficient water jets.

Further down the line are propulsion systems that do away with propellers and rotors altogether. Gas injected into the water can be used to propel a vessel. The problem facing developers of these systems is in how to control the gas flow and thus the boat. The gas can be either steam or gas that is generated in a similar way to that used in a gas turbine by adding fuel to compressed air; the attraction of these systems is that there are no moving parts under water.

Into the Future

Much of the modern development of fast boats has been in craft designed for leisure use. Now marine professionals are seeing that fast boats can be both effective and reliable. The military is using patrol boats with speeds up to 100 miles an hour. Fast boats are invading many traditionally conservative areas of commercial use, and are seen as pilot boats and even fishing boats.

Fast-boat development tends to go in cycles. Hull design improves, but engine development lags behind. Then the engines catch up, and it is the level of crew comfort that is the limiting factor. Engine development has now overtaken hull development, and all the power you need is available in lightweight and economical packages. It looks like we are due for some significant improvements in hull design, ones that will make life more comfortable for the crew as well as elevating the performance of boats at sea.

As I travel the world, I see many wild and wonderful new concepts for obtaining high speed on the water. In many cases the designer or inventor has focused on speed in calm water. If you ignore the need to operate in waves, fast boats are easy to design and develop. The real challenge comes in designing fast boats to operate in the actual conditions a boat will face at sea. The sea can be a good friend when you work with it, and a harsh enemy when you challenge it. History has shown that with fast boats, the best approach is evolution, not revolution, pushing the boundaries slowly and steadily toward higher speeds and better seakeeping.

Index

*Numbers in **bold** refer to pages with illustrations.*

A
advection fog, **156**
aerodynamics, 36–37
aluminum boats, 39
antennas, 65, **218**, **233**
Arneson drive, 90, 92
autopilot steering, 225–26

B
ballast systems, 126–**27**
barrel roll, **183**
batteries, 78–**79**
beam, stability and, 30, 31, 33
beam seas
    breaking waves, avoiding, **171**,
        172–73
    driving in, 169–73, **170**,
        171
    matching speed to waves,
        170–71
    steering in, 171–72
    throttle control, 171–72
boat construction materials
    aluminum, **39**
    carbon fiber, 38
    composites, 37–39, **38**
    Kevlar, 38, 39
    resins, 38
    rigid inflatable boats (RIBs),
        39
    vinylester, 38
boat construction methods
    aluminum, **39**
    molding systems, 38–39
    sandwich construction, **38**
    weight of the boat, 37

bow shape
    buoyancy, 33
    cathedral hulls, 22–**23**
    deep-V monohulls, **10**, **11**
    following seas and, 175–**76**
    head seas and, **176**
    rigid inflatable boats (RIBs), 50
bow thrusters, 99
breaking waves
    in beam seas, 172–73
    characteristics of, 132, **134**,
        147–**49**
    in following seas, 178
    in head seas, 168–**69**
    in inlets, **179**–80
    land features and, 142
    in shallow water, **136**, 137–39,
        138
broaching, 176–**77**
buoyancy, 31–34, **35**

C
Callan 55 (stepped deep-V mono-
        hull), **18**
capsizing, 238–39
carbon fiber materials, 38
catamarans
    cavity hull designs, **246**
    comparison of hull designs, **7**
    design of, 24–**25**
    future developments, 241–43
    limitations of, 28–29
    stability of, 25
catamarans, types of
    displacement, **7**, **25**–27
    foil-assisted, **7**, **28**, 243
    planing, **7**, **26**, 27
    racing, 36, **188**, **191**, **194**
    wave-piercer, **7**, 28, 241–**42**

cathedral hulls
    bow shape, 22–**23**
    characteristics, **7**
    design of, **22**
    in following seas, 175
    limitations of, 22
    versatility of, 23
cavity hulls, 244–**45**, **246**
cell phones, 234
center of buoyancy, **32**–34, 36
center of gravity, 31–33, **32**, 126
charts, 208, **211**–13. *See also* elec-
        tronic charts
chines
    chine flats, **14**–15
    hard-chine hulls, 8
    reverse chines, **14**, **15**–16
    ride comfort and, 14–16
    stability and, **16**
    stepped chines, **14**–15
clapotic waves, 132, **145**, **147**
cleaver propellers, 88–**89**
clothing, 193–95
    eye protection, 195
    gloves, 194
    headgear, 195
collisions
    with debris, 237
    radar use to avoid, 221–**23**
COLREGs (International Regula-
        tions for Prevention of Colli-
        sions at Sea), 221, 229
communication at high speed,
        233–34
communication systems
    cell phones, 234
    internal, 192–93
    VHF radios, 232–**33**, 234
composite materials, 37–39, **38**

computer-controlled ride systems, **248**–49

cooling systems, 74–**76**

crew
    as ballast system, 127
    fatigue, 201–2
    ride comfort and complaints, 187–89
    role on a fast boat, 191–92

cross-seas, **135**–36, 142, 144–**45**

currents, 137, 140

D

deadrise angle, 10, 11, **12**, 13

deep-V monohulls
    advantages of, 8–11
    bow shape, **10, 11**
    characteristics, **6**
    choices and compromises, 18
    deadrise angle, 10, 11, **12**, 13
    Hunt design, **9**
    improvements to, for high speed, 10–11
    lifting strakes, **13**–14, **15**, 16
    lines plans, **9**
    lower-speed designs, 11, **12**, 13
    planing surfaces, **12**, 31
    spinout, **183**
    stability of, 33
    weight, 16–18

diesel engines
    efficiency of, 68–69
    future developments, 249
    stern-drive propulsion and, 82
    throttle response, 68, 69, 72, 73, 106–7
    turbochargers, 68, 72–73
    and water-jet propulsion system, **69**

directional stability
    deep-V monohulls, 17, 124
    hull design, 30
    power trim effects, 124–25
    semidisplacement monohulls, 20

shaft-and-propeller drives, 125

surface propulsion, 125

two-speed gearboxes, 125–26

water-jet propulsion, 125

displacement catamarans, **7**, **25**–27

driving a fast boat
    in beam seas, 169–73, **170**, **171**
    breaking waves and, 147–**49**
    communication, 192–93, 232–34
    concentration skills, 182, 184, 189
    crew's role, 191–92
    driver's role, 189
    fatigue, 201–2
    in following seas, **150**, 173–78, **176**, **177**
    in head seas, 149–50, **159**–69
    navigator's role, 190–91
    at night, 184–85, 225, 228–29
    performance reserve, 158–59
    pre-departure checklist, 207
    response time and speed, **2**–**3**
    running an inlet, 178–80, **179**
    sea conditions and, 146–47, **149**–50, **151**, 157–58
    trip planning, 185–86
    waves, reading, 184

dynamic lift, 34–36, **35**

dynamic steering, 121–23, **125**

E

electrical systems, 78–**79**, 80, 238

electronic charts
    display placement, 63–64, **217**
    navigating with, 213–**15**, 229
    programming, 207–**10**
    route modifications, 216

elephant trunks, 51

emergency position-indicating radio beacon (EPIRB), 239

emergency situations, 235–36
    broaching, 176–**77**
    capsizing, 238–39
    colliding with debris, 237

fire, 237–38

grounding, 237

engines
    future developments, 249
    power curve, 72
    throttle response, 71–72, 73
    Yanmar 500 hp engine performance curve, **72**

engine support systems
    cooling systems, 74–**76**
    electrical systems, 78–**79**, 80, 238
    fuel systems, 76–78, 237–38
    maintenance, 74
    maintenance checklist, 75

engine types
    comparison chart, 67
    diesel engines, 67, 68–**69**
    gas turbine, 67, 69–**70**
    inboard gas engines, 67–68
    outboard gas engines, 67, 70–71

EPIRB (emergency position-indicating radio beacon), 239

exhaust systems, wet, 75–76

eye protection, 195

F

fast boats
    defined, 1
    future developments, 240, 250

fatigue, 201–2

fetch, 151, **152**

fire, 237–38

five-point harness, **61**

fixed-shaft surface drives, 89–**90**, **91**

flaps. See trim tabs

flying machines. See wing-in-ground (WIG) vehicles

fog
    advection fog, **156**
    making landfall in, **230**–31
    navigating in, 155–56, 228–**29**
    radiation fog, 156

foil-assisted catamarans
   characteristics, **7**
   design of, **28**
   future developments, 243
following seas
   bow shape, 175, **176**
   breaking waves, avoiding, 148,
      178
   broaching, 176–**77**
   driving in, **150**, 173–78, **176**,
      177
   matching speed to waves, 131,
      174–75
   steering in, 176
   throttle control, 175
   trim tab adjustments, **111**, 112
footrests, 58–**59**, 199–200
fuel consumption, **77–78**
fuel filters, 77
fuel systems, 76–78, 237–38
fuel-transfer ballast system,
   126–27

G
gas turbines
   design of, **70**
   future developments, 249
   limitations of, 69–70
   throttle response, 73–74
gearboxes
   controls, **102**, **103**
   electronically controlled, 98
   operation of, 98
   outboard gas engines, 81
   purpose of, 97–98
   stern-drive propulsion, 81, **82**
   trolling valve, 99
   two-speed, 98–99, 125–26
Gill bracket, 51–52
gloves, 194
GPS (global positioning system)
   accuracy of, 216
   antennas, 65
   navigation with, 205, **214**
   steering by, 224–25

gravity, 31–34, **35**
ground-effect craft. *See* wing-in-
   ground (WIG) vehicles
grounding, 237
gull-wing hulls. *See* cathedral hulls

H
handholds, 53, **54**, 59–**60**, **198**–99
headgear, 195
head seas
   breaking waves, avoiding,
      168–**69**
   driving in, 149–50, **159**–69
   matching speed to waves,
      160–63, **165**
   ride comfort, 167–**68**
   throttle control and, 163–67,
      164, **165**, **166**
   trim tab adjustments, 110, **111**,
      112
helm stations, 63–**64**, **102**, **103**,
   190–91
hovercraft, 244–**45**
hull designs. *See also* catamarans;
   cathedral hulls; cavity hulls;
   monohulls; rigid inflatable
   boats (RIBs); trimarans
   choices and compromises, 5, 8
   comparison chart, **6–7**
   dynamic lift, 34–**35**
   planing surfaces, 30
   ride comfort and, 35–36
   stability and, 34
   wetted surface, **35**
hull pressure, 37
hull resistance, 34–35
Hunt, Ray, and deep-V hulls, 8, 9
hybrid marine engines, 249
hydrofoils, 243

I
inboard gas engines
   advantages of, 67–68
   design of, 67, **86**
   limitations of, 68

rigid inflatable boats (RIBs), 52
   throttle response, 67, 72, 106
inlets
   conditions, **143**
   running, 178–80, **179**
inshore waves, 136–37
interceptors, 112–**15**
International Regulations for Prevention of Collisions at Sea
   (COLREGs), 221, 229

K
keel, 17, 20, 30
Kevlar, 38, 39

L
landfall, 229–31, **230**
land features
   effects on tides and currents,
      142, **143**
   sea conditions and, 150, **151**
   trip planning, 185–86
   waves and, 142, **143**, **145**, **146**,
      147
   wind and, 142, **153**
life jackets, 200–**201**
lift, **32**, 33, **35**, 36
lifting strakes, **13**–14, **15**, 16, 96
long, thin monohulls. *See* very
   slender vessels (VSVs)
longitudinal stability, 18, 19, 30, 33

M
making landfall, 229–31, **230**
moderate-V hulls, 11, **12**, 13, **17**
monohulls. *See also* deep-V monohulls; stepped deep-V monohulls; very slender vessels
   (VSVs)
   comparison of hull designs, **6**
   future developments, 240–41
   moderate-V hulls, 11, **12**, 13, **17**
   semidisplacement monohulls, **6**,
      20
   shallow-V monohulls, **6**, 8

N

navigation, 204–6. *See also* electronic charts; radar
  under difficult conditions, 231
  electronic, 205–6
  in fog, 155–56, 228–**29**
  making landfall, 229–31, **230**
  at night, 225, 228–29
  paper charts, 208, **211**–13
  potential error, **211**
  with radar, **219**, **220**, 222–23
  route modifications, 215–17
  route planning, 206–7
  route plotting, 208–9
  route reversing, 231–32
  visual, 205, 209–10, 214–15, **226–28**
  waypoints, 207–9, 213–**15**
navigator's role, 190–91
negative lift, 36–37
night driving, 184–85, 225, 228–29

O

oscillation waves, 132–34, **133**
outboard gas engines
  advantages of, 71
  design of, 70, **86**
  four-stroke engines, 70–71
  gearboxes, 81
  Gill bracket, 51–52
  lower units, 82–83
  multiple-engine installation, **84**, **85**
  operation of, 80–81
  power trim effects, 117, **119**
  rigid inflatable boats (RIBs), 51–52
  steering, 122
  throttle response, 71, 72, 106
  trim and tilt functions, 83
  twin-engine installation, 83–84
  two-stroke engines, 70–71

P

paper charts, 208, **211**–13
passive steering, 120–**21**
performance reserve, 158–59
personal flotation devices (PFDs), 200–**201**
planing catamarans, **7**, **26**, **27**
planing surfaces
  beam of boat and, 30
  deep-V monohulls, **12**, 31
  dynamic lift, 34–**35**
  hull design, 30
  theory behind, 29–30
porpoising (bow movement), 117
power trim
  operation of, 116
  outboard gas engines, effects on, 117, **119**
  stern-drive propulsion, effects on, 116–**17**, **118**
  surface propulsion, effects on, 120
pre-departure checklist, 207
pressure waves, 132, 139–40
propellers
  cavitation, 85, 107, 160
  cleaver propellers, 88–**89**
  semi-tunnel installation, 85, **87**
  size, 73, 107
  torque reaction, 85–86, **87**
propulsion systems. *See also* propellers
  design of, **86**
  diesel engine and water jet, **69**
  engine and propulsion packages, 79–80
  future developments, 249–50
  outboard gas engines, 80–**84**
  shaft-and-propeller drives, 84–**86**, 107
  stern-drive propulsion, 80–84, **81**, **82**
  surface propulsion, 86–95, **88**, **90**, **91**, **92**, **93**, **94**, 107
  throttle response, 107–8
  water-jet propulsion, 95–97, **96**, 108
pyramid waves, 142, **144**, 170

R

racing catamarans, 36, **188**, **191**, **194**
radar
  antennas, 65, **218**
  for collision avoidance, 221–**23**
  display placement, 63–64, **217**
  importance of, 217–18
  limitations of, 220–21, 223
  navigating with, **219**, **220**, 222–23, 229
  north-up displays, 219–20
  setting up, 210–11
  split-screen displays, **219**, 220
  thunderstorm avoidance, **154**
  true motion computers, 219
radiation fog, 156
rain, 153
resins, 38
response time and speed, **2–3**
Revenger 34 (rigid inflatable boat), **43**
reverse chines, **14**, **15**–16
ride comfort
  balance and, 128
  boat weight and, 17
  chines, 14–16
  crew complaints, 187–89
  deep-V monohulls, 31
  hard-chine hulls, 8, 10
  in head seas, 167–**68**
  hull design and, 35–36
  rigid inflatable boats (RIBs), 44
ride-control systems, 246–49, **248**
rigid inflatable boat (RIB) tubes
  bow tubes, 50
  double-skin inflatable tubes, 46, **47**
  as fenders, 45
  foam-collar tubes, 45, **47**
  hybrid tubes, 45–46, **47**
  inflatable bladder tubes, 46, **47**

inflatable tubes, 39, 42–44
tube attachment, 44–45, 47–50, **48**, **49**
tube pressure, 43–44
rigid inflatable boats (RIBs)
boat construction, **39**
bow shape, 50
cabin design, 41–42
control consoles, 55
design of, 29, 40–**42**, **43**, 46–**47**, **51**, **52**
elephant trunks, 51
fendering, 45
in following seas, 175
handholds, 53, **54**
in head seas, **160**, **162**
inboard engines, 52
limitations of, 40, 41
outboard engines, 51–52
ride comfort, 44
seating, 41, **53**–55
seaworthiness of, 41, 46–47, **48**
self-draining systems, 50–53
stability, 42–43
variable geometry, 44–45
ripples, 132
rooster tail, **91**, 93
rough seas
boat weight and, 17
driving in, 146–47, **149**–**50**, **151**, 157–58
performance reserve, 158–59
surface propulsion operation, 93–95
rudders, 120–**21**
running an inlet, 178–80, **179**
running strakes. *See* lifting strakes

S
safety. *See also* emergency situations; seating
antennas, 65, **218**, **233**
clothing, 193–95
communication, 192–93, 232–34

crew complaints, 187–89
crew's role, 191–92
driver's role, 189
fatigue, 201–2
footrests and toe straps, **57**, 58–**59**, 199–200
handholds, 53, **54**, 59–**60**, **198**–99
helm stations, 63–**64**, **102**, **103**, 190–91
life jackets, 200–**201**
navigator's role, 190–91
seasickness, 202–3
seat belts, 60–**61**
windshields/wind deflectors, 61–63, **62**
sea clutter, 217
sea conditions. *See* rough seas
seamanship, 2–3
seasickness, 202–3
seat belts, 60–**61**
seating
bolster seating, 57, 196, **197**
foam materials, 58
rigid inflatable boats (RIBs), 41, **53**–55
saddle seating, **53**–54, 56–**57**, **196**
spring seating, 57–58
self-draining systems, 50–53
semidisplacement monohulls, **6**, **20**
shaft-and-propeller drives, 84–**86**, 107, 125
shallow-V monohulls, **6**, 8
shallow water, 137–39, **138**, 142, **143**
skeg, 17, 20, 30
slow-speed maneuvering, 99–100
speed
in beam seas, **170**–71
in following seas, 174–75
in head seas, **160**–**63**, 165
by hull design, **6**–**7**
nautical miles covered, 205

response time, **2**–**3**
responsibility and, 1
slow-speed maneuvering, 99–100
steering at high speeds, 123
throttle response, 72, 102–3, 107–8
wetted surface and, **35**
spinout, 122–23, 180–**82**, **183**
squalls, 154–55
stability
ballast systems, 126–**27**
beam of boat and, 30, 31, 33
of catamarans, 25
chines, **16**
of deep-V hulls, 33
hull design and, 34
keel, 17
lifting strakes, **13**–14, 16
of rigid inflatable boats (RIBs), 42–43
skeg, 17
of stepped hulls, 30–31
wings, 36
stability, types of
directional, 17, 20, 30, 124–26
longitudinal, 18, 19, 30, 33
transverse, 33
standing positions, 58
steering a fast boat
autopilot steering, 225–26
in beam seas, 171–72
beam wind and, 123–24, **125**
bias, 223–**24**
challenges of, 223
dynamic steering, 121–23, **125**
in following seas, 176
by GPS, 224–25
at high speed, 123
outboard gas engines, 122
passive steering, 120–**21**
potential error, **211**
rudder steering, 120–**21**
stern-drive propulsion, 122
trim and, 123–**24**, **125**

steering a fast boat *(cont.)*
    trim tab adjustments, 111–12
    twin-rudder steering, 121
steering wheel, 63
stepped chines, **14**–15
stepped deep-V monohulls, **19**
    advantages of, **18**–19
    characteristics, **6**
    spinout, **183**
    stability, 18, 19, 30–31
    theory behind, 19
stern-drive propulsion
    design of, **86**
    diesel engines and, 82
    gearboxes, 81, **82**
    lower units, 82–83
    operation of, 80, **81**
    power trim effects, 116–**17**, **118**
    steering, 122
    trim and tilt functions, 83
    twin-engine installation, 83–84
stern thrusters, 100
surface propulsion
    balanced rudder steering, **121**
    cleaver propellers, 88–**89**
    development of, 87–88
    directional stability, 125
    efficiency of, 86, **88**
    fixed-shaft surface drives,
       89–**90**, **91**
    future developments, 249–50
    power trim effects, 120
    propeller size, 107
    rough-sea operation, 93–95
    slow-speed maneuvering, 99
    theory behind, 86–87
    throttle response, 107
    trimmable surface drives, **86**,
       89, 90–**93**, **94**
swells, 135

T
throttle control
    beam seas and, 171–72
    following seas and, 175

head seas and, 163–67, **164**, **165**,
    166
    trim and, 108–9
throttle control levers
    electronic engine controls, 105
    foot, 103–4
    importance of, 101–2
    location, **102**, **103**
    separate-lever, 97–98, **102**, **103**,
       105–**6**
    single-lever, 97, 103, **104**–**5**
throttle response
    balance and, 128
    to control trim, 108–9
    diesel engines, 68, 69, 72, 73,
       106–7
    engine responsiveness, 71–72,
       73
    gas turbines, 73–74
    inboard gas engines, 67, 72, 106
    outboard gas engines, 71, 72,
       106
    propulsion systems, 107–8
    speed, 72, 102–3, 107–8
    surface propulsion, 107
    turbochargers, 72–73
    water-jet propulsion, 108
    weight of the boat, 108
thunderstorms, 153–**55**
tides and tidal currents, 137,
    140–42
toe-in, 84, **85**
toe straps, **57**, 58–59
towing operations, 239
transverse stability, 33
trim. *See also* power trim; trim
    tabs
    balance and, 128
    ballast systems, 126–**27**
    interceptors, 112–**15**
    purpose of, 83
    steering and, 123–**24**, **125**
    by throttle control, 108–9
trimarans
    characteristics, **7**

design of, 23–**24**
future developments, 243–44
trimmable surface drives, **86**, 89,
    90–**93**, **94**
trim tabs
    adjustments to, **110**–**12**
    balancing a boat with, **112**
    head sea adjustments, 110
    operation of, 109–10
    purpose of, 110
    water flow with, **113**
trip planning, 185–86
trolling valve, 99
turbochargers, 68, 72–73
turbo lag, 73
twin-rudder steering, 121

V
venturi effect, 142
very slender vessels (VSVs)
    characteristics, **6**
    design of, 20–**21**
    driving challenges, 22
    future developments, 240–41
    seaworthiness of, 21
VHF radios, 65, 232–**33**, 234
vinylester, 38
Virgin Atlantic Challenger (cata-
    maran), **90**
visual navigation, 205, 209–10,
    214–15, **226**–**28**

W
water-jet propulsion
    advantages of, 97
    availability of, 96
    design of, **86**
    directional stability, 125
    future developments, 249–50
    hull design for, 96
    lifting strakes, 14, 96
    limitations of, 97
    operation of, 95, **96**
    reversing technique, 115–16
    slow-speed maneuvering, 99

steering control, 95–96
throttle response, 108
waterspouts, 155
wave-piercer catamarans
characteristics, **7**
design of, 28
future developments, 241–**42**
waves
crests, 130, **131**
cross section of, **134**
currents and tide patterns, **141**
direction of travel, **133**
fetch, 151, **152**
gradient, 130, 131–32
height, 130, **131**, 132, 151, **152**
height and strength, 133
land features and, 142, **143**, **145**,
146, **147**
period, 130
reading, 184
refraction, **145–46**, **147**
significant wave height, 152
speed of, 130, 131, **152**
statistics, 131, 147, **148**
strength and height, 133
swells, 151–52
troughs, 130, **131**, 136

wavelength, 130, **131**, 132, **141**
wave trains, **135**, **144–45**
wind and, 129–30, **151–53**
waves, types of
breaking, 132, **134**, **136**, 137–39,
138, 142, 147–**49**
clapotic, 132, **145**, **147**
cross-seas, **135**–36, 142, 144–**45**
inshore, 136–37
oscillation, 132–34, **133**
pressure, 132, 139–40
pyramid, 142, **144**, 170
ripples, 132
in shallow water, 137–39, **138**,
142, **143**
swells, 135
waypoints, 207–9, 213–15
weather conditions. *See also* fog
rain, 153
squalls, 154–55
thunderstorms, 153–**55**
waterspouts, 155
weather forecasts, 151–53
weight of the boat
boat construction considerations, 37
deep-V monohulls, 16–18

ride comfort and, 17
rough seas and, 17
throttle response, 108
wet exhaust systems, 75–76
wetted surface and speed, **35**
white caps, 134
white horses, 134
wind
beam wind and steering,
123–24, **125**
land features and, 142, **153**
negative lift, 36–37
venturi effect, 142
waves and, 129–30, **151–53**
windshields/wind deflectors,
61–63, **62**
wing-in-ground (WIG) vehicles,
245–46, **247**
wings, 36, 37

Y
Yanmar 500 hp engine performance curve, **72**